Jane Goodwin Austin

Cipher

A Romance

Jane Goodwin Austin

Cipher
A Romance

ISBN/EAN: 9783744674751

Printed in Europe, USA, Canada, Australia, Japan

Cover: Foto ©Thomas Meinert / pixelio.de

More available books at **www.hansebooks.com**

CIPHER:

A ROMANCE.

—"Like a 0, which means much or nothing, as you use it."

BY JANE G. AUSTIN

NEW YORK:
SHELDON & COMPANY.
1869.

Entered according to Act of Congress, in the year 1869, by SHELDON & COMPANY, in the Clerk's Office of the District Court for the Southern District of New York.

A FEW WORDS PREFATORY AND DEDICATORY.

My Dear L:
Do you remember standing with me upon the bridge, and tossing chip boats into the river, and how eagerly we watched to see which should drift ashore, or wreck themselves against the stone pier, or remain idle and motionless in the eddy pool, and which should glide safely through the arch and down the smooth stream beyond?

Come, now, and help me launch another venture, the little craft called "Cipher," whose construction you have watched with such ready sympathy and interest, and to whose freight you have so largely contributed. What is to be its fate? Will it be stranded, or shattered, or left idly in the pool, or run down by heavier craft, or sunk by the missiles of those wicked boys upon the other bank? Shall we call to the boys and deprecate their attack by a confession that our little boat is not an iron-clad war vessel, much less our final idea of an elegant yacht, and that even for a chip boat she has been almost spoiled by over-whittling? No, never mind the boys; let us say nothing at all to them, but, standing hand in hand, watch together the fortunes of our little craft, thanking God that, should she sink or should she swim, she does not carry our lives or our happiness with her.

J. G. A.

Concord, Mass., April, 1869.

CIPHER:

A Novel.— Part First.

CHAPTER I.

MR. GILLIES'S FIRST LETTER.

"'J. Q. A. GILLIES, Post-Office.' Why, here's a letter for Mr. Gillies. First one that ever I see!"

The scene was the interior of a city post-office, the speaker a carrier or postman, who stood at one end of a long table assorting a heap of letters thrown there for him to arrange and distribute.

The clerk whom he addressed paused a moment in his occupation of cancelling the stamps upon a mountain of outward-bound letters and glanced at the one in the hand of the carrier.

"For Gillies, sure enough, and as you say, the first one I ever knew of his getting. There he is, making up the northern mail. You'd better hand it over."

"Let's see what he'll say to it," remarked the carrier, crossing the office and approaching another table covered with letters and packages, where stood a middle-aged man, with stooping shoulders and the sallow complexion peculiar to men and plants grown in the shade.

He was busy in folding small parcels of the letters before him in wrappers, announcing their contents at the same time in a voice whose sonorous sweetness contrasted even grotesquely with his appearance, while a clerk opposite rapidly entered the list thus dictated in a large volume, and two assistants tied and "backed" or docketed the little packages.

"Barnstable, N. H., twenty-seven, nine, three."

"Biddeford, Maine, six, two," intoned the yellow man.

"A letter for you, Mr. Gillies," interposed the carrier, tossing it upon the table.

"Not for me. Never have letters. Benson, Vermont, twelve, four"—chanted the clerk.

"You're J. Q. A. Gillies, I expect, aren't you?" asked the carrier, a little indignantly, as he caught up the letter and thrust it under the eyes of the impassive Gillies, who was already reciting,

"Carrington Centre, Vermont, three, twelve, three."

As the letter was thus abruptly interposed between his eyes and the package already completed beneath his nimble fingers, he cast a hurried glance and then a steady look at it, while an expression of astonishment, even of alarm, crossed his face.

"John Q. A. Gillies, yes, that's my name, but it can't be for me. I never have letters,' said he, reluctantly.

"Three, twelve, three unpaid," murmured the entering clerk, repeating the last call and glancing impatiently from the long rows of unentered letters to the clock above his head.

"You've got one now, anyway. There it is," and the carrier tossed it again upon the table, while Mr. Gillies hurriedly called,

"Charlestown, N. H., thirty-six, twelve, nine, I would say nine, Mr. Blodgett."

"Nine," echoed the entering clerk, and with one eye upon his book he cast the other in astonishment at Vance, the "backer." Mr. Gillies for once had made a mistake, and Blodgett and Vance felt a natural satisfaction in the occurrence.

The entering went on, but not so serenely as before. That thick yellow letter with its bold address lay upon the table, staring into Mr. Gillies's face so persistently that he could not choose but return its glances, and even when the course of operations had carried him half way down the table, his eyes travelled incessantly to the end where it lay alone and conspicuous.

"Montpelier, Vermont, twenty-one, seven."

"John Q. A. Gil— I beg your pardon, Blodgett. I meant Merrifield, Vermont, six, two," called Gillies, hurriedly.

Blodgett and Vance tittered, and the first suggested, good-naturedly,

"You're thinking of your letter, sir, aren't you!"

"It's not for me. I never have letters. Attention, Vance."

"Rockport, Maine, six, two."

And from this point John Q. A. Gillies no longer suffered his attention to wander beyond the business in hand, but kept himself and his assistants so closely to it that the northern mail on that Friday evening was made up at least five minutes before its usual time. Gillies closed and locked the bag, and watched, in an abstracted sort of way, the porter who took it upon his back and carried it to the entrance, ready for the expressman.

Then he turned, still thoughtfully, and taking up the letter, studied the address as if it had been a hieroglyph; examined the post-mark; looked for a seal, and found none, and finally murmured,

"A drop letter. If I open it I can tell who it's for, perhaps. It isn't me."

But yet he threw it down again, and looked about to see if his services were not needed somewhere; if some one was not coming to speak to him; if some other John Q. A. Gillies was not looming up from the horizon. No such deliverance was at hand, however, and, with a sudden flutter of womanish curiosity, the middle-aged clerk, who had hardly in his whole life seen a letter addressed to himself, tore open this one.

The contents were brief and sufficiently clear :

"If Mr. John Q. A. Gillies will call at the rooms of Jones, Brown & Robinson, solicitors, at his earliest convenience, he will hear of something to his advantage."

CHAPTER II.
AN OLD MAN'S LAST ODDITY.

At nine o'clock of the next morning a dubious knock upon the outer door of Messrs. Jones, Brown & Robinson's chambers elicited a gruff "Come in," from Robinson, who being the youngest and worst paid of the firm, was expected to give the most time and do the most work.

"It's not for me, of course, but "—confided Mr. Gillies to the door, as he pushed it open and stood dumb before the gruff-voiced Robinson, who was chafing his numb fingers over the stove.

"Good morning, sir. Are you looking for one of the firm? I'm Robinson," announced the lawyer, concisely, for the tall yellow man with the dubious look did not strike him as a good investment for much politeness.

"Yes, sir. I was looking for one of the firm, although I'm sorry to trouble you for nothing—"

"Heavens! what a voice the fellow's got. A splendid baritone. Should like to hear him try '*Suoni la Tromba*,'" thought Mr. Robinson, who was a bit of an amateur in musical matters. But he said:

"No trouble; no trouble, sir. Take a seat. You were saying—?"

"I got this letter last night. It is directed in my name, but I suppose there is some mistake. I can't think that anybody knows of anything to my advantage. *I* don't."

Mr. Robinson's professionally quick eyes traversed the face, figure, and outward adornment of the person so quietly uttering this forlorn sentiment, and then fell upon the letter in his hand.

"Oh, yes. Mr. Gillies, I presume?"

"My name is Gillies," admitted the clerk, dubiously.

"Of course. And this is your address?" pursued the lawyer, rustling the letter.

"Yes. That is, I am in the post-office, and my name is John Q. Adams Gillies."

"Certainly. I made a few inquiries of Mr. Postmaster —— before sending this letter. It's all right, Mr. Gillies, I assure you. Step this way."

And Mr. Robinson led the way to the inner office, pointed to a seat beside the desk, and disposed himself in the arm-chair before it.

John Gillies looked troubled and anxious. For five-and-forty years he had led an existence so completely isolated, his life had been so barren of any tie or interest beyond his own welfare that even the slight excitement of receiving a letter could, as we have seen, unnerve and distress him, and now the matter seemed assuming an importance that terrified him. He wished for no news, good or bad; he wished for no meddling eyes and fingers in his affairs, even though they promised advantage. The man felt, in the hands of this shrewd lawyer, as an oyster should, into whose shell a lobster insists upon thrusting a claw, with promise that the interference shall result in nothing but good.

"I don't think I'd better sit down. I am sure it is some other Gillies that you mean."

"No, it's not. Sit down, sit down, sir, and I'll give you the whole story in a nutshell," insisted the lawyer, and the clerk slipped into the designated seat as if it had been a dentist's chair.

The lawyer opened his note book.

"Perhaps you remember, Mr. Gillies, one very icy day last winter, when an old gentleman passing up the post-office steps in front of you, slipped, and in falling fractured his collar-bone. You helped him up, called a carriage, and at his desire drove with him to his hotel. You then, still at his request, sent a surgeon, and in the evening returned to inquire for him."

"Mr. Vaughn, you mean."

"Reginald Vaughn, Esquire, late of——"

"He's dead then? Excuse my interruption."

Mr. Robinson bowed stiffly, implying that he excused, but did not approve of it, and after a significant pause, as waiting for further remarks from the client, continued,

"You called twice afterward by Mr. Vaughn's express desire, and went with him to the steamer when he left for Europe. He died in London six weeks ago, and just before his death dictated an instrument bequeathing all his property to John Q. Adams Gillies, clerk in the post-office of this city. That gentleman is undoubtedly yourself, and you will please receive my congratulations upon your accession of fortune."

John Gillies leaned his sallow face upon his hand, and looked moodily into the fire.

"It was contrary to my usual habit to make these calls. I only did it because I was asked, and the old man said something about being lonely and deserted. As for picking him up and taking him home, I couldn't help that, of course."

"Why, surely, man, you're not sorry for having induced Mr. Vaughn to think of you as his legatee?" asked Mr. Robinson, rather impatiently. "If it is your situation in the post-office that you are regretting, I see no necessity for your resigning it. Probably, too, you can sell the estate. Stop, I should give you this packet forwarded with the will, and addressed to yourself. In a letter to us, written at the same time, Mr. Vaughn speaks of it as containing important conditions connected with the inheritance. Here it is."

"Another letter," muttered John Gillies, as he reluctantly took a sealed envelope from the lawyer's hand.

The letter it contained was not a long one, but Mr. Robinson had time to lose and regain his patience and to lose it again, before his new client, slowly re-folding the paper, placed it in the envelope and the envelope in his pocket.

"Well!" said the lawyer at length, for Mr. Gillies, his chin buried in his hand, seemed less and less likely to break the silence.

"Well!" echoed he, rather irritably. "But it is not well. If I accept this property under the conditions imposed upon me the consequence will be an entire revolution of my life. I am to make this estate of Cragness my home, and for company——"

The lawyer waited for the next word, but John Gillies's dry lips closed over it before it could escape, and when they unclosed it was to say,

"You were Mr. Vaughn's legal adviser, were you not?"

"Yes. Our firm has managed the affairs of the Vaughns for fifty years."

"Probably, then, you can give me some history of the family."

"Legal and medical advisers do not generally gossip of the affairs of their clients," said Mr. Robinson, drily.

"Certainly not, but if I assume this property, I assume with it a trust requiring as minute an acquaintance with the history of the Vaughn family as I can acquire."

"Does the late Reginald Vaughn desire you to apply to me for this history?' asked Mr. Robinson, cautiously.

"In so many words."

"Will you show me the letter expressing this desire?"

"I will show you that sentence. The body of the letter is intended for my private eye."

"An odd man—a *very* odd man was the late Reginald Vaughn," muttered the lawyer, as John Gillies again drew the envelope from his pocket, and slowly unfolding the letter, doubled it so as to leave only two lines fully exposed to view.

"Nothing could be odder than his putting this trust and this property upon me, and I had far rather have been left quiet where I was," said the clerk, moodily. "But even though I refused the whole affair, and went back to the post-office as poor as I left it, the mischief is done. My ideas have got a wrench that has unfitted them for their old groove. I should always be wondering why I didn't accept fortune when it came to me, and fancying a thousand pleasures it might have brought with it. And then this—this trust—interests me."

He paused rather abruptly, and the lawyer ventured,

"It is a secret trust, you say."

"Entirely a secret trust," assented Gillies, gravely, "and as such I accept it, and with it the bequest of Reginald Vaughn, and the utter change of life involved in it. Here is the letter."

Mr. Robinson took the paper and read—

"If you wish for such help as is to be found in a history of my family, you may obtain it from either member of the firm of Jones, Brown & Robinson, our solicitors for many years."

"That is quite sufficient, Mr. Gillies, and I will gladly place such knowledge as I have at your service," said the lawyer, returning the letter.

Mr. Gillies simply bowed with the reluctant air which had accompanied him through the interview, and the solicitor, after a moment of thought, began the following narrative.

CHAPTER III.
CRAGNESS AND BONNIEMEER.

"THEY are an old family, these Vaughns, and as proud of their honors as other old and well-to-do families. They have a genealogical tree at Bonniemeer as tall as one of those California pines, and a crest on the silver, and all that. Something more than a hundred years ago, Egbert Vaughn, a younger son of the English family of that name, came to this country and built the old house you have inherited, giving it the name of Cragness. He died, leaving one son, also called Egbert, who in due time married a cousin upon the Vaughn side, and became father of two sons, named Egbert and Alfred. His first wife died when these boys were twelve and fourteen years old; and he married again, but lost his second wife in the first year of their marriage. She left one son, named Reginald, who died in London six weeks since."

"He was this Mr. Vaughn?" asked John Gillies, tapping with his dry forefinger upon the letter in his hand.

"He was that Mr. Vaughn," assented Robinson; "but while Reginald was still a child the two elder brothers grew to be men, and very quarrelsome men, too. At least, they could never agree with each other, or with their father, who favored sometimes one and sometimes the other of them, but fixed all his affections upon Reginald, whose mother he had doted on with an old man's fondness.

"Matters finally came to a crisis among them, and, after a violent quarrel, Alfred Vaughn left Cragness, and subsequently died abroad. At the time of his disappearance, his father came to town and executed a bill bequeathing the estate of Cragness and the personals to his youngest son, and all the remainder of his property, principally derived from the first wife, to Egbert, his eldest son. Alfred was barely mentioned, and received no bequest. Soon after this, Egbert was married; and, persuading his father to make over to him his promised inheritance, he built a handsome house upon the property of Bonniemeer, and settled there, keeping up but little communication with the father, who, with his youngest son, lived for a few years at Cragness in a very secluded manner, and then died, leaving Reginald in possession.

"He, then a young man of two or three-and-twenty, went immediately abroad and spent many years in travel. Finally, however, he returned home, stayed a short time at Bonniemeer, and then retired to his own estate, where he lived a very secluded life until a year or so before his death, when he came to town and sent for our Mr. Jones, who had an interview with him at his hotel, and who expressed himself not surprised at Mr. Vaughn's recent disposition of his property."

A slight smile wrinkled John Gillies's yellow cheeks. He saw that the younger lawyer was piqued at the preference thus shown to his partner.

"Mr. Jones desired, however, that either Mr. Brown or myself should see you when you came," continued Robinson, "and declined an interview on his own part, so whatever private clue he may have to Mr. Vaughn's motives does not seem likely to benefit your researches."

"And what became of Mr. Egbert Vaughn?" inquired John Gillies, tenaciously clinging to the point.

"Excuse me, Mr. Gillies, but are not you a Scotchman?"

"Excuse me in turn, Mr. Robinson, but had not we better finish the Vaughn genealogy before we begin upon mine?"

Mr. Robinson glanced with increasing disfavor at his new client, but answered, coldly:

"You are quite right, sir. Mr. Egbert Vaughn married, as I have said, and became the father of several children, who all died young, except a daughter, now married to Alfred Murray, Esq., of this city, and a son, named Frederic, who, at his father's demise some years since, inherited the estate of Bonniemeer, where he at present resides with his wife, a young lady from the Southern States. He has as yet no children."

"Then this Mr. Frederic Vaughn and his sister are the only representatives of the family now alive?"

"So far as I know, they are," assented the lawyer.

"How far apart are the houses of Bonniemeer and Cragness?"

"About two miles, and each of them nearly that distance from Carrick, the nearest village. They are both secluded enough. I believe I have now given you all the information in my possession regarding this family, Mr. Gillies. Can we be of any further service?"

"I thank you, sir. I may very possibly require your help in this affair before long;" and the cloud of perplexity upon the clerk's face grew still darker. "I cannot tell—at any rate you will, if you please, take whatever legal measures are necessary for establishing this will, and putting me in possession of the property I shall be glad to consider your firm as my legal advisers."

"Certainly, Mr. Gillies, if you feel inclined to honor us with your confidence,' said Robinson, formally.

"You mean that I have not yet done so," retorted Gillies, as drily. "You are quite welcome to all I know of myself, which is just this. I was selected from the inmates of a foundling hospital by a man named Gillies, a bachelor, with not a friend or connection in the world, so far as I know. He did not seem to care very much about me, although he treated me kindly and sent me to a public school until I was twelve years old. At that time I entered the post-office where Gillies was a clerk. He died soon after, and I rose through regular gradations until I reached my present position. I am now forty-five years old, and, as I told you before, have never been out of the city bounds except for a country walk, which wearied and disgusted me. I am fond of only one thing in the world—music. I dislike nothing. You have my history."

Mr. Robinson looked at him in astonishment.

"And you are going to live at Cragness?" asked he.

"I am going there. Farther I cannot say."

"But how will a man of your tastes and habits content himself in a solitary sea-shore house. How will you amuse yourself?"

"I will have an organ," said John Gillies, softly, as a tinge of color rose to his sallow cheek, a sign in this impassive nature of rare and overpowering emotion. "The one wish of my life has been to possess a fine organ. I will have the best in Germany."

"Shake hands, Mr. Gillies. I am a musical enthusiast also, and you must come to my house to-night; we have a few friends and a little concert. I think you will be pleased with some of the voices."

"Thank you, but I never visit," said Gillies, slightly touching the proffered hand, and rising to go.

"As you please, of course; but I should have been glad to see you," and the lawyer showed his new client to the door, with a smile upon his lips and a curse in his heart.

CHAPTER IV.
THE MERMAID'S CAVE.

THE village of Carrick was a place of few excitements. The departure or arrival of the three fishing schooners whose several firms embraced every person of consequence in the hamlet; an occasional wreck upon the ragged reef forming the harbor; a small jubilation on election or "Independence" day; these were its principal public events.

A smaller but more frequent interest, however, centred in the semi-weekly arrival of the mail coach forming the only communication between Carrick and the outer world. Even to see it whirling down the sandy street was something, but the knowledge that it bore the lean mail-bag, perhaps a passenger, perhaps some dim report of news affecting, it might be, the fishing interest, it might be the less vital affairs of state, was sufficient to attract every male idler of Carrick to the tavern of the Mermaid's Cave, where it stopped for change of horses; while every woman in town paused with her pies half in the oven, her baby yet unwhipped, her coffee "on the bile," to rush to the door and stand on tiptoe staring down the street as if the Possibility, for whose advent most of us wait all our lives, were booked to her by that especial coach.

Never, perhaps, had the constancy of these idlers been more severely tested than on the afternoon of a certain dismal December day when the coach, delayed by a furious storm of snow and hail, so far passed its usual hour of arrival that the dinner prepared for the passengers was, as Mrs. Burroughs, landlady of the Mermaid's Cave, remarked, "dried to a skillington, and had no more taste left in it than last year's seaweed."

"The worse for them as has to eat and pay for it," retorted her lord, philosophically. "But keep it hot, Jemima, she'll be here yet. Billings never failed to get through somehow, and whoever he brings will be hungry enough to eat biled hake 'thout gravy."

"There's the supper horn for some on us," said one of the loungers about the bar-room stove, as the blatant tones of a fish-horn pierced the gathering darkness without, and angrily seemed to demand an answer.

"Reckon it's mine," remarked Reuben Brume, with a somewhat uneasy grin. "But I'll hold on a spell for the stage. She can't be much longer, and I guess my woman 'll keep a bite and a sup for me."

"More like she'll give you the bite without the sup," retorted Burroughs, who like most magnates was fond of a joke at the expense of his courtiers.

A general laugh followed his present jibe, for Nancy Brume's proficiency as a scold was well known throughout the village.

"What's the joke? I don't see none," asked Brume, angrily. "Some folks laughs as a loon squawks, jest to make a pooty noise."

"It takes wit to see wit, Reub. You'd better jest laugh when other folks do, 'thout trying to see why," replied the landlord, with a wink to his neighbor.

Brume, far from mollified by this suggestion, was still cudgelling his dull brain for a retort, when the door was thrown open and a smart young fellow, whip in hand, entered the room and strode up to the bar.

"A glass of toddy, Burroughs, as quick as you've a mind to make it. It's cold enough outside to freeze your mermaid's tail off. Don't you hear her screeching?"

The dismal groan of the sign vibrating upon its rusty pintles accompanied the question, and Reuben Brume, finding the laugh diverted from himself, gave up the desperate search for a retort, and asked, instead,

"Did you see anything of the stage, James?"

"Yes, it's lumbering into the village. I brought down a horse for Mr. Vaughn to ride home. It wasn't worth while to try wheels nor yet a sleigh, such going as we've got to-night."

"Is he coming in the stage?" asked the landlady, in some excitement.

"Yes. He drove the horses up three days ago, but said if it stormed bad he should come down in the stage and I was to meet him here with a cutter. Here they come."

A shout and the crack of a whip were heard at this moment, and the inmates of the bar-room rushed in a body out upon the stoop at the front door, in time to see the driver check his reeking horses and clamber stiffly from his box.

"It's some cold, Billings, ain't it?" suggested Burroughs.

"You put this old concern down to Wylde's to-night, and see if ye're as chirk when you git there as you be now," retorted the driver, grimly, while he threw open the coach door and turned down the step.

"Carrick. Stop for dinner," briefly announced he, and then leaving his horses to the stable boy, and his passengers to the landlord or to fate, he pushed through the group of idlers, and entering the deserted bar, mixed himself a stiff glass of spirits and water.

From the coach descended first a well-formed and handsome young man, apparently about twenty-five years old, who, nodding good-humoredly to the spectators, followed the driver into the house. Close behind him appeared the stooping figure, yellow face, and rounded shoulders of a tall man, who, slowly extricating himself from the coach, and rising to his full stature, remained an instant staring disconcertedly about him.

"Won't you walk in, sir?" asked the landlord, rubbing his hands and shivering a little. "A nice fire in the bar, and dinner all ready."

"This is the town of Carrick, is it?"

"Yes, sir, this is Carrick. Was you going to stop here?" And at the implied possibility the idlers paused in their retreat toward the fire, and gazed with revived interest upon the stranger, whom a lucky chance had perhaps delivered over to them.

"Yes. Is this the hotel?"

"Yes, sir," replied Burroughs, with a little hesitation. "The Mermaid's Cave, stage tavern, post-office, and hotel."

At this new assumption of dignity on the part of their magnate, some of the courtiers drew themselves up with a sense of increased consequence, some nudged each other with sly smiles, and the disaffected Brume openly remarked,

"Fust time I ever heerd the old tahvern called a ho-tel. Burroughs 'll be setting up for 'the gen'lemanly lan'lord' next."

At this moment the discordant tones of the fish-horn sounded again through the whirling snow, and Reuben, now left alone upon the stoop, paused a moment in doubt of the expediency of disobeying the summons. The supper hour, however, was already passed. To return now was to suffer all the penalties and reap none of the advantages of further delay, and after a momentary hesitation, Reuben, with a defiant grimace in the direction of his home, followed his comrades into the bar-room, and joined the silent ring about the stove, every man in it bending his entire attention to the conversation between the landlord and the stranger. Mr. Vaughn stood a little apart, questioning his groom as to the state of the roads, and the best mode of travelling them. At another time this interrogatory, now reduced to by-play, would have constituted an ample evening's entertainment for the frequenters of the Mermaid's Cave, but to attend to more than one thing at a time was never a fashion of the men of Carrick, and Mr Vaughn they had seen and heard before, while the stranger fell among them as a human victim to sharks long confined to a fish diet.

"Cragness! Why that's the old Vaughn place," said the landlord, just as Reuben Brume edged into the circle.

"Yes. I wish for a sleigh, horse, and careful driver to take me there immediately after dinner," said the stranger.

"But there ain't nobody living there now. The Square went off to Europe or somewhere last winter, and there's only an old man—old Laz'rus Graves—in the house."

"I know it. Can I have the sleigh?"

"Wa-al"—and Mr. Burroughs looked helplessly about the circle for competent counsel in this unprecedented case.

The courtiers stirred each in his place as expressing sympathy and interest, but no man yet ventured to suggest the appropriate question which should at once arrive at the point next to be ascertained, namely, the motive of this mysterious stranger in thus seeking conveyance to a deserted and lonely house, haunted, too, as every babe in Carrick could testify.

"Wa-al," repeated Mr. Burroughs, and again his rolling eyes traversed the circle. This time they fell upon the figure of Mr. Vaughn, who, having finished his instructions to the groom, now approached the fire. A brilliant idea illuminated the publican's brain.

"Here's Square Vaughn can tell you all about the old place," said he. "I guess you don't fairly know what sort of craft you're shipping in, agoing there, and maybe he'll give you some light. Square, this gentleman wants to go to Cragness to-night."

"Indeed?" And Mr. Vaughn, with somewhat cold politeness, turned to the stranger, who, in their long day's journey, had not offered one remark to him, or vouchsafed more than the curtest replies to his own attempts at conversation.

"I am afraid you will find the old place somewhat desolate on such a night as this," said he.

"Possibly. But I am not sensitive to such matters. Are there no horses to be hired here, can you tell me?"

"Why, yes. I suppose, Burroughs, you could let this gentleman have your own horse and a saddle, couldn't you? My man says the road is impassable for wheels or runners on account of the drift."

"Whitefoot ain't agoing out to-night," whispered a sepulchral voice from the kitchen door into the landlord's ear, who, starting a little, answered slowly,

"Wa-al, Square, I'd like to 'commodate the gentleman, of course, and I've got my own horse in the barn as you say, but I guess he'd better stop there to-night. I couldn't send no one to 'fetch him back, and like enough it'll storm worse to-morrow, and maybe the gentleman never would get to Cragness, and I'd be awful sorry to lose Whitefoot."

"I suppose, then, I must stay here until the storm is over," said the stranger, glancing somewhat ruefully about the dingy room.

"We'll 'commerdate you the best we can, sir, though winter time, so it's rather hard to have everything shipshape," said Burroughs, casting a dubious side-glance toward the kitchen door.

"I can suggest a better course, perhaps," interposed Mr. Vaughn, with a little hesitation, "if you will ride my servant's horse and accompany me to Bonniemeer, I shall be most happy to offer you a bed, and so soon as the roads are practicable, will send a man to show you the way to Cragness. Burroughs, you will let James ride Whitefoot, won't you? I promise you shall see the old nag safe to-morrow."

"Yes" echoed from behind the kitchen door, and "Yes," replied the landland, with some added phrase of confidence in the "Square's making it all right if anything came to the horse."

All eyes now turned upon the stranger. His first impulse was, evidently, to refuse Mr. Vaughn's proffered hospitality, but a second thought held him a moment irresolute, and he finally said,

"I thank you, sir, for your invitation, but it may make some difference to your feelings to know that I am John Gillies, heir to your late uncle, Reginald Vaughn."

The listeners gasped for breath. Such a mine of interest as was opened by this announcement sufficed to engulf all Carrick for many a day.

Mr. Vaughn smiled frankly, and extended his hand.

"Very happy to give you a neighbor's welcome, Mr. Gillies," said he; "and I only wish I could congratulate you on your accession to the property. But 'the home of my fathers,' as the school girls say, had never much attraction for me, and I infinitely prefer you should be its proprietor to owning it myself. You will come home with me, I trust?"

"Thank you. Yes," said Mr. Gillies, almost cordially.

"Then we will set out at once and dine at Bonniemeer," suggested Vaughn.

"But you'd best take something to keep out the cold, gentlemen," interposed the landlord. "The iron's in the fire, and we'll have some flip ready before you'll get your horses round."

"It's churlish to refuse a stirrup cup, I suppose," said the younger gentleman, laughingly, and Mr. Gillies gravely bowing, said not a word, but watched somewhat curiously, while the landlord drawing a tankard of ale, mingled with it sugar, spirits, and spices, and then pulling from the glowing coals a short iron bar fitted with a wooden handle, stirred the compound in the tankard, until a rich spicy odor from the heated liquid rose in clouds, and caused the souls of the courtiers to momentarily retire from eyes and ears to centre in their noses.

Each gentleman drained a glass of the flip thus compounded, and the host joined them in another, saying, as he raised it to his lips,

"Here's wishing you good healths, sirs."

"A prosperous journey were more to the purpose just now, Burroughs," said Mr. Vaughn, gaily. "Are the horses ready, James?"

"All ready, sir," replied the groom, rather sulkily.

"Then get your own share of the flip, and follow us," said his master, and the two gentlemen mounting the impatient horses held by the stable boy at the door, rode away as rapidly as might be, while James, upon the landlord's broken-winded nag, followed as best he could, comforting himself with several remarks not to be here repeated. The idlers of the Mermaid's Cave attentively watched them out of sight, and then returned to the bar-room to digest the events of the evening, aided by Billings, who had decided the weather and the roads to be unpropitious to farther progress that night.

CHAPTER V.
THE OMEN OF THE DUNES.

As the closing door of the bar-room shut off the stream of ruddy light, which had hospitably marshalled the travellers to their saddles, John Gillies looked about him in dismay. No such scene as this had ever entered his experience.

The twinkling lights of the hamlet already lay behind him, in front, the dark expanse of an angry sea, its breakers thundering on the beach, and rolling up in great white crescents to his horses' feet, or in their retreat dragging down to the depths the rattling pebbles the next wave was to return. To the right lay a long range of sand dunes glimmering ghostly white through the darkness, while the wind chasing the storm through their mimic gorges and shifting tunnels, and up and down their treacherous slopes, shrieked and yelled in its awful glee. Across the scene a broad white track bordering the black waters showed the crescent curve of the beach, a sort of terrene milky way.

The snow now turning to sleet, beat furiously into the faces of the travellers with a feel like powdered ice. No such scene had John Gillies encountered in all his intermural rambles, and he was inwardly strengthening himself against an impertinent doubt of the wisdom of his own course, when his companion shouted in his ear,

"A wild night, even for the coast."

"Very likely," said Mr. Gillies, curtly.

"I am taking you by the beach. It's a little more open to the storm, but my man says the other road is drifted very badly," continued the master of Bonniemeer.

"I leave it entirely to you, sir," replied his guest, and neither the weather nor his company encouraging further conversation, Mr. Vaughn relapsed into silence, broken only by an occasional phrase of encouragement to his horse, while for nearly an hour the three men struggled on, often reduced to a foot pace by the violence of the storm, now directly opposed to them, and blowing at times with such fury that the horses, restrained from their natural impulse to turn from it, reared impatiently, as if to overleap a tangible obstacle.

The night, now fairly set in, was as dark as is ever known in the immediate vicinity of a large body of water, and it was only by keeping close behind his leader that the stranger was able to follow the road as it finally left the coast and struck in among the sand dunes.

Suddenly, Mr. Vaughn's horse swerved, paused, and uttered a shrill neigh.

"What now, Thor!" exclaimed the rider, as he bent from the saddle to search for the object of the creature's alarm or surprise.

Something like a garment partially buried in a snow-wreath, rose and fell stiffly as a blast of wind swept through the dunes.

"Good heavens! some one is lying here, frozen perhaps. What is to be done?" exclaimed Mr. Vaughn, throwing himself from his horse.

Mr. Gillies unclosed his lips to suggest a watchman, but recollecting himself, was silent. James and Whitefoot were far in the rear.

"It's a woman, I should think, and she has something—yes, it's a child—wrapped in her cloak. Do you hear me, sir; here's a poor creature and her baby freezing to death at your horse's feet!" exclaimed Vaughn, impetuously, as his comrade quietly began to dismount.

"I understand, but I don't know what to advise. There is no station-house near by, I suppose, where we might apply for help."

"Station-house! good heavens, no! My own house is the nearest; but how are we to get her there?"

"I cannot suggest," said Mr. Gillies, calmly, and in the darkness lost the look of disgust bestowed upon him by his companion.

"She's gone, poor creature, I'm afraid," and the younger man softly raised one of the stiff hands, and then replaced it beneath the cloak.

"James! He's out of sight and hearing," continued he, impatiently. "Well, Mr. Gillies, if you will mount again I'll give you the child to carry, and contrive to get the woman upon my own horse. They can't be left here."

"I cannot carry tne child. I never touched one," said Mr. Gillies, in solemn alarm.

"O, very well. I shall wait for my man to take it, then. I do not know that he is more experienced than yourself, but I presume he will not refuse to make the attempt, when life and death are at stake."

"A plan suggests itself to me," said John Gillies, slowly.

"Indeed; what is it?" asked his companion, with scarcely-concealed disdain.

"I will stay here with the woman until your servant comes up, when I will direct him to place her in front of him. You, meantime, will hasten home with the child, as every moment of continued exposure is a chance of life lost to it."

"You will stay here? Possibly, James may not come up at all. I shouldn't wonder if that old nag had foundered, and he walked back to town," said Mr. Vaughn, doubtfully.

"In that case, I shall, after satisfying myself that no life remains in this body, leave it, and trust to the horse to carry me to his home. I have read that their instinct in such cases is a sure guide."

"But why not let me now put the body in front of you, and come at once?" asked Mr. Vaughn, in a more amicable tone.

"I do not wish to touch it," replied the impracticable Gillies.

"Then I will accept your own proposition. I dare say the horse will come straight home, and, as you say, the life of this child depends on immediate relief."

Mr. Gillies, as his sole reply, seated himself in the snow at a short distance from the body.

"Good heavens, man! you'll be asleep in five minutes, and freeze to death in fifteen. I did not actually think of leaving you, of course; but you are so very self-possessed I could not help a little trial to see if you were in earnest."

"I am always in earnest," said John Gillies, solemnly; and Vaughn, with an imperceptible shrug, replied:

"How delightful! But here is James; now we are all right at last. Here, James, come and put this poor creature's body in front of me, and then take the child yourself. Who is that behind you?"

"Thomas, sir. He was sent down to Carrick just after I started, and got to the tavern a few minutes after we left. So he came along the beach."

"Was sent!" exclaimed Vaughn, in a changed voice. "Is anything wrong at home?"

"Mrs. Vaughn is sick, sir," said the groom, hesitating; "and Thomas says Mrs. Rhee seemed a good deal frightened when she sent him."

"Thomas! what message did Mrs. Rhee send to me?" asked the master, impatiently.

"She said, sir, ride for life if you wanted to see your wife again," said Thomas, huskily.

A deep groan burst from Vaughn's lips, and, throwing himself upon his horse, he struck spurs into his sides with an energy that made the fiery creature plunge and rear, and then dart forward as if borne by the wind itself.

Even in that moment of agony, however, the humane and hospitable instincts of the man asserted themselves.

"James," cried he, "I depend upon you to bring the woman, the child, and this gentleman safely to Bonniemeer."

The next instant he was gone.

CHAPTER VI.
BONNIEMEER.

WITH some difficulty, the grooms succeeded in placing the body of the woman upon one of the horses, and while one man mounted and held it there, the other, with the little child in his arms, regained his own saddle, and, calling upon Mr. Gillies to follow closely, they took the same road their master had done.

The violence of the storm would have rendered communication difficult had it been desired, and not a word was exchanged until, at a sharp turn of the road, the servants pausing to see that the stranger was close beside them, turned in at a gate sheltered and nearly concealed by a dense growth of evergreens.

At some distance, and a little higher than this entrance, appeared the glancing lights of a large building dimly outlined against the stormy sky.

A few moments later the horses paused at the foot of some broad steps, and James, with the infant, carefully dismounting, carried it in at the hall door, and presently returned followed by two or three female servants, who, with much outcry and many questions, helped him to take the body of the woman from the stiffened arms of Thomas, who avowed himself "chilled to the marrow," and carried it into the house.

Then, and not till then, James, who had privately resented more than he thought safe to express Mr. Gillies's resolute non-interference in this work of humanity, said,

"Will you get off your horse, sir, and walk into the house. I will speak to Mrs. Rhee, for I suppose Mr. Vaughn won't be able to see any one to-night."

Mr. Gillies remained immovable.

"I will give any man here a dollar, or as much more as we may decide upon, to show me the way to my own house of Cragness," said he, at length.

"Cragness, sir! There isn't a man or horse about the place that could reach Cragness to-night. There's no choice but for you to stop here. Won't you please walk into the house," replied James, with respectful impatience.

With undisguised reluctance, the visitor dismounted and followed his guide up the steps.

"I had rather go to my own house," persisted he.

To this remark James offered no reply; but, pushing open the heavy door, ushered the guest into a hall, whose warmth, light, and the fragrance from some large flowering shrubs, offered a charming contrast to the wild weather without.

The door of a room at the right of the entrance stood open, and James pushed it a little wider.

"Walk into the library, sir, and sit down," said he. "I will speak to the housekeeper."

"I am sorry I could not go to Cragness," murmured John Gillies, as he advanced into the quiet room and looked about him. The lamps were not lighted, but a fire of bituminous coal blazed in the grate and fitfully illuminated the frescoes of the ceiling, the rare marbles and dim, lettered bindings of volumes rarer than any marbles, the carved blazonry above the fire-place, the moss-green carpet, and furniture.

"A man of letters and art—a proud man and a luxurious," commented shrewd John Gillies, as his eyes wandered over these details. "And not a musical instrument of any sort," added he, with a hard smile of contempt, as he turned his back upon the room, and stood looking into the glowing coals.

"Shall I show you to your room, Mr. Gillies?" said a voice at his elbow.

He turned, and found a woman beside him. A woman, perhaps thirty-five years old, with one of the most singular faces he had ever seen. Not a trace of color lay beneath the pale olive of the skin, except a deep scarlet in the lips. The large eyes, dark and full as those of a stag, had swept one rapid glance at him when she first spoke, but fell before his own could fairly meet them. Heavy masses of black hair were swept away from a low forehead, and half covered the small ears. The figure was slight and graceful, the hands small, the dress quiet, but handsome. It was in none of these, however, that the peculiarity of this woman's appearance lay; it was in the latent expression of the whole, a sort of terrible intimation of something just beneath the surface, hidden for the moment by an unnatural quiet, but ever watching for a moment of weakness in its guardian to burst from her control.

Something of this the acute physiognomist, John Gillies, felt, but failed at the moment to reduce the perception to thought.

"Shall I show you to your room, sir? I am Mrs. Rhee, Mr. Vaughn's housekeeper," said the woman, finding her first appeal disregarded.

"Thank you. I am sorry to intrude upon strangers at such a time as this, but am informed it would be impossible to reach my own house to-night."

"Quite, sir. It is a terrible night for any one to leave a happy home and go all alone into the storm."

She shivered convulsively as she spoke, and moved toward the door.

Both words and manner were strange, and catching rather at their hidden than their obvious meaning, Mr. Gillies said,

"The woman we found to-night, will she recover?"

"She is dead," said the housekeeper, briefly, as she began to ascend the stairs.

"And Mrs. Vaughn?" asked Gillies, doubtfully.

Mrs. Rhee paused, and clung a moment to the banister before she answered, in a whisper,

"She is dying."

"A terrible night for any one to leave a happy home and go all alone into the storm," echoed through John Gillies's brain, but he said nothing, and the housekeeper recovering from her sudden emotion, passed swiftly up the stairs and threw open the door of a bed-chamber, warmed, lighted, and luxurious.

"You will find a bell at the head of the bed, sir, and dinner will be served in half an hour," said his attendant, briefly, as she closed the door.

The guest stood looking after her a moment, and then drawing a chair to the blazing fire, seated himself and stared absently into its depths.

"A terrible night," murmured he; "I wonder if what is left of those two women will know what sort of a night it is. I wonder if that housekeeper was very fond of her mistress, or if she is what they call nervous. I wonder if this man sitting before this fire is the man who twenty-four hours ago had never been out of the city where he was born, had never seen one of these curious people. I wonder if they keep going on in this way all the time."

Half an hour later, the servant sent to summon Mr. Gillies to dinner, found him sitting in the same position still staring vacantly into the glowing coals.

"Mr. Vaughn begs to be excused from dinner, sir. He cannot leave his wife," said Mrs. Rhee's subdued voice, as the guest entered the dining-room.

The dining-room door again opened, and a small man with quick bright eyes, and a close mouth, entered, and advanced toward the table.

"Mr. Gillies, Doctor Roland," said the housekeeper, briefly.

The two men bowed, and seated themselves at table. Some trifling conversation upon the weather, and upon the peculiarities of the sea-shore in winter, ensued, but the housekeeper did not speak, except in performing the duties of the table, nor did either food or wine pass her lips. Only as they were about to rise, Mr. Gillies noticed that she asked for a glass of ice water, and drank it with feverish rapidity.

Returning at last to his own room, he paused on hearing satified grons from a corridor just beyond, and, looking down it, was startled to see a dark shapeless figure lying upon the floor at the farther end, and writhing to and fro as if in agony. Cautiously approaching until he stood directly above it, Mr. Gillies still failed in the dim light to discover more than that it appeared to be a woman suffering intensely.

"What's the matter?" asked he, hesitatingly. "Can I help you in any way?"

The sounds of distress became more violent, although evidently suppressed as much as possible, but still the figure neither rose nor spoke.

Gillies, unwilling either to abandon or to urge his proffer of sympathy, stood irresolute, when a door softly opened, and Mrs. Rhee appeared, closing it behind her.

"Chloe!" said she, sternly, and stooping down, she whispered a few words, and then said aloud,

"Get up, Chloe, and go to my room to wait till you are called. Mr. Gillies, I will show you the way to your own chamber."

"I know the way to the chamber I was in before dinner," said Gillies, composedly. "I came here to see what was the matter with this person."

He paused, as he spoke, to look at the uncouth figure now standing erect before him. It was that of an intensely black negro woman, dwarfed in stature, and so malformed that her head, bent upon her breast, could only be turned from side to side, forcing her in addressing any person to give them a sidelong upward glance indescribably elfish and peculiar.

"She is Mrs. Vaughn's nurse, and she feels—"

Mrs. Rhee paused abruptly. The negro woman who had moved away a few steps, turned impulsively, and catching the housekeeper's skirts, buried her face in them with a dumb moan of anguish more pitiful than words. For an instant Mrs. Rhee stooped as if to throw her arms about her, but restraining herself, said imperiously,

"Come with me, Chloe. Mr. Gillies—"

"I have no intention of farther intrusion upon the domestic affairs of this house, ma'am," said Gillies, coldly. "I should not have been guilty of it in this in this instance had not humanity—"

But Mrs. Rhee had not paused for more than his first words. Already she had disappeared through a door at the end of the corridor, followed by Chloe.

Mr. Gillies walked meditatively to his own room, and gave no further clue to his feelings that night, than to say as he stepped into bed. "I wish I could have gone to Cragness."

CHAPTER VII.

THE HOUSEKEEPER'S HAND.

THE next morning dawned clear and cold. Mr. Gillies, arising at his usual early hour, approached the window with some curiosity, and very few preconceived ideas either of the situation of Bonniemeer or of scenery in general, his experiences in this direction having been limited to half a dozen ascents to the cupola of the State House of his native city.

Fancy the revelation to such a man of a view like that lying now beneath his eyes!

At the right, miles of evergreen forest " clothed the wold and met the sky," its dense green flecked with the snow clinging to the level branches, and softened by the snake-like tracery of the naked birches fringing its margin. To the left abruptly rose a rocky headland, crag piled upon crag in majestic outline, tossing scornfully from its broad shoulders the snow which gently sought to cover it, and raising its fearless crest to meet the morning sun that paused to crown it brother monarch, while yet the valley lay in twilight.

Across the front swept the ocean, curving broadly to the horizon line, and giving the idea of limitless extent, the satisfaction of soul only to be obtained by the introduction of ocean into a picture.

The satisfaction of soul! for if the horizon closes with a mountain, a plain, a broken country, who has not felt the impulse to place himself just at the vanishing-point and see what lies beyond? It is an unfinished continuity, and excites more craving than content. But the gaze, which after traversing leagues and leagues of shining water, broken only by the grand curve of the globe itself, sinks at last into the vague brightness of the horizon line, the dissolving-point where sea is sky and sky is sea, lingers there content. Beyond lies space, eternity, God, and humanity quails from the encounter.

Behind that crag at the left hand, although Mr. Gillies did not know it, lay his future home. The wood at the right sheltered the hamlet of Carrick, and the beach lay glistening a mile from the window whence the post-office clerk took his first look at Nature.

A servant presently summoned him to breakfast. At the head of the table sat Mrs. Rhee, and John Gillies's first impression in looking at her was, that she had shrunk farther into herself since he saw her last. Surely her eyes were not so hollow, her lips so thin, her temples so sunken, the night before. Even the hands, busy among the teacups, looked withered and pinched, and the observer noted that a ring upon the first finger, which he had watched sparkling in the lamplight at dinner-time, was now slipped round by the weight of the stone, as if it suddenly had grown too large.

The table was laid for two only, and the housekeeper, motioning Mr. Gillies to the vacant place, said, in a low voice,

"Mr. Vaughn will not come to breakfast, and the doctor has gone."

"And Mrs. Vaughn—"

"She died at midnight."

Mrs. Rhee turned away her face as she spoke, but Gillies could see the deadly pallor that overspread even the slender throat and little ear, the quiver of suppressed anguish that trembled through every curve of the graceful form, and while he looked and wondered, the phrase of the night before went sighing through his mind like the burden of a half-forgotten song.

"A terrible night to leave a happy home and go out all alone into the storm."

The meal was a silent and a slight one, Mrs. Rhee merely performing the duties of the table, while her guest, naturally abstemious, found his appetite materially lessened not only by his situation, but by the absence of his accustomed viands.

As they rose from the table, a servant entered with a message from Mr. Vaughn, desiring the housekeeper to attend him, and Gillies, awaiting her return, strode impatiently up and down the room, asking himself again and again, what concern of his was the grief and loss oppressing this household, and how or why it should become his own so much as it had done.

The servant quietly cleared the table, and he was left alone. Throwing himself into a chair beside the window, he sat drumming upon the sash, when the door opened noiselessly, and Mrs. Rhee entered. Gillies's quick glance involuntarily searched her face for the result of her interview with her master, and found it in a renewal of the strange expression he had noticed at their first interview. The same concentrated firmness about the mouth, the same painful constraint upon the brow, while the secret of the dilated eyes looked from them so eagerly, lay so close beneath the surface that John Gillies bent his brow and held his breath, waiting to see it fully revealed. But, conscious of his observation, the woman turned hastily away, and approaching the fire, held her hands so close to the blaze that it caught upon the lace about her wrists. She neither started nor made any exclamation, and when Gillies, springing toward her, caught and wrapped her hands in a cloth snatched from the table, she only murmured indifferent thanks as for a courtesy that might as well have been omitted. But the incident had diverted those searching eyes from her face, and, conscious of the relief, she spoke hastily:

"Mr. Vaughn desires me to apologize for him. He does not feel able to see any one, but hopes that you will make use of the house, the servants, and the horses at your pleasure."

"I am much obliged to Mr. Vaughn, and I should be glad of a conveyance and a guide to my own house as soon as possible, if you will order it," said Gillies, with undisguised satisfaction.

Mrs. Rhee rang the bell and gave orders that James and two horses should attend Mr. Gillies immediately.

"You will be obliged to ride, sir," said she. "The roads are not broken for a sleigh yet."

"Very well, ma'am. I came here on a horse and I presume it will not be more dangerous or disagreeable to ride to-day than it was last night. I do not like it, but can endure it," replied Gillies, reflectively.

"Mrs. Vaughn's funeral will be the day after to-morrow," continued the housekeeper, in a voice whose measured coldness betrayed the emotion it covered but did not conceal. "The woman who was found on the beach will be buried at the same time, and Mr. Vaughn will be gratified by your presence."

"By no means!" exclaimed Gillies, hastily. "I never went to a funeral in my life, and I probably never shall."

The housekeeper replied by a look of some displeasure, and Gillies abruptly inquired,

"Did the child die, also?"

The look of displeasure changed to one of surprise as Mrs. Rhee coldly inquired:

"Do you refer, sir, to Mr. Vaughn's daughter?"

"Good Heavens, no!" exclaimed Gillies. "I thought—that is to say, ma'am, I have been informed that Mr. Vaughn had no children. I was asking about the dead woman's baby."

"Mrs. Vaughn died in giving birth to an infant," said the housekeeper, fixing her ominous eyes upon him, and dropping the words from her white lips as if they had frozen them.

"But, the other child," persisted Gillies.

"Mr. Vaughn will keep it to be educated with his own daughter—he says." And with the last words the speaker's voice dropped to an accent of bitter scorn and jealousy, as incomprehensible to her listener's ear as any other of the mysteries surrounding this strange house and its inmates. He stood for a moment looking her steadily in the face, and then, glancing out of the window, said, abruptly:

"I see the man and the horses. Good morning, ma'am."

"Good morning, sir," replied the housekeeper, coldly, and with no more leave-taking, Mr. Gillies hastened to the outer air, and in reply to James's respectful salutation and remark upon the coldness of the weather, he muttered,

"Cold enough, but better than in there. Two dead women, two babies, and a witch for a housekeeper. Ugh!"

CHAPTER VIII.
"CRAGNESS, SIR."

THE new proprietor looked up, and found himself at the foot of a considerable eminence standing boldly out into the sea, which, in the high spring tides, washed three sides of it, and had year by year encroached upon its area, until now its farther advance was resisted by the solid granite foundations of the little peninsula, washed bare of all disguise, and frowning defiantly down at the waters which dashed angrily upon it, and withdrew only to return yet more vehemently.

Upon the crest of the promontory stood a low stone building of peculiar architecture, the main body of the house describing a parallelogram of no considerable extent, but throwing out toward the sea a long and narrow gallery, terminating in a circular tower of only one story in height, with a domed roof.

The thick walls and narrow windows, combined with the chill air of abandonment hanging over all, gave the place a peculiarly gloomy appearance.

John Gillies sat on his horse perfectly quiet, and surveyed his inheritance and future home.

A mighty struggle was going on in his mind. This dreary house, this savage scenery, this imperative mystery, all were as diametrically opposed to any wish he had ever formed, as to any experience he had ever known. The forty prosaic and methodical years of his life rose up before him, each one summoning him to turn his back upon these strange new claims, and to return to the life that he knew, and the assured future it promised him.

On the other hand lay the obstinate pride of the man, his stubborn adherence to any course or opinion he had deliberately adopted, and with these mingled, though Heaven only knows whence in that sterile nature it had sprung, an impulse to abandon himself to this mystery so unexpectedly involving him, to plunge into the new life and new interests, alien to his habits though they were, with the same energy and dominance of will, which had for years given him the first place among those with whom he had been associated.

Two minutes John Gillies sat in the sharp north wind, staring up at the old house of Cragness, and in those two minutes he had passed the crisis of his life, and decided not only his own destiny, but that of a number of other persons.

Or was it perhaps that his destiny decided him?

James meantime had ridden up the hill, and was now knocking vigorously at a door in the back of the house.

"It's no good to go to the front, sir," said he, as Mr. Gillies drew rein beside him. "There's a door there, but it's never opened, and old Lazarus burrows this way somewhere, I believe. Here he comes."

Slow steps were heard approaching along the passage, and then the harsh cry of rusty bolts withdrawn by a feeble hand. The door presently opened, and an old man, small of stature, with long white hair, faint blue eyes, and a skin blanched as if by long exclusion from the sun and air, stood upon the threshold.

"How are you, Lazarus Graves?" said James, heartily. "Here's the new master of Cragness, Mr. Gillies, come to take possession. Stir yourself, old man, and show him in from this freezing cold."

The old man looked attentively in the groom's face until he had finished, and then said,

"Mr. Reginald is not at home to-day. You had better call again."

"Not at home! No, nor he won't be, old Lazarus. Don't you remember Mr. Robinson came down here last week, and told you he was dead, and had left the place to Mr. Gillies? This is the gentleman, and you had better let him in, and get a fire and some dinner going as fast as possible."

The dim blue eyes wandered painfully from one strange face to the other, and then suddenly overflowed with tears.

"Mr. Reginald dead!" said he. "Why, I carried him in my arms when he was a baby and I had boys of my own. O, no, he couldn't be dead, and poor old Lazarus Graves left alive."

"He's more broke than I thought, sir," said James aside to Gillies, who stood staring perplexedly at the old man. "It's the news of his master's death has been working on him. He was quite smart before that. Hadn't you better come back to Bonniemeer, sir? I am sure Mr. Vaughn would wish it. You can't be comfortable here."

"To Bonniemeer!" repeated Gillies, quickly. "Certainly not, James. I shall do very well here, I have no doubt, if this old man can be got to let us in."

"That's easy done," said the self-assured groom, stepping into the passage and taking Lazarus by the arm.

"Come, father," said he, "take us to the fire wherever you keep it. This is the kitchen, isn't it?"

And he pushed open the door of a cavernous brick-floored apartment, in a corner of whose wide chimney a handful of fire withered away, leaving but small impression upon the sepulchral air. A broken chair, and a simmering saucepan hinted at the occupancy and uses of the place.

"Cold comfort, sir, I'm afraid," said James, standing aside for Mr. Gillies to enter. "But I suppose there isn't a spark of fire in the house besides."

"Fire! There's fire in the library. Mr. Reginald might come any time you know, so I'm always ready, and so is his dinner," interposed Lazarus, eagerly.

"Well, then, suppose he has come, that's all," said James. "Here is Mr. Reginald, a little changed by his life in foreign parts, but wanting the fire and the dinner just the same as if you remembered him."

The old man looked bewildered. Gillies, ill-pleased with the position, but hesitating how to assume his proper place in his own house and in the conversation, frowned slightly, and moved toward the fire. The eyes of the old servant followed him, and returned dissatisfied to the smiling and assured face of the groom, who, without being in the least superior to his condition of life, had the art, so useful in every condition, of organization.

"It's all right, I tell you, Lazarus," said he. "There's Mr. Reginald come back to stay awhile, and you must just go on as you used to when he was here before. Now bring us to the library."

The old man shook his white head dubiously, but turned to leave the kitchen. James approached Mr. Gillies.

"I hope you won't think me forward, sir, but I have known Lazarus Graves a good many years, and I thought perhaps I could humor him into doing as he'd ought to better than you could. He's so broken that I don't believe he really knows whether you are Mr. Reginald Vaughn or not."

"He's crazy. I don't like crazy people. It's a very irregular way of doing business to make him think I am some one else. Besides Mr. Reginald Vaughn is dead, and I don't like using a dead man's name," muttered Gillies, discontentedly, as he walked toward the door.

James shrugged his shoulders, and followed.

Pursuing the echoing foot-falls of their guide, the two men traversed a long passage, mounted some steps, and found him unlocking a small door deep sunk in the thickness of the wall.

"Hope you'll excuse me, sir, but I wouldn't let the old fellow keep the key of this door," whispered James. "He'll lock you in, and forget all about it, and may be die in a fit and leave you to starve."

Gillies nodded, and, the door being at last opened, followed the old janitor into a dark passage, which he concluded to be the gallery noticed as connecting the rotunda with the main building.

It was pierced with several windows, closed by shutters, and admitting the light only at small openings in the form of crosses. At the end of this gallery, Lazarus Graves unlocked another door, and, throwing it open, said in a cheery voice,

"There, Mr. Reginald, I've kept it dusted and aired, and since the cold came, I've had a fire in it mostly, to keep the chill off in case you came sudden.'

Without reply, Mr. Gillies passed in at the open door, and looked about him.

The room was large and lofty. As the exterior promised, the form was circular, the ceiling domed.

Walls and ceiling alike were panelled with a rich dark wood, and the floor was of oak, partially covered with a heavy Eastern carpet. In the stone fireplace smouldered a fragment of drift-wood, relic of some forgotten wreck, above it hung rusty arms surrounding an heraldic device like that holding a similar position at Bonniemeer. Opposite to the door the circular form of the room was broken by a deep bay window containing a small table, a chair, and footstool.

Approaching this window, Gillies saw that it faced, and, indeed, overhung the sea, being thrown out beyond the face of the precipice from whose verge sprung the outer wall of the tower.

"I've kept your chair in the old place, Mr. Reginald," piped Lazarus. "You didn't use to like to have it moved, so I've been careful, and that's the same book you left on the table. I'd a notion once to put it up, but thought better on it."

Gillies raised the little volume from the reading-desk beside him. It was "The Philosophy of the Supernatural." He threw it down, and shivering a little, walked toward the fire.

"I've dusted the books once in a while, but the rats have been at them some, I'm afraid," pursued old Lazarus, too much engrossed in discharging his conscience of its trust to look attentively at his recovered master. Approaching the wall, he drew back first one panel and then another, showing that the space between them and the outer wall had been finished in sunken book-cases, well filled with volumes, most of them in the dark leather or ghastly vellum of the antique bindings.

"That will do," said Mr. Gillies, speaking for the first time. "You can go now, both of you."

Lazarus Graves turned, and fixed his watery eyes upon the speaker with a startled expression, and the slow cloud of perplexity settled again upon his face. He turned to James, who, standing respectfully near the door, waited to be dismissed.

"What did you say about Mr. Reginald, young man?" asked he.

"Why," said James, slowly, "what I meant to tell you was, that Mr. Reginald isn't coming back any more, but that this gentleman is in his place. Mr. Gillies is his name."

The old man shook his head positively.

"He'll come back," said he. "His last words were, 'Keep everything just as it is, old Lazarus, and I'll be back some day before you know it.' And I've been very careful to keep everything as it was, and he'll be back, you may depend upon it."

"Well, till he comes, he wants you to treat this gentleman just as if it were himself," said James, slightly changing his tactics. "You're to do the best you can, and treat Mr. Gillies as if he were the master."

"Did he send that word?" asked Lazarus, hesitatingly.

"Yes, just those very words," replied the groom, promptly.

"O well, then, its all right," and the cloud vanished from the troubled old face, as Lazarus hobbled out of the room, and returned to his kitchen.

"Can I do anything for you at Carrick, Mr. Gillies?" asked James, with the door in his hand. "I shall be there with Burroughs's horse this afternoon."

Mr. Gillies considered a moment, and then said, "You may ask the landlord to send me some provisions at the same time with my trunks, and you may ask if there is any person not an idiot or a lunatic who will come here and do the necessary work of the house."

"A man or woman, sir?" asked James, innocently.

"A man, of course," replied Gillies, promptly, adding, under his breath, "A woman indeed!"

"Yes, sir; I will see to it. Good-morning, sir."

"Good-morning, and here, James, is something for yourself."

"No, I thank you, sir. Mr. Vaughn pays me well, and never wants any of us to take presents. Good-morning." And James left the room with quite the air of a Brutus.

CHAPTER IX.

RUYLLYE AOL OLUDLU.

LEFT alone, Mr. Gillies's first movement was to fasten the door, his next to open every one of the sliding panels and narrowly examine the recess within, to make sure that none of them covered a hidden entrance to the room. Then he seated himself in the reading chair occupying the bay window and looked out. It was like looking from the windows of a ship in mid ocean, for, owing to the peculiar construction of the opening, no sign of land was visible from it; only a world of waters stretching wide and blue to the horizon, with the pale gold of a winter sun flecking their surface and glittering on their white-maned crests.

John Gillies looked long and earnestly, then sadly shook his head.

"I doubt if I ever like it," muttered he, and turned the chair with its back to the window. Then, in a reluctant fashion, as one who approaches an imperative but repulsive duty, he drew a note case from his pocket and selected from its contents a paper carefully folded, and docketed

"LETTER OF INSTRUCTIONS FROM R. VAUGHN."

Spreading this upon the table before him, Mr. Gillies slowly read—but not aloud, for, to have afforded gratuitous information upon his affairs even to the walls and the sea, would have been to do violence to his nature—these words:

You will probably be much surprised, Mr. John Gillies, at finding yourself appointed my heir, and the explanation I am about to give of my choice, will leave you as bewildered as before; nevertheless, it would defeat my own purpose were I to be more explicit.

Several years ago, when I returned from Europe and took possession of my meagre patrimony of Cragness, I found my brother Egbert comfortably established at his seat of Bonniemeer, and happy in his family and position. The fraternal friendship that sprung up between us was pleasanter than I can say, to me, a man without ties of family or affection other than those binding me to him and his. I made a home of his house, and resolved in my own mind to bequeath my small property to one of his children.

This state of things endured for years, and then in one day these relations and this determination were destroyed. I withdrew to Cragness, and have lived there until now, a lonely and unhappy man. My motive in thus destroying the happiness of my own life has remained up to this moment a mystery to all connected with it. My brother, in trying to solve it, met with so decided a repulse that he left me in displeasure, and, with the implacable spirit of our race, never allowed himself, from that day to the day of his death, to again approach the subject or to exhibit any desire for a renewal of the brotherly intimacy whose loss was nearly as severe to him as to me.

To you, John Gillies, I give the explanation I refused to my nearest friend. I had discovered a secret relating to our family affairs whose announcement would have ruined at a blow all that fair structure whose corner-stones were my brother's honor, his wife's peace, their children's future. Should I have been the one to bring desolation to the home that had opened to me with such welcome and such promise? And yet might I keep this thing to myself and feel that the traditional honor of the Vaughns had suffered no taint?

For years I have vainly sought in my own heart for an answer to these questions, and yet they remain unsolved. While I have waited, Time has moved steadily on. My brother is dead, his wife is dead, of all the pretty children who used to group about my knee only two remain, but those two stand in their father's place, and to them I still owe the duty I owed to him.

I feel that my own departure draws nigh, and the question that was too mighty for the vigor of manhood is not to be solved by the feeble and timorous mind of age. I dare not carry the secret I have discovered to that other world where I may meet those who will demand account of it; I dare not speak it out and bring dishonor and perplexity to my brother's house. I have decided to commit it to Destiny, and I choose you as the agent of Destiny. Why you, why exactly you and no other man, are the man I choose as this agent, is another secret belonging only to myself and to you, and its solution is bound up with that of the great and principal one which has tortured me to my death, and which I now bequeath to you couched in a cipher peculiar to my own family and unknown beyond it:

EDAOLU OE OLUDLUV.

In the interpretation of these three words, you have the clue to a mystery so portentous that it has crushed my life beneath its weight, and now haunts my death-bed with a terrible doubt of my own guiltlessness in so long withholding it.

And yet I cannot speak it out; I cannot. Take it as I give it you, John Gillies, and with it take the consciousness that, folded in this mystery, you hold the peace, the honor, the comfort, the very life and name of a proud and ancient family. Remember that you, of all men, are the one best fitted for this responsibility, and it was only when I decided to find and confide in you that even death seemed a possible end to my entanglement; for, as I before said, I should never have dared to carry it to meet those who wait for me beyond the dark river.

You will not refuse me, you dare not, for it is from the grave I speak to you, and charge it upon you as a living man to obey the voice of the dead. Accept my bequest, accept my secret, and both under these conditions:

You are to make Cragness your home, spending the most of your time there, and using the library as your usual sitting-room.

You are to make the most faithful endeavor to compass the secret partially confided to you, and, if discovered, you are to use it in the manner which honestly seems best to your own mind, or at your option to destroy all evidence of it, and allow matters to remain as destiny has arranged them.

You are upon no account to confide any particular of these arrangements to any member of the Vaughn family, although you are allowed to use your own judgment in selecting an adviser outside of that circle; your natural reticence of disposition being guarantee that this permission will not be abused.

If you wish for such help as is to be found in a history of my family, you may obtain it from either member of the firm of Jones, Brown & Robinson, our solicitors for many years.

As to your testamentary disposition of the property bequeathed by me to you, I say nothing more than that I shall expect it to be guided by the result of your researches.

And now I leave the matter to Destiny and to you. If the infirm purpose and vacillating will which have been my bane through life have misled me at the last, may God pardon me and inspire my successor with more wisdom. REGINALD VAUGHN.

"In this room," muttered Gillies, finishing and folding the letter. Then he rose and surveyed the room as an athlete measures the foe with whom he is about to grapple in deadly conflict. A room of mysteries, he felt. A room whose every object looked at him with wary eyes and close-shut mouth, as who should say, "I have the secret, and I shall keep it." A look answering line for line to the stubborn determination of his own face, and, indeed, as room and man stood confronted, an observer could not fail to perceive one of those subtle likenesses by no means unusual between men and things, resulting now in attraction, now in repulsion. In the present instance, the relation threatened to become antagonistic, for the stubborn and reticent man demanding the secret which the equally stubborn and reticent room refused to yield, would inevitably come to hate the thing that too successfully resisted him, and a room so personal as this library of Cragness would be at no loss for means to make itself odious to the man who defied it.

Some vague perception of this strange relation between himself and the place must have stirred in John Gillies's own mind, when, with clenched hand and frowning brow he turned his cold eyes once more to every side, and muttered,

"I'll have it yet!"

A sudden chill seemed to fall at the words from roof and walls, and in at the broad sea-window. An involuntary shiver ran through the flesh and blood which it assailed; but the man's will neither shook or faltered.

Striding to the fire-place, he threw another fragment of the old wreck upon the embers, and then standing upon the hearth, his back to the room, applied himself to seriously consider the heraldic achievement before him, an object to which he had hitherto paid but small attention. The shield was a proud one. Upon an azure field it bore a knight in golden armor, his lance couched for the the onset, his left hand guiding his sable war-horse. The crest was an argent passion-cross, upborne by angels' wings. The motto enwrought in golden letters upon a fanciful scroll was—

Dieu, le roy, et le foy du Vaughn.

The whole was surrounded by the quaint and many-colored arabesques known to the heralds as the lambrequin.

This device John Gillies examined in detail, with the same grave attention which he bestowed upon everything; but even here found cause of discontent.

"The knight has his face covered, and the motto is in a foreign language," said he, and taking a book from the mantel-shelf he resolutely began at the title-page and read until the gathering dusk warned him that night was approaching.

Then, suffering the book to fall to the floor at his feet, and, leaning back in the old chair, he allowed his mind for the first time to turn upon the strange circumstances surrounding him.

The sound of footsteps and a feeble knock at the door aroused him, and opening he found old Lazarus upon the threshold, with a broad-shouldered, awkward fellow behind him.

"There, I told you there was no one here but Mr. Reginald," said Lazarus, peevishly.

"That ain't Mr. Reginald, you old simpleton—it's Mr. Gillies, the very man I was asking for," retorted the stranger in a loud whisper; and then, stepping forward, he said, with the mixture of awkwardness and conscious independence peculiar to the American rustic and to no other class of men beneath the sun:

"My name's Brume. I live down to Carrick, and see you last night when you came in the stage. Jim Powers, that stops to Frederic Vaughn's, was down to the tavern awhile ago, and said you wanted your things fetched up, and would like a man to stop awhile, and sort of help along a little. So I thought, as I'd nothing particular to do just now, and it's sort of tedious sitting round all day, I'd fetch up the things, and, if we suited each other, I might stop."

"As a servant?" enquired Gillies, calmly.

"O waal, cap'n, we don't need to call no names about it. I know how to take hold of most anything; been to sea for cook and steward, and are what they call a jack-of-all-trades. I'll do pretty nigh as you'd like to have me; but I can't begin, going on forty, to call any man master, or myself servant."

"So long as you perform service you are a servant," said Mr. Gillies, positively; "but the name under which you perform it makes no difference to me; if it does to you, choose what suits you best. I will make enquiries about you in Carrick, and if the answers are satisfactory I will engage you, at such wages as we may decide upon. Do you wish to stay on these conditions?"

"Well, yes, cap'n; I expect I might as well," said Reuben, rather doubtfully:

"I shall require very little of any one," added Mr. Gillies, "and shall choose to see as little as possible of any one. This old man is to stay, and be treated with consideration."

"Old Lahs'rus! Oh, sartin. He's one of the old stand-bys, and I shouldn't never think of setting up agin him," said Mr. Brume, with an approving slap upon the shoulder of the old man, who, with one withered finger at his lips, was staring uneasily from one speaker to the other, and again past them both into the library, whence he seemed to expect the momentary appearance of one who should, assuming his rightful place in the house, drive out these vexatious intruders and reëstablish the old order of things.

"At present," said Mr. Gillies, coldly, "I should like some dinner. You may see, if you please, if anything is to be found in the house."

"There, now," said Reuben, with a sudden illumination of countenance, "I guessed right for once, I'll bet a cent. Jim told me how matters wos up here, and that he didn't b'lieve Lahs'rus would make out anything of a dinner for you. So I told Burroughs he might put up a basket of vittles, and I'd fetch 'em along. Even if you'd got something, I thought they might work in handy; for I'm pretty hearty to eat, myself, and if you wasn't a mind to take 'em, why I told him I'd pay for 'em out of my own pocket. I reckon 'twouldn't break me, though I don't pretend to be a Creshus."

"You did very well, although ordinarily I do not wish any one to make purchases for me without orders," said Mr. Gillies. "I will eat here. Bring in what you have prepared, and then see about my bed and your own."

"All right, cap'n. I reck'n we'll keep her before the wind, though we be rather light-handed," said Reuben, cheerily; and, taking possession of old Lazarus, he withdrew, closing the door behind him, while his new master, returning to the fire-place, stirred the brands until a river of sparks flowed up the broad chimney, and great billows of light surged into every corner of the dark room, and flashed from the oriel-window out upon the waters, so that the bewildered mariners thought to have discovered a new Pharos upon the dangerous coast.

CHAPTER X.

THE GOLDEN SERPENT.

It was the day after the double funeral had taken its sad path from the gates of Bonniemeer, and Vaughn sat alone in his study, helpless under the sense of lonely desolation which no words can paint to him who has never known it, which no time can efface from the memory of him who has.

One of the commonest impulses of this condition of restless misery is toward flight—a flight terminating often like his of the song, who, fleeing from his househo.d demon, heard it call to the wayfarers from the loaded wain, "Aye, we're all a-flitting!" and so turned back to wrestle with it beneath his own rooftree, rather than in the open world.

This impulse toward flight now possessed the widowed Vaughn, and, yielding to it upon the moment, he rang a bell, and summoned Mrs. Rhee to his presence.

She came, and stood within the door, pale, haggard, wasted, her eyes faded with incessant tears, her mouth tremulous with ill-suppressed emotion.

Vaughn glanced at her, carelessly at first, then with a steady scrutiny. The housekeeper returned the look, and the Secret—THE SECRET that lay between them, spoke from eye to eye, imploring, refusing, appealing, denying, until the woman hid her face within her wasted hands, and Vaughn, springing from his seat, trod as impatiently up and down the room as though he could thus trample out of sight a past that would not be left behind.

Presently, commanding himself, he said, with measured calmness,

"Sit down, Anita. I wish to speak with you on matters of business alone."

The housekeeper mutely obeyed.

"I am going abroad, it may be for some years," pursued Vaughn, no longer looking at her, but hastening to place his resolution in words binding upon them both.

"I shall leave business matters in the hands of my lawyers, one of whom will be appointed my agent here, but to you I wish to entrust the affairs of the house and the care of the child—of Gabrielle's child. You should be a second mother to her, Anita."

He paused, and looked at her with strange significance and yet a strange reluctance.

She looked as steadily at him, and said,

"You may trust me. I will be a mother to the child of Gabrielle, and—you. I, who have no child, can pity this motherless baby, can love her in place of my own."

The unutterable pathos of her voice reached his inmost heart and roused not sympathy alone, but such a storm of conflicting emotions as swept his very soul before it and bowed him to the earth. He turned from her, hiding his face, and through the heavy silence of the room was heard a dull throbbing sound as of some hidden clepsydra. That sound was the beating of Anita's heart, as standing with her hands clasped above it, her figure inclined forward, her lips parted, her eyes glowing, her color faded to an ashy pallor, she watched the man before her—watched till the crisis should be past and the tenor of her future life declared.

Suddenly Vaughn turned and looked at her. She read his face eagerly as one might read the page of futurity held open in a wizard's hand. She read there pity, sympathy, and an inexorable resolution—a resolution based upon the very foundations of the man's nature, and no more to be overthrown. She read, and with a bitter, bitter moan she turned away, the thin hands clasping yet more fiercely the throbbing heart whose every bound seemed like to be its last. Could she have doubted his face, the first tones of his voice would have proved to her that she had not deceived herself.

"If the future looks cold and barren to you, Anita, remember that it is to be conquered by your own effort. So far as physical well-being is concerned, I can assure it to you—the rest you must do for yourself. We all have our own fight to make in one way or another."

He waited, but she would neither speak nor look, and he went on, resolutely,

"I may be gone a long time. You will hear from me through my business agent, and I shall wish you to write, through the same medium, of matters connected with the child or the house that you may wish to communicate."

He hesitated a moment, and approached a little nearer to where she stood with drooping head and downcast eyes, one hand resting lightly upon a chair, the other hanging nervelessly beside her.

"There is one thing that you must promise me, Anita. The child must never know, must never suspect even so remotely. Can you do it?"

"I promised the same thing two years ago, when you married Gabrielle," replied the housekeeper, half scornfully. "Have I ever broken that promise?"

"Never, as I firmly believe. But now you will be alone, and you will love this little child so much that it will be hard."

"Is it the only thing in my life that is hard?" asked she, sharply.

"No. I have told you that we have all our own fight to make. If yours is a hard one through act of mine, may God and you forgive me. Do not fear that I shall not suffer the full penalty of my own misdoings. Do not doubt that my own conscience has said and will say all and more than you, or Gabrielle, or even this new-born child has a right to say. If you suffer, Anita, you do not suffer alone. And now I will have no more of this. From this moment we speak together in only our obvious relations. You quite understand my wishes in regard to the child."

"Quite, sir. Am I to address her entirely as Miss Vaughn, or will you give her a Christian name?"

Putting aside the sarcasm without notice, Vaughn replied,

"Certainly she must be named, and she shall have a name expressing her birthright. Call her Franc; it means free."

"Not Gabrielle?" asked the housekeeper, impetuously.

"No; Franc, or perhaps Francia is better. Let her be called Francia."

"Yes, sir," said the housekeeper, her voice as coldly submissive as his was coldly determined.

"Chloe, of course, will be her nurse, and you will guarantee Chloe's silence, as heretofore, I presume."

"Yes, sir."

"I believe that is all, then. I shall see you again upon some household matters not yet decided."

"What is to be done with the other little girl, sir? The child of the woman found dead on the beach."

"Ah. I had forgotten. Is she an intelligent and well-formed child, healthy and bright?"

"Yes, sir, I should judge so.

"Let her be educated with Francia, then, and precisely in the same manner. Regard her as my adopted daughter, and make no difference between them in any way. I will never commit the cruelty of rearing a child beneath my roof to a condition of dependence and sycophancy. The finest nature must become debased or crushed by such a life. Educate her in every respect as if she were Francia's sister, and let her story be kept a secret from her as long as possible. Look to this, if you please."

"Yes, sir."

"She must be named, also."

"She is named already, sir. At least the word Neria is pricked into her shoulder with Indian ink, and I take it to be her name," said Mrs. Rhee, somewhat contemptuously.

"Neria? The mermaids must have named her before they left her on the shore. Well, it is a pretty name. Let it belong to her. Was there nothing about the mother to tell who she was or where she came from?"

"Nothing, sir. She looked like a lady, although her clothes were poor and worn. She had a wedding ring, and wore a curious bracelet, but neither of them were marked, nor were any of her clothes. James has inquired at Carrick, but no one saw her pass through, except an old man, who remembers that some one asked if Mr. Vaughn lived near here, and he directed her to this house; but it stormed so that he did not notice much how she looked, or ask any questions as to where she came from, or anything."

"Probably she wanted help, and had been referred to me," said Vaughn, quietly settling in his own mind a question that should not have been so readily answered. "Where is the bracelet of which you speak?"

"Here, sir. I brought it to give into your own charge, as it appears very valuable."

She laid it in his hand as she spoke. A golden serpent, his scales delicately wrought in the old Venetian style, and so subtly jointed as to writhe at every motion with all the graceful convolutions of his kind. The flattened head was set with an emerald crest and diamond eyes, while between the distended jaws flickered a flame-like tongue carved from a single ruby.

Vaughn, who had a luxurious fancy for rare gems, looked with delight at the exquisite toy coiled upon his hand, vibrating with every throb of its pulses, and flashing back the sunlight from its diamond eyes with a cold glitter half diabolical in its life-likeness.

"It must be an heir-loom of some old family," said he. "Our paltry goldsmiths do not conceive such exquisite fancies. And the workmanship is the Venetian style of the last century—genuine, too; it is no modern imitation. Is there no mark upon it of any kind?"

"No, I believe not," replied the housekeeper, wearily, while through her mind glanced the question,

"Can he really care more for this toy than for the anguish devouring my heart!"

"Yet, but there is. See here." And unheeding the swimming eyes that sought his own, Vaughn showed where, upon the serpent's throat, one scale was marked in tiny characters with the initials "F. V., 1650." Upon the scale above was traced the outline of a crest, but so faintly that Vaughn failed to make it out by the minutest scrutiny.

"'F. V.' Why, those are my little Francia's initials," said he, musingly.

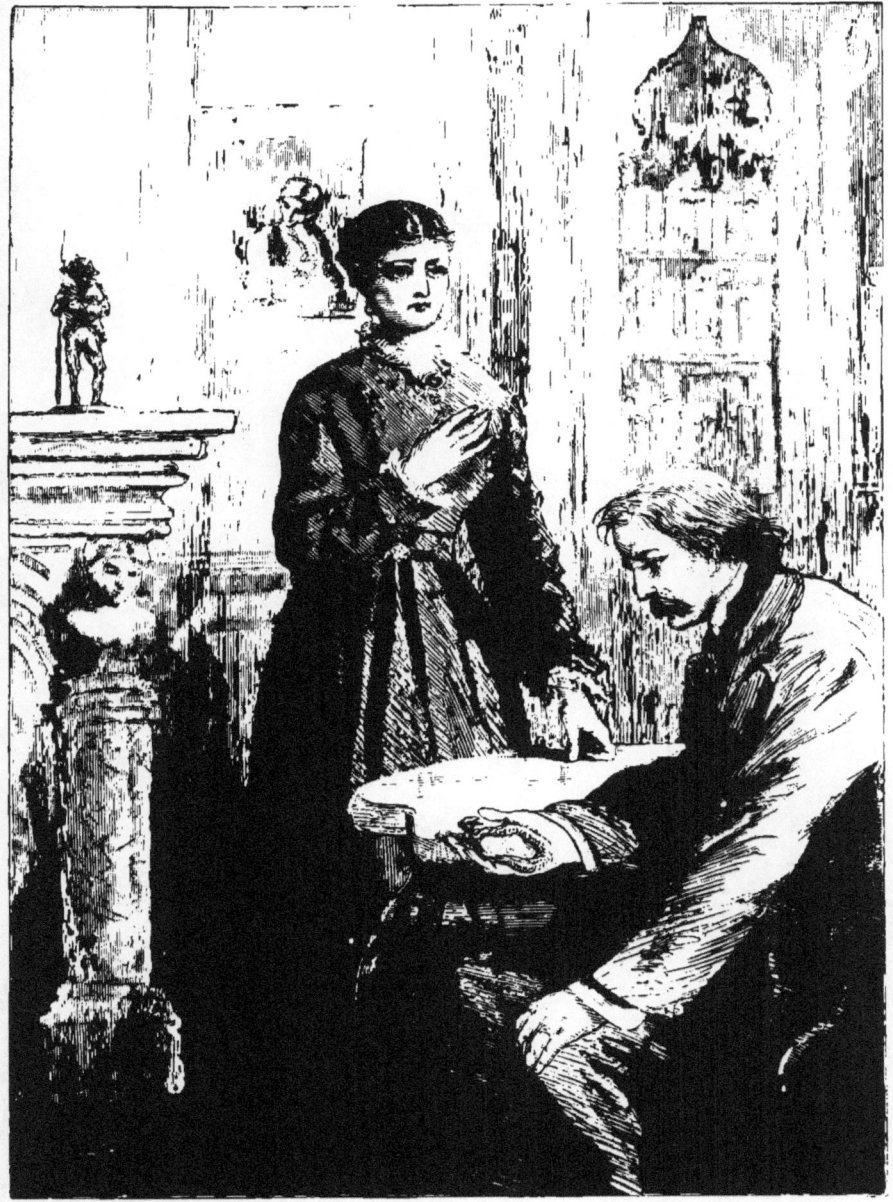
"IT MUST BE AN HEIR-LOOM OF SOME OLD FAMILY," SAID HE.—

"Who knows but this precious bracelet is actually a family jewel of our own. You say the woman was inquiring for me. I must see the old man you speak of before I leave."

"He knows no more than I told you, sir. I have seen him myself. I did not suppose you would be able to speak with him so soon——"

She glanced at him half reproachfully as she spoke, and a shadow crossed his face.

"Yes, I know," said he, hurriedly, "I do not forget my loss in caring for the living. This child is now my charge, and I shall attend to her interests as carefully as to those of my own daughter. The bracelet I shall put away until Neria is old enough to wear it; and before leaving home I shall make all possible inquiries concerning her mother's story. And now, Anita, good-by. I shall not see you alone again until time has done so much for both of us that we need not fear to meet."

He took her hand, looked down into the dark eyes raised to his with such an ocean of anguish in their depths, and then, half drawn by them, half impelled by his own tender nature, he stooped and kissed her.

A vivid scarlet stained her cheeks, a wild joy lighted her eyes; and as she slowly withdrew her hand and left the room, every line of her supple figure, every motion of her graceful head, so expressed the new life burning in her veins that Vaughn, watching her, muttered, as she closed the door,

"It was folly, it was inconsistent. But it is the last. Never again, Anita, never again."

And Fate, listening, smiled a scornful smile, whispering,

"Yet once more Frederic Vaughn, yet once more, and in your own despite."

CHAPTER XI.

TIGER TAMING.

IN pursuance of the intention expressed to his new retainer, Mr. Gillies took an early opportunity of ascertaining Reuben's reputation in his native village.

"O, there ain't no harm in the fellow," said Mr. Burroughs, to whom his first inquiry was addressed. "I guess the worst that's to say of him is that he's sort o' slack, and had rather luff and bear away than to keep her right up in the wind's eye. But he's handy, Reub is, and can do first rate if he's a mind to. I shouldn't wonder if he answered your purpose, Cap'n, as well as a better man. But what does Nance say about it?"

"I do not know to whom you refer," said Mr. Gillies, in his driest manner.

"Why, Reub's wife, Nancy Brume. If she hain't gi'n her consent, it won't do no good to ship him. She'll be after him, and get him, too."

Mr. Gillies looked puzzled and disgusted, but made no reply.

"Tell you what, Cap'n," pursued the good-natured publican, "why don't you jest step over there, and speak to Nance about it yourself. It seems a pity you shouldn't have Reub, and I tell you now, Nance is skipper of that concern, and is the one you've got to reckon with first or last. If you don't go and see her, she'll be up to see you before many days are over."

"Heaven forbid!" ejaculated Gillies; and after a moment of consideration, briefly added,

"Very well, I will go. Where does she live?"

Stepping out upon the porch, Burroughs pointed to the little cottage from whose door the fish-horn had been so vigorously blown upon the evening when Mr. Gillies was first introduced to the village of Carrick.

"That's the house, and I guess you'll find her to home. Don't be scared if she's kind of rough at first, Cap'n. Her bark's worse'n her bite."

To this friendly advice, Mr. Gillies deigned no answer whatever, but stepping off the porch, walked briskly in the direction indicated.

The door of the cottage stood open, and the visitor paused a moment before it, in some doubt how best to make his presence known, when a sudden uproar arose within, and a boy, dressed in a fisherman's coarse clothes and heavy boots, fled out of the door and down the street, pursued by a tall wiry woman holding a large fish by the gills, which novel instrument of punishment she heartily applied about the boy's head and shoulders whenever she could reach him, shouting at the same time,

"I'll teach ye to fetch me a hahdock agin, ye young sculpin! Didn't I tell ye I wanted a cod, and what d'ye s'pose I care how many they took up to Fred Vaughn's. Think I'll be put off with a hahdock while other folks eats cod? Take that, and that, and that!"

And as little else than the head of the offending haddock now remained in the fair epicure's hand, she seized the lad by his shock of wiry hair, and bending his head back upon her arm, scrubbed his face with the remnant of fish, until the luckless fellow, screaming with mingled rage and terror, broke away and rushed down the street.

Mrs. Brume looked after him a moment, and then slowly turned toward home, wiping her hands upon her apron, and muttering to herself invectives, mingled with self-gratulation.

Mr. Gillies stood upon the door-step with a face of unmoved gravity.

"Does Mrs. Brume live here?" inquired he, as the virago approached.

"Yes, I'm Miss Brume," replied she, in an uncompromising manner.

"I should like to speak to you, then, for a few moments."

"Well, you can come in." And Mrs. Brume led the way into a vigorously tidy kitchen, and after setting a wooden chair for her guest, retired to a back room to remove the traces of her late encounter. While she was gone, Mr. Gillies cast an observant glance about the room. Everything was as clean, as orderly, and as uninviting, as hands could make it. The white floor was scoured and sanded, the stove blackened and polished, the windows as nearly transparent as the green and wavy glass could be made. Even the cat blinking in the sunny corner had a wan and subdued expression, as if her natural depravity, and with it her vitality had been nearly cleansed away.

Mrs. Brume returned, her face and hands red with ablution and excitement, her hair, also red, smoothed, and a clean white apron tied tightly about her waist. Seating herself in a chair opposite her guest, she opened the conversation by saying,

"Like enough you thought strange to see me so mad with that young one, but he hadn't no business to bring me a hahdock when I spoke for a cod, and I ain't one of them kind as puts up with everything and never says a word. I'm apt to speak my mind, specially if I'm a little riled, and I'd as lief one man would hear me as another."

To this ingenuous confession Mr. Gillies responded by a slight bow, and then said,

"I called to let you know, Mrs. Brume, that your husband thinks of remaining with me for the present. My name is Gillies, and I live at Cragness, the estate of the late Mr. Reginald Vaughn."

Mrs. Brume's color rose, and she twitched at the strings of her apron, but as she raised her eyes they met the cold grave look steadily bent upon her, and with a very unusual effort to suppress her rising wrath, she asked,

"How long does he think of stopping?"

"As long as I wish to employ him," returned Gillies, coolly.

"O—h!" replied Mistress Brume, slowly, while an ominous pallor settled about her lips, and her hands flew to her hips.

"And if I might ask without offence, Mr. Gillies, I'd just like to know how long you calc'late to keep a honest woman's husband away from her?"

"So long as he wishes to remain," replied Gillies, in the same imperturbable manner, and beneath that manner and that steady gaze Nancy Brume found her usually unfailing powers of invective mysteriously checked and subdued. She bravely tried to rally her forces.

"O well," said she, bridling, "I don't suppose its of no consequence to either one of you what I think about it. A poor weak woman hain't got no chance when the man as had ought to look out for her can get them as calls themselves gentlemen to back him up and help him along in trampling onto her feelings—"

But these same feelings of Nancy Brume's, denied full expression in their usual manner, found sudden vent in another form, and she burst into tears, sobbing from behind the white apron.

"I don't know, I'm sure, what I ever did to you, sir, that you should come and take away my husband this way, and then set there as cold as I don't know what, and—make from fun of me, and all."

"Make fun of you, ma'am!" exclaimed Mr. Gillies, indignantly, and indeed the phrase by which Dame Brume had sought to express the unsympathizing and unassailable manner of her guest was ludicrously inappropriate, although sufficiently significant of a jealousy almost universal in her class toward its social superiors. Nancy, unable to defend her position, with feminine quickness changed her base of operations.

"I'm sure I've been as good a wife to that man as there is in Carrick. His house has been kept tidy and his vittles has been cooked reg'lar, and if his clo's hain't always been whole and neat, it wasn't my fault, but his'n, which he wouldn't leave 'em off—"

"Mrs. Brume! will you stop and listen to me!" interrupted Mr. Gillies, so decidedly, that the white apron suddenly dropped into Nancy's lap, disclosing a scarlet but attentive face.

Mr. Gillies glanced at it and then away. Poor Nancy's beauty was not of the exceptional style to which tears are an added charm.

"What I wish to say is simply this," continued the guest, rising to depart. "I have taken your husband into my service for an indefinite period, and thinking it proper you should be informed of the fact, I called here to mention it. With your matrimonial virtues or faults I have, of course, no concern, and merely came here to-day lest you should think it necessary to seek your husband at Cragness."

"I don't know but I've been kind o' ha'sh, sometimes," pursued the wife, more attentive to her own course of thought than to the cold words of her guest, "but I've set more by Reub than he knowed, I guess, and though I did put him out and lock the door t'other day I never thought he was going off for good. I wish't you'd let him come home and have a talk 'long o' me, Mr. Gillies, 'fore you fix it all off."

"I have no reason to suppose he wishes for such permission," said Gillies, with grim humor.

"You don't think he's give me up altogether," cried Nancy, in sudden terror, and again the white apron went over her head, and she rocked to and fro in a paroxysm of grief. The guest silently walked toward the door.

"Stop just a minit, please, sir," sobbed the deserted wife, and as Gillies reluctantly paused, she wiped her eyes, and looking up in his face with a piteous smile upon her hard mouth, said,

"I wish't you'd take me, too, sir."

Gillies recoiled.

"Take you, too!" exclaimed he, in solemn horror.

"Yes, I'd do all the work of your house, and keep it real nice and tidy, too. Reub can't do that, nor—though he can cook pretty well, he can't come up to me, and I'm a first-rate washer and ironer, too, and I'll do just as you'd like to have me. Do take me 'long o' Reub, Mr. Gillies, for it don't seem as if I could make up my mind to part with him. I'll come real cheap, too, it won't hardly cost more for both than one, and I'm awful saving about a house."

There was a pathos in the rude tones and sharp face of the wife thus pleading for leave to work at her husband's side, to which no man could have been quite insensible, and the shrewd arguments by which she supported her proposition produced their full effect upon the mind of her listener.

He considered for a moment, and then said,

"But your husband came to me with the intention of separating from you. I cannot refuse him my protection."

"O, I'll settle with Reub," said his spouse, with feminine confidence in her own conciliatory powers. "He sets by me, same as I do by him, more'n either of us let on. He kind o' calc'lates on me, too, to push him along and hold him up straight. Reub'll agree fast enough."

Gillies considered again.

"Your plan has its advantages, Mrs. Brume," said he, at length, "and if I find Reuben is satisfied with it, you may come to Cragness on trial, and under one condition, but that a stringent one."

"And what's that, sir?" asked Nancy, beamingly.

"That you shall never raise your voice above its present tones while upon my premises, and that you never scold your husband in any tones. When you find the vivacity of your temper beyond your control, I will always give you permission to come to Carrick, and expend it either upon the fisher boy or in any other manner you see fit, but while under my roof, I shall expect it to be held in perfect control. I am a quiet man, and strongly object to disturbance of any kind, especially discordant noises."

"I'll do my best, sir," said Nancy, meekly.

"That will not be sufficient, unless your best comes up to my requirements," returned Gillies, coldly. "And I wish you to come with the understanding that unless my conditions are fulfilled, I shall expect you to retire from my house, leaving your husband there so long as he wishes to stay."

"I ain't used to being beat by anything, and if I once tackle my own temper,

I reckon I can get the upper hand of it same as I would of anything else," said Nancy, with the calm confidence of a habitual conqueror.

"Then I will speak to Reuben, and, if he wishes for your society, he may come down to-night and tell you so. Good-morning, Mrs. Brume."

"Good-day, sir."

As Mr. Gillies walked away, he smiled, in his own dry fashion, and said, in his own mind,

"Surely, no man in his senses will voluntarily place himself in that woman's power, after having once escaped from it."

But, probably, Reuben Brume's ideas of sanity differed from those of his master; for the very next day saw Nancy installed in the kitchen of Cragness, and commencing an indignant but noiseless raid upon its many crypts and by-places, while Lazarus, seated beside the fire, watched her vigorous movements with dire astonishment; and Reuben obeyed her numerous mandates with cheerful alacrity.

"Looks kind o' good, arter all, to see you round, Nance, specially when you're so good-natered," said he, in the course of these operations; and Nancy, womanlike, retorted:

"Yes; and I was a big fool not to let well enough alone, and leave you to muddle along here, best way you could."

But Mrs. Brume, besides being a woman of quick temper, was a woman of powerful will, and the resolution she had taken in coming to Cragness she kept as perfectly as the faulty nature of humanity would permit; and the occasions when her husband was forced to enquire if he should "speak to Mr. Gillies" became so rare that Reuben privately blessed the day of his emancipation, and looked upon his master with the admiring awe due to a moral Van Amburgh.

CHAPTER XII.

"THE MAIDEN TO THE HARPER'S KNEE."

THE sun of a summer's day had just sunk beneath the horizon, leaving the western sky a-flood with a golden glow unflecked by clouds, while sea and earth lay hushed beneath the grand calm that ever falls with such a sunset. Clouds, gorgeous though they may be, cannot but detract from this calm—cannot but disturb the unity, the conviction of eternity, that fills the heaven and crowns the earth in its presence. The cloudy sunset is a grand spectacle of nature—the golden glow that seems to draw us into itself and on to Eternity, is Space illumined by Divinity. Against this sunset the trees crowning the summits of the western hills lined themselves almost leaf by leaf, while Mount Lion, standing sharply out in the foreground, loomed black and forbidding as the impious height reared by Titans who would fain clamber to that glory's source. Higher, the gold melted through a belt of tender green into the clear blue of the zenith, while all the East was veiled in an amethystine mist, as rare as it was lovely in its tint.

Out of the slumberous sea rose a moon rounded to its perfect circle, and with her splendor fell upon earth and sea a benediction:

Peace, O Earth! be still, O Sea! for He that made us, reigneth.

The tide was out, and upon the grey-ribbed sands lay many a wonder of the deep. Shells, pebbles, mosses, of every delicate dye and graceful form, quivering jelly fish and awkward insects, lobsters, crabs, horse-shoes, and one malevolent squid or cuttle fish, who seized upon everything within his grasp, tearing and crushing it to atoms.

Among these marine curiosities strolled a party of four young people, three of them girls varying in age from twelve to seventeen, the fourth a lad of sixteen, who divided his attention pretty equally between his companions and a fine spaniel answering to the name of Otter, who seemed to ask no better amusement than to obey his master's many and somewhat imperious mandates, frisking now into the water, now up the rocky shingle at the head of the beach, now forward and now backward, as he was ordered.

"Hark! There is music, an organ, I should think; where can it be?" asked Claudia, a glowing brunette beauty, and the eldest of the three girls.

"Why, it is Cragness! Who would suppose we had come so far?" said Francia, looking about her. "Just round that rock you will see the library window, Claudia, built out over the water. That is all you can see of the house from the beach."

"Let us go on, then, and listen to the music. Does that old scarecrow of a Gillies play like that?" asked her cousin, in contemptuous surprise, as she led the way onward and paused at last directly beneath the deep bay window of the library of Cragness.

The others followed, Francia skipping along beside Claudia, narrating in a tone of lively gossip such particulars as were current in regard to Mr. Gillies's mode of life, and adding comment and suggestion from her own merry wit.

Behind them walked Neria, a tall, slight girl, of a face and figure promising, through the immaturity of their thirteen years, a development of rare loveliness. With bent head, and eyes fixed upon the ocean and the rising moon, she seemed to care as little for the lively chat of the girls in front as the rude play of the boy and dog behind her.

Claudia, who had the sensuous love of music befitting her temperament, paused beneath the window, and, imposing silence upon her companion, seated herself upon the rocks to listen. Francia wandered down upon the sands, collecting brilliant pebbles, in the next moment to be thrown away, and about midway between them stood Neria, her hands locked together, her head drooping, her dreamy eyes fixed upon the water, and a faint smile stirring her sensitive mouth.

Beneath the hands of its master, the great organ poured out its soul in music, exalting like the archangel who soars undazzled to the foot of the throne, piling chord upon chord in massive harmony until great billows of sound swept out upon the breathless air and surged up to the open gates of heaven. The solemn ecstasy reached its height, and fell, through fine gradations, to a single silvery melody, pure and sweet as the song the shepherds sung upon the heights of Bethlehem; then wandered on through dreamy variations until of a sudden, perhaps because the level rays of the rising moon now shot into the great bay window, the wandering notes changed to a well-known strain, and a fine tenor voice rolled out the notes of "Casta Diva;" while, combining with the severe purity of the melody, the managed instrument rendered such complicated orchestral effects that one could hardly believe one pair of human hands the only media between human ears and the world of harmonious melody suddenly opened to them.

The aria ended, the organist fell again into his dreamy fantasia, and now the great organ wailed and sobbed as if the banished peri breathed forth her longing and her sorrow through it; and tears, not to be withheld or explained, sprang to the eyes of the listener. A quick transition, a handful of minor chords, deep discords resolving into strong, hard tones, and a storm of passion, an infernal rebellion, a contest of demons, was hurled out to the summer night, and swelled wilder and louder, faster and fiercer, until Claudia rose to her feet, her cheeks flushed, her eyes wide and bright with emotion, her lips arched and quivering.

Neria had sunk upon her knees, her face buried in her hands, and her slender form shaken with irrepressible sobs.

"I must see this man—now, at once," said Claudia, imperiously. "Neria, come with me."

But Neria did not move or speak, and Claudia, the impetuous, hastily climbed the tortuous path leading to the brow of the cliff, and a moment after knocked at the same door that, twelve years before, had been opened by Lazarus Graves to admit the new master of Cragness to his lonely home. It was now opened by a gaunt, middle-aged woman, who eyed the visitor with surprise and distrust.

"I wish to speak to Mr. Gillies," said the young lady, briefly.

"Do? Well, I'll tell him, but I don't know as he'll come," replied Nancy Brume, curtly.

"No; I will go to him; he is playing on the organ, and I wish to hear him."

"Hear him! You don't expect he's going to play with you a setting by, do ye? Why, if he could help it, he wouldn't let the rats and mice in the old walls hear him. I dursn't do it," said Nancy, with a tone of awe in her voice, engrafted there by her twelve years' residence under Mr. Gillies's roof.

"Nonsense; show me the way directly," retorted Claudia, imperiously. "I will explain everything myself."

Without further remonstrance, Nancy turned and led the way up the long passage, muttering,

"Have your own way and live the longer; but 'tain't the way gals acted when I was young."

Arrived at the door of the gallery dividing the library from the house, she paused and, with the curt direction, "Straight ahead," waited until Claudia had entered, and then, closing the door upon her, went back to her own domain.

The young girl hesitated a moment, and then, with heightened color, passed on, and, softly turning the latch of the library door, entered and stood within the gloomy chamber.

The musician turned at the sound of the opening door and sat looking in mute wonder at the brilliant apparition so suddenly vouchsafed him. And indeed Claudia had never looked so beautiful as now, when a touch of maiden shame softened the lustre of her eyes, trembled on her proud lips, and bowed her regal head. So, as she stood, her white draperies and glowing beauty thrown forward from the dusky shadows crowding up behind her, a tremulous half-motion vibrating through her slender figure, her whole presence instinct with youth's beautiful enthusiasm, she might have been the spirit of music evoked and embodied by the artist's longing soul and magic touch.

John Gillies gazed speechless, and his very consternation restored to his guest the advantage she had for a moment lost. She laughed a little rippling laugh, and advanced to the centre of the room.

"Indeed, I could not help it, Mr. Gillies," began she; "and if you often make such music here by the sea as has drawn me hither, you must be too well accustomed to visits from mermaids and nixies, or whatever spirits haunt these old grey rocks, to wonder that a mere mortal was unable to resist the spell. My name is Claudia Murray, and I am niece to Mr. Vaughn, of Bonniemeer. I love music better than I do life, and I never heard such music as has floated from this window in the last half hour. Now please sit down again and play to me."

She threw herself as she spoke into a great arm chair beside the fire-place, and

——turned her sumptuous head, with eyes
Of shining expectation fixed

on the musician.

In silent obedience, he seated himself before the organ; but now the tones were feeble and confused, expressing as faithfully as before the emotions of the musician's soul, and therefore painful and unsatisfying. He ceased suddenly, and, rising, closed and locked the doors of the instrument.

"I cannot play to listeners," said he, half in humility, half in anger, as he came and stood before his guest.

Claudia looked up and smiled.

"But you must learn," said she, "for I am always coming to listen to you.

If I may not come here, I will sit outside upon the cold rocks beside the sea; but listen I must."

Gillies stood and looked at her with the same terrible wistfulness that we have all seen in the eyes of some dumb creature struggling for the utterance which nature has denied him. To borrow the distinction of a subtle psychologist, the John Gillies as his Maker knew him experienced emotions which John Gillies as men knew him could not express, and which John Gillies as he knew himself could only half define. So he looked at Claudia and opened his lips, but no words came.

Again the woman drew assurance from his discomfiture.

"You won't forbid my coming to hear you sometimes?" asked she, with a bewildering smile.

"If I know you are here, I can never play," said Gillies, hesitatingly.

"But you might—O, Mr. Gillies, if only you would!" and the listless figure sprang upright and stood, with clasped hands, looking up into his face.

"If I would—" repeated he, perplexed.

"If only you would try to teach me a little."

"I teach you!" and John Gillies turned pale and trembled visibly.

"Yes. I can play on the piano pretty well, I believe, and I know about music—the mechanism, you know—but O, I never dreamed it had a soul till I heard you just now."

The shadows lifted from the musician's face, as his mind reverted to his own most usual subject of thought. He forgot the strange and beautiful vision before him, in contemplation of a beauty fairer, higher, sweeter than anything of earth. The passion of his life swept away the admiration of a moment.

"It is only when we learn that music has a soul that we can interpret it to the soul of another," said he, serenely.

"But how learn it?" asked Claudia, passionately. "I have all my life studied music, but never felt it until to-night."

"Probably you have all your life studied an instrument and the technicalities of science. If you had studied music as an art, you would have found her soul long ago," said the musician.

"Yes, that is it. I have studied the piano, I have never studied music; I have never found any one to teach me this art. O, sir, will you?"

Dark eyes swimming in tears, curved lips tremulous with feeling, clasped hands, and a face pale with genuine emotion. Powerful agents, these, to work upon the will of a man; but the eyes of the artist fell upon them now as calmly as upon his own reflection in the mirror.

"I will try," said he, briefly. "But if I find that you are incapable of receiving the ideas I shall try to communicate, I shall stop. No man can do more for another than to show him the path. Each must tread it for himself."

"I understand," said Claudia, humbly; "and, though I may be stupid and unappreciative, at least you shall not find me ungrateful."

If she hoped to extort words of flattery from those dry lips, the wily coquette was disappointed; for Mr. Gillies did not even glance at her as he said,

"I will try. Your may come here to-morrow at four o'clock. But do not expect too much."

"I will come, and I do expect a great deal," said Claudia, joyfully, and, with a graceful gesture of farewell, took her leave.

END OF PART I.

CIPHER:

A Novel.—Part Second.

CHAPTER I.

A SUMMER NIGHT.

EIGHT more years had etched their almost imperceptible wrinkle upon earth's furrowed brow, and the moon of a summer's night dreamed softly upon sea and shore, upon the grey and grim old walls of Cragness, within whose shade John Gillies and the Secret still watchfully confronted each other upon the still fair waters of Bonniemeer, the lakelet that gave its name to the estate, and upon a pretty pleasure-boat drifting across its placid waters.

The occupants of this boat were Neria and Francia Vaughn, Claudia Livingstone, a bride in her honeymoon, and her brother Fergus Murray, a young man whose five-and-twenty years had done for him the work that fifty fail to accomplish for many men.

Let him who would read faces aright watch them when exorcised to truth by the magic of such a night; and when we remember that madness is but undisguised sincerity, and that a lunatic is but too fervent a lover of that fair moon who first entices men to sleep beneath her kisses and then stabs them to the brain while they dream of her, we see at once that to submit to her influence, to meet her smile, is to voluntarily enter upon the first stage of madness by allowing the deepest emotions of the heart to become patent upon that bulletin-board, the face.

Watch we then by moonlight, these, the principal characters of our story, as each slips idly through his fingers the white and grey thread that Arachne twists as pitilessly in the moonlight as in the dark, while we smile as we weep, while we trust in her, as after we have learned to sneer.

Claudia, tall, elegant, and Circean in her beauty, reclined in the stern of the boat, gazing now at her own reflection in the water, now at the diamonds upon her white fingers.

At her feet sat Neria, her hands clasped upon her lap, her eyes upraised in absorbing reverie, her pure profile clear cut against the background of dark woodland, her attitude as graceful as it was unconscious.

In the bows, Francia, smiling to herself, wove with nimble fingers a wreath of dripping water-lilies, glancing as she wrought at the handsome head of her Cousin Fergus, who, with his back to her, found amusement now in lightly dipping the oar that he held, so as to shatter the image Claudia watched with so much satisfaction, and now, in gazing at Neria's wonderful loveliness.

The wreath was done, and Francia lightly placed it upon the head of the unconscious oarsman, who started slightly, and then catching the hands still busy about his temples, drew them to his lips, and lightly kissing them, said,

"That is too much honor, little cousin, and besides the decoration is not appropriate. Give it to Neria, who in the moonlight looks like the spirit of the lake, or," and releasing the hands, the young man turned toward his cousin and lowered his voice. "If we want a veritable Undine, I know where to find her."

"Undine before she found her soul?" asked Francia, archly.

"Before she was married, yes," replied Fergus.

"The idea that a woman must necessarily be improved by being married. I don't believe it—there's Claudia now."

"I believe we won't discuss Claudia's affairs. I don't approve of meddling with what don't concern me," said Fergus, with a shade of severity in his voice. Francia drew a little back, and silently averted her face, while a rich, lazy voice asked, from the stern of the boat:

"What's that about Claudia?"

"Claudia has admired herself sufficiently for once," replied Fergus, resuming his seat and his oars, and must now go to relieve the anxieties of her friends on shore."

"Whether she will or no?" asked Claudia, half rebelliously. Her brother made no reply, and in a few moments the keel of the little boat grated upon the white sand of the beach. At the sound, three gentlemen rose from a bench, where they had been sitting, and came down to meet the voyagers.

In the first, a fine-looking man, bearing his forty years as Time's seal of perfected manhood, we recognize Frederic Vaughn, the master of Bonniemeer.

The shorter, stouter, more florid man beside him, is John Livingstone, the bridegroom of Claudia Murray, and the tall, thin, grey-haired, and grey-faced gentleman behind them is her father, the widowed brother-in-law of Vaughn.

Without waiting for the hand her father stepped forward to offer, Francia sprang lightly to the shore, and passed hastily up the path leading through the wood to the house. Fergus, stepping more deliberately from the boat, drew it up on the beach, and after carefully handing Neria out, impatiently called:

"Come, Claudia, we are waiting for you!"

But Claudia lingered, adjusting her draperies; and when, at last, she stepped upon the gunwale, placing her hand in that of Fergus, he seized it so hastily that Claudia stumbled, tangled her feet in her long dress, and was only saved from falling by the destruction of the gauzy fabric.

"Take care!. Did you tear your dress? It is not a fit one for a boating party," said Fergus, hurriedly passing the boat-chain over the post set for it, and hastening after Neria, already disappearing in the sombre woodland path.

"There, Mrs. L, that's fifty dollars gone, I suppose," remarked Mr. Livingstone, as Claudia ruefully gathered up her ruined dress.

"I wish you wouldn't call me Mrs. L.," retorted the lady, pettishly. "You know that I detest it."

"Don't get mad, young woman. It wasn't me tore your dress, and I guess it won't break Livingstone Brothers to furnish the funds for a new one," said the husband, good-humoredly, as he tucked his wife's arm under his own, and led her up the path.

Mr. Vaughn and his brother-in-law slowly followed.

"Livingstone makes Claudia a very good husband," said the latter, complacently.

"He seems very good-natured," assented Vaughn, with reserve.

"Yes, and that is a great deal. Then he is perfectly willing to leave her to her own pursuits and companions, and has both means and inclination to indulge all the costly whims which nearly ruined me while I had the honor of supplying her purse."

Mr. Vaughn slightly smiled, but said nothing; and, after a little pause, his companion added, positively:

"A very good husband, and a very good match."

"I am glad you are so well pleased," said Vaughn, finding an answer imperative.

"Humph! Your aristocratic prejudices won't allow you to be reasonable, Vaughn. You don't like my son-in-law because he's in trade, and because his father had no idea of a grandfather or a coat-of-arms. But, as for the last, I assure you, Livingstone has imported the very finest one in the Heralds' College, and Claudia has got it engraved on everything in the house."

"Your satire is more honest than your praise, Murray. You are more of a conservative at heart than I," said Mr. Vaughn.

Murray slightly smiled.

"My practice is for myself—my theories for others," said he. "I have a theory that Mr. John Livingstone is an admirable husband; but in practice I see him as little as possible."

"But Claudia is your daughter, and may be supposed to have the same tastes and prejudices as her father," pursued Vaughn.

Mr. Murray's sarcastic smile deepened.

"Claudia," said he, slowly, "is a young woman of uncommon good sense. She considered this matter well, and decided for herself, and, as I think, wisely. There was a young man, good-looking, well-mannered, romantic, and all that, whom she preferred, no doubt; but he was just out of the medical school, and was beginning on the thankless course of gratuitous practice incumbent at this day upon a young physician. In ten years he may be able to marry and live in a small way; but he never will be able to provide the sum Claudia expends each year for pin-money. Mr. Livingstone and he offered themselves on the same day. The girl dutifully came to me and asked advice."

"And you counselled her to accept the richer?" asked Vaughn.

"I said to her, 'My dear, look past the next five years into the forty or fifty which I hope await you beyond, and consider whether you will roll over them in a barouche, or plod through on foot, dragging a baby-cart after you.' She looked me in the eye a minute, turned as pale as a ghost, and quietly laid Dr. Lutrell's letter on the fire. That was all."

Vaughn's lip curled, but he made no reply; and the two men walked on through the rustling wood, where the moonlight quivered down, to make a diamond of every swinging dewdrop, and to light the rendezvous of amorous fays.

Vaughn stopped and looked about him. Twenty years before, he would have said:

"Can worldliness assert itself in such a scene as this?" But at forty one has learned, if ever, that "speech is silvern and silence is golden."

Mr. Murray cast a vacant eye upon the moony sky, the dreaming earth, the swinging blossoms, and whispering trees, and then said:

"You like this sort of thing, Vaughn?"

"Yes."

"Why don't you take a wife and settle down, then? You havn't spent a month here since Gabrielle died; have you?"

"Only the summer we all spent here five years ago," said Mr. Vaughn, quietly.

"O, yes; the last summer of Mrs. Murray's life—poor Catherine."

Again, silently, Mr. Vaughn considered whether the ruthful epithet was best applied to Mrs. Murray dead or Mrs. Murray living; and the unconscious widower resumed:

"But why don't you marry again, Vaughn."

"I have no inclination at present," returned his companion, coldly.

"Perhaps not; but you will do it yet, and, unless you look out for yourself, you will be drawn into a very foolish thing. It is not my affair, and I know so well the reward of friendly interference that I would not have risked speaking except from the very highest regard for your welfare."

"I am extremely grateful, my dear fellow," replied Vaughn, in good-humored astonishment, "but I haven't an idea what you're driving at."

"Of course, you'll laugh, and, possibly, will be offended; but, once for all, I tell you that little ward of yours, Neria, is falling in love with you," said Mr. Murray, in a matter-of-fact voice. Vaughn stopped and stared at him.

"Neria in love with me!" exclaimed he.

"Falling in love, I said," returned Murray. "It is only a few weeks that you have been at home, you know; and since she saw you last she has grown from a girl to a woman, and is, womanlike, all ready to fall prostrate at the feet of the first idol that chance sets before her. She is fascinated by your appearance and manners, and the *savoir faire* resulting from your wide travels appears to her the wisdom of a God. She is devoting herself now to the building of an altar for this god; and, presently, when the incense begins to rise, you may find it more intoxicating than you imagine."

Vaughn walked thoughtfully on for some moments, and then said,

"The caution is kindly meant, Murray, and, I assure you, kindly taken; but I don't think you quite know me, and neither of us knows more of Neria than her exquisite beauty. Perhaps, then, we had better not try to look into the sacred mysteries of a virgin heart, or discuss, as probabilities, ideas which seem to me the wildest of chimeras."

Mr. Murray stoically accepted the delicate rebuke, and said,

"O, very well. I only wished to open your eyes; and now have no more to say, except to rather demur at your phrase, 'exquisite beauty.' To my mind either Francia or Claudia is far handsomer than Neria. She is too cold and lifeless, has too little color and curve for my taste. She always reminds me of the winter sea that washed her up."

"You have not seen her as I have," said Vaughn, quietly; "and perhaps never could. And to compare her with Claudia and Francia, or them with each other, is unjust to all three, for while each is an almost perfect type of a special form of beauty, the three forms are as wide apart as the sea and the sun. I saw women like Claudia in Spain, in Italy, in the Ionian Isles; I have found Francias in England, in Germany, and here at home, but there are no more Nerias."

He smiled dreamily as he spoke, and Mr. Murray shrugged his shoulders.

"I should think in Norway, Sweden, Russia, anywhere near the North Pole, you might find plenty of them," said he, slightingly.

"Plenty of complexions as pure, and once in a year, perhaps, features as delicately moulded, a form as exquisitely proportioned—but the peculiarity of this girl's beauty is one that I have never before encountered. She is transparent. The body is beautiful enough, although men like you might call it cold and inanimate, but the real beauty is within, and only once in a while takes possession of the body and transfigures it, absolutely changes it to another."

Mr. Murray shook his head.

"Just as romantic as ever," said he, compassionately. "More of a boy than my Fergus ever was. Now, I suppose in common every-day parlance, you mean by this transfiguration and 'possession' that Neria has a very expressive face. Well—"

"No, that is not what I mean," interposed Vaughn. "I mean that under strong emotion or deep interest, she becomes another person. Her eyes, which ordinarily are a clear, light grey, deepen to the color of the sea beneath a thunder sky; her lips glow with a vivid scarlet, and ripen to an exquisite fulness; her cheeks bloom with the rare tint that Titian strove all his life to embody in color; her very hair deepens from its pale gold to an aureola of glory; her slender figure dilates and rounds itself to the perfection of womanhood. It is marvellous—absolutely marvellous, and no one who has never witnessed this change should speak of Neria's beauty, for it is a thing he cannot understand."

Mr. Murray plunged his hands into his pockets, and looked askance at his brother-in-law.

"I had better have held my tongue," said he. "I had no idea you were in this condition, or that you had turned your forty years to so little account."

Vaughn slightly frowned, then smiled.

"It is I who should have held my tongue," said he. "You and I never looked out of the same eyes, Murray, and you do not see that I am admiring this lovely ward of mine just as I admired the Madonnas of the Sistine, the Psyche of Florence. She is to me another embodiment of beauty, that is all— another reason to praise God, who gave me eyes and brain to admire His works."

"And that is all?" asked Murray, incredulously.

"That is all," assented Vaughn, with a grave and steadfast look into the furtive eyes of his companion.

"Wait awhile," said Mr. Murray, dryly, and they ascended the broad steps to the terrace, where Claudia sang passionate love-songs to her guitar, while her husband, with a handkerchief over his head, sat upon the sill of the drawing-room window, and Francia wandered restlessly up and down, looking every moment toward the garden where Neria's white dress floated through the long alleys with a dark shadow at its side.

Light and shadow presently came toward the house, and Francia, who had been for some moments immovable at the end of the terrace nearest to the garden, hurried to the other end, and seated herself upon the shaded steps, with a cruel little pang at the thought that she should not be missed. Without turning her head, she heard the merry talk that sprang up at the farther end of the terrace, heard some one ask for herself, and Claudia's careless answer that she had gone into the house, perhaps to rest. Then she heard a firm quick tread along the marble walk, and drew still further into the shadow as Fergus approached, paused, and sat down beside her.

"What is the matter, Francia?" asked he, with a little impatience and a good deal of tenderness mingling in his voice.

"Nothing's the matter," said Francia, pettishly.

"Yes, but a good deal's the matter when you speak in that way, little girl,' retorted her cousin, taking in his own one of the listless hands that only half-tried to evade the capture.

"Now tell me, Franc, what is it?"

Half yielding to the tender and imperious tone of this demand, Francia spoke, but, womanly, left the most unsaid.

"You were so cross in the boat!"

Fergus laughed aloud.

Now, Franc, aren't you ashamed of yourself? Very likely I spoke too sharply, but was that a thing worth pouting over for hours? What I meant was that you and I have no right to judge, or even discuss other people's affairs. You were beginning a remark about Claudia's marriage, you know, and I thought it was something of which you should not talk. I could not explain then, but you ought to have understood."

Francia looked up with a smile in her blue eyes.

"You are so fastidiously honorable," said she.

"And you are such a little goose," retorted her cousin, meeting the smile half way.

"Come, Franc, we are going in," called Claudia from the window, and with a little reluctant sigh, the girl obeyed the summons, slowly followed by Fergus, who, instead of entering the house, sought again the garden paths and wandered there until "Orion, low down in his grave," showed that the night had changed to morning.

CHAPTER II.

SIEUR.

HOLD to Genesis if we may, to Hugh Miller if we must, for the story of the creation; but who that has seen a summer morning upon the sea-shore can doubt that there was once an Eden whose echoes yet haunt the earth? The hush, the dreamy melancholy, the mystery of night, is gone, the soul no longer sighs to escape from earth and float unfettered into space; but rather it incorporates itself more closely in the body, giving to a man almost the afflatus of a God, saying to him, Up and be doing, for what limit is there to our capacity? And one no longer treads the common earth with weary feet, but feels himself upborne upon invisible wings above the garden where angels walked with men and infused new strength into their souls with every word.

Such a morning dawned upon Bonniemeer, and Neria, alone upon the terrace, stood looking over sea and earth, and dreaming the pure, bright dreams that such scenes should stir in a young and virgin heart.

Not dreaming, but humming a blithe hunting song that suited well his active and virile mien, came Fergus, striding rapidly up the avenue, until catching sight of Neria, he stopped, half in admiration of her attitude and the glorified beauty of her eager face, half shame-faced in remembering his disordered appearance and the dripping towel in his hand.

At the same moment Vaughn, appearing in the doorway, paused to look at the two, and especially at Fergus, trying to see him with a young girl's eyes. "A handsome fellow," thought he, with a strange reluctance in making the admission, "and with a certain air of pride and resolution that should have its weight. Not highly intellectual, perhaps, certainly not fanciful or romantic, although not free from the sentimentality of youth. Bearing the impress upon his face of a clear and well-trained mind, of high principle and fastidious honor, of elegant tastes and habits—a man whom a girl must admire, might easily love, should he love her," concluded Vaughn, just as his nephew sprang up the steps, giving him a gay good-morning, and he replied, a little coldly,

"Good-morning, Fergus. You have the advantage of us in your early walk."

"Yes, sir, and also in my dip into the surf. A splendid morning for a bath."

And the young man passed on, with one sidelong, wistful glance at Neria, who smiled a greeting, but did not speak. At the same moment Vaughn approached and greeted her.

"Good-morning, sir," said she, half shyly extending her hand.

Vaughn took it and held it for an instant, examining the slender, rose-tipped fingers.

"And what a morning!" continued Neria, turning to meet a little wave of fresher air, one of Ocean's ponderous love-sighs that just then grazed her cheek.

"Yes," replied Vaughn, absently, and then asked,

"Of what were you thinking, Neria, just before Fergus came up?"

"I was thinking of you, sir," replied Neria, quietly.

"Of me!" echoed Vaughn, too startled even to be flattered.

"Yes, sir. I was thinking that a man born and brought up in face of such grandeur and beauty as this, must of necessity be noble and pure, and wise as—"

"No, do not say it, child!" cried Vaughn, in terror. "Do not put me to shame by reminding me of opportunities, incentives, aids to a nobler life, that have been showered so freely upon me, and which have been so miserably, miserably neglected."

The clear eyes looked into his with such wonder, almost such fright, that the pain melted from his brow in a tender smile as he said,

"Do not look so much shocked, either. I did not mean to represent myself as an ogre, or even as a man stained with some dark crime; but who is, then, worthy to live, as you say, in the presence of such beauty and such grandeur as this? What man, I mean? If one looks among women—"

He paused, and with a smile half playful, half in earnest, looked deep into the transparent eyes still raised to his.

"But, Neria, tell me something," added he, drawing her hand through his arm and walking up and down the shady terrace. "Why have you given me no name since I came home? It is three weeks now, and you have not once called me anything but sir. Five years ago, you said papa, as Franc does now."

Neria looked a little troubled, and then suddenly relieved.

"I am glad you spoke of it, sir," said she, "for now I can ask you what I had better say. I do not like to say papa or father, because you know you are not my father, and it is claiming a right and a place which do not belong to me."

"Do not belong to you, dear?" asked Vaughn, in pained surprise. "Have you felt any want of affection or consideration in me, or in any one? Has Francia ever shown a feeling of jealousy or assumed—"

"O no! no!" interrupted Neria, anxiously. "Pray do not think of such a thing. Franc does not know I have thought of these things. She has forgotten, I believe, that I am not her very sister."

"And how came you to know it?" asked Vaughn, half smiling at the childish expression, and yet with an ominous frown gathering in his dark eyes.

"It was long ago," said Neria, dreamily, "when we were quite little girls, that we had some dispute, Franc and I; and although I gave up to her, I said she had no right to try to force me to, for she was in the wrong, and was really the one to yield. Then Mrs. Rhee, who was by, said something about everything being more Franc's than mine; and when we asked what she meant, she said I was an orphan whom you had taken in out of pity, and though it was no fault of mine, it should make me humble and less forward to speak of rights and to contend with Francia about trifles. I thought about it a good deal, and although Mrs. Rhee never would say any more, and seemed to wish it were forgotten, I made old Chloe tell me, little by little, all about it."

"All about what?" asked Vaughn, quietly.

"About your finding me on the sea-beach, in the arms of my poor dead mother—"

Neria paused, and stood for a moment looking out toward the sea with a wistful yearning in her eyes, as if the memory of that dead mother were to her forever associated with that other mystery beside which she had lain. A look so full of inexpressible longing of lonely grief, that Vaughn, gazing down upon it, would fain have clasped her to his heart and kissed the darkening eyes and quivering lips to peace and trust; but he could not do it, as he should, he would not, as he wished.

"I always thought about it while I was little," continued Neria, drearily; "and sometimes it made me sad—made me feel as if I did not quite belong here, and really had not the right to resist if Francia did not agree with me. But since I have grown up it seems different. I feel as if you really wished I should be your daughter, and did all you could for me, and it was ungrateful not to keep the place you had put me in. Besides, I cannot—I do not think it right for any one to give up what they know to be true and just, even if some one else has rights which they have not. I could not tell Francia that I thought as she did, if I did not, or even be silent when she or any one said what I did not think the truth. But I hope I am not ungrateful or quarrelsome, and indeed I love Franc as if she were my mother's child, and you, sir, as if you were my father."

No cloud, no doubt, dimmed the candid eyes which Vaughn questioned with the keen interrogatory of a man's selfishness, no maiden timidity made them droop before his own. He slowly withdrew his gaze, half pleased, half pained.

"But still," pursued Neria, "I do not like to call you father, because you are not in very truth my father, and so I should do nothing to make it appear so."

"Perhaps you are right, Neria, although, as I have always considered you a child of my own, your scruples seem to me excessive. .But, after all, it is as well to change this paternal title for one that will express no more than the exact truth. Will you call me guardian?"

"Yes, sir, if you like it."

"But not 'sir!' little ward! That is too formal."

"Francia says 'sir,' and so does Fergus," suggested Neria, hesitatingly "And I was thinking if you liked it, that *Sieur* is the very name I would like to call you best, as if you knew you were the king and I the orphan ward for whom you cared."

"Ah, you do not leave out the romance when you read history," said Vaughn, smiling. "Well, then, call me *Sieur* if you will, and the name so resembles your usual address that no one will notice the change, and so our little secret shall be our own."

"I don't like secrets very much," said Neria, apprehensively.

"Child, you are morbidly sensitive on this matter of candor. It is right and just that every heart should keep some things locked safely away from the world. So only do we preserve our individuality," said Vaughn, gravely; and his ward answered with docility,

"Then this shall be a secret."

"Come, good people, come to breakfast, we are all waiting for you," called Claudia from the window, and Neria turned to her so winsome a face, that the young matron smiled as she had not done for many a day.

CHAPTER III.

A CONFESSION.

"AND now what?" asked Mr. Livingstone, as the party rose from breakfast.

"A ride," said Fergus, decisively. "Neria and Franc, get on your habits, and I will order the horses; Claudia, I suppose you don't care to ride?"

"No, it tires me too much. I am going to drive, by-and-by, with Mr. Livingstone," said the bride, languidly.

"But I should be very happy to ride," exclaimed Francia, with a brilliant smile.

Fergus silently looked at Neria, who had not spoken.

"I cannot go this morning," said she, "I have something to do."

"Pshaw! Put by your something, and come. There is not such a day once a month," expostulated Fergus, in a low voice.

Neria smiled, but shook her head.

"You and Franc must enjoy it enough for me too."

"What is your something? What are you going to do?" asked Fergus, pettishly.

"O, something."

"Something you won't tell me?"

"Not just now," said Neria, beginning to look a little troubled.

"You will spoil my ride—in fact, I won't go."

"That would be unkind to Francia, who wishes to go," said Neria, quietly.

"It will be your fault if she is disappointed."

"As it was my fault that the squirrel bit me?" asked Neria, smiling meaningly.

Fergus colored indignantly.

"I did not think it was in you to be so ungenerous, Neria," said he, rising and walking to the other end of the room, where the others were gathered in the breezy bay window.

"Shall we go, Fergus?" asked Francia, timidly; for she had learned to read her cousin's face, and now saw displeasure and disappointment in it.

"Yes, if you please," said he, coldly; and, as Franc moved slowly toward the door, he stepped out of the window, without glancing toward Neria, and went to order the horses.

Half an hour later, Claudia, lounging in a great Indian chair, saw Neria coming down the stairs in her walking dress, and, with a sudden impulse, advanced to join her.

"Stop a minute," called she, "I will go a little way with you, if you are for a walk."

Neria hesitated, and then said:

"Come, then, a little way."

"How far are you going?"

"I will tell you as we walk along."

"Charming little mystery! Where is my veil? O, here; tie it behind for me, please. This sea air is so trying to one's complexion, and it's quite a mistake to suppose brunettes don't tan. Goodness, child, you are never going to wear that little hat and no veil? You will be a squaw by the time you come home."

"I never tan or burn, and I never wear a veil," said Neria, quietly, as she put the little hat, with its drooping white plume, upon the top of her airily-folded, shining hair.

"Yes, it is very becoming, I admit," said Claudia, half envious; adding, as she glanced at Neria's stainless skin, "and such a complexion as yours is heaven's last, best gift to man."

"Not to man, exactly," retorted Neria, putting aside, as ill-judged, an impulse to suggest to her companion some better cause for thankfulness to heaven.

"And now, where are we going?" asked Claudia, as they walked under the rustling lindens in the avenue, amid whose golden blossoms innumerable bees hummed with a murmur like surf breaking on the distant shore.

"I will tell you now. You remember Mr. Gillies?"

"Yes, indeed! The charming old hermit who infected me with his own music-madness that summer, five years ago. Do he and his old tower with the glorious organ still exist?"

"Yes; but, Claudia, I think he never has been just the same since that he was that summer," said Neria, dubiously. "When I used to go with you to take your lessons, you know how animated and enthusiastic he was about music—how dry and reserved on everything else?"

"Yes, I know," said Claudia, with a cunning smile.

"Well, after you went away, Francia and I used to go sometimes and listen from the beach to his playing, just as we did the first night; and after a while he found us out, and one night he asked us in. So we went, and, though Franc thought it rather fearful to sit in that old library in the dark and listen to such solemn music, I enjoyed it; and, when he asked us to come again, we got leave from Miss Boardman, and used to go often. Sometimes he would ask a few questions about you, but generally he said very little, unless we spoke to him. At last, one evening, I don't know how it was, but I found myself standing close beside him, and crying as hard as I could. He was playing something of his own, then, and I never heard such sorrow and loneliness as he conveyed in that music; he never could have said it in words—"

"No," interrupted Claudia, softly; "like dumb people, he expresses himself through his fingers."

"Well, he turned suddenly and saw me, and caught my two hands in his, and looked at me! Claudia! there is a picture of Landseer's—of a stag hunted to death, and turning to look at the hunters, who come crowding up the hill toward him—he looked just like that: so piteous, and so dumb."

"You romantic child," said Claudia, adding, a little uneasily,

"Well, what did he say?"

"Not a word; and, after a minute, he closed the organ and left the room. But the next time we went he asked me if I would learn of him to play. I said that nothing could make me happier. So he began at once."

"But it did not succeed, I imagine," said Claudia, with another smile.

"What, the teaching? O, yes, I learned quite easily."

"No; I don't mean the teaching. The poor old hermit did not find his homœopathic idea of curing the disease by reproducing its cause, successful?"

"I don't understand." said Neria, with a puzzled look.

"Well, never mind. So you took lessons? For how long?"

"Three or four years—till Miss Boardman, who used to go with me, left us, and Mrs. Rhee said it was improper for me to go alone; so, as Franc wouldn't go, and there was no one else, I left off."

"But you are going now?"

"Yes; within a few months Mr. Gillies has been quite ill and very dull. We heard of it through his housekeeper, and one day Francia and I called to see if he needed anything that we could send him. He asked to have us come in, and said if I would sit down and play for him, it would do more good than anything else. I did it, of course, and, when I was going, he thanked me with so much feeling that I asked if I should not come again. He said so much in reply that I was quite ashamed to hear him; and ever since I have been over, at intervals, and am going now. Now you are all here, I am more occupied at home, and have only been once in three weeks; but this morning (on the terrace) I resolved to go before dinner, let what would stand in the way. I have done wrong not to do so sooner."

The two girls walked on in silence. Presently Claudia stopped, and, looking far away to the point where, beneath a silvery shimmer, the sea seemed to melt into the sky, she said in a low voice,

"It was like me."

"What?" asked Neria.

"Why, child, you were too young and too innocent to see what went on beneath your eyes that summer. I was curious to know if that hard, cold man, with his one passion, had any heart. I searched till I found it, and—I broke it."

Neria looked at her, with a slow horror gathering in her eyes.

"O Claudia!" was all she said; but as she turned and walked on alone, the remorseful woman who had met those eyes and heard that tone, sank down upon the beach and wept as she had not wept since the fatal day that first saw her glide beneath John Gillies's roof.

CHAPTER IV.

MR. GILLIES DISCHARGES HIMSELF OF HIS TRUST.

ARRIVED at Cragness, Neria was at once admitted to the library, and found its master seated at the open window, looking listlessly out over the water. He rose as his guest entered, mutely greeted her, and then feebly sank again into the great arm-chair. The years had wrought upon John Gillies in a fashion characteristic of himself. His tall figure was not bowed, but seemed to have dried away to a skeleton, thinly covered with indurated flesh and ashen skin; his grey hair was no thinner than it had been twenty years before; his dry lips closed as firmly, his shaggy brows drew together as keenly, but in the eyes themselves there was a change. Those grey eyes no longer looked on men and things with the shrewd suspicion, the crafty watchfulness, of their youth, but had taken a dreary, introspective softness into their depths—a pain, a doubt, a longing, inexpressibly mournful to Neria, who looked now at her old friend with a new appreciation of the silent story of his life.

Almost without a word, Mr. Gillies unlocked the organ and motioned the young girl to seat herself at it. As silently, she complied; and presently stole out upon the hushed air, not the pain and sorrow of the human heart aching in the musician's breast, but a tender melody, rising and deepening to a noble anthem—tones of lofty hope, of aspiration and prophecy—a strain that bore the listener from the grief of earth to the content of heaven; that, in language high above speech, told of the grand unities of creation, of the eternal harmony in which all discords shall yet be resolved, and the incompleteness and vagueness of life shall be satisfied, by the Master's hand striking the grand chord, embodying in its fulness the key-note of every man's soul.

The solemn joy died away, and Neria sat, with bowed head and dreamy eyes, her fingers idly wandering over the keys, and drawing from them faint whispers, dim echoes—hints of the murmuring sea that swept up beneath the open window, of the summer that glowed in sky and shore.

A thin, hard hand, laid lightly upon her arm, roused her, with a start.

"I have something to say to you, Miss Neria," said John Gillies, and walked stiffly back to his seat in the window, where Neria followed him, and silently sat.

But the recluse seemed to relapse into his usual reticence. Leaning an elbow on the table and his chin upon his palm, he sat looking far away to the horizon line, where, like the wings of a great bird, the sails of a distant ship glanced and wavered in the sunlight.

"You are not quite well yet, Mr. Gillies," said Neria, at length, fancying herself forgotten.

The dreamy eyes came back from the white-winged ship now sinking below the horizon, and fixed upon her face.

"Not well? I can hardly say that; but I am going away, Miss Neria."

"Away from Cragness?"

"Away from everything. I don't say, going to die, because I don't know what that means; but I am soon to make the great change, and I have an unfulfilled trust holding me back. This trust I wish to make over to you, if you will have it; but first I must tell you what it has done for me. Then you shall choose."

Again he paused, and in his fixed eyes dim shadows of the past slowly gathered and darkened. When he spoke again, it was in a weary and hollow voice,

"I made the grand mistake of my life in coming here. I did not know myself as I now do, or I never should have accepted Reginald Vaughn's bequest. My nature, unlike that of other men, had but one passion—one point open to romance or idealism—and through this one narrow channel poured all the impulses of my life, leaving the rest to be guided by reason, method, habit.

"The combination, if unusual, was effective. The vehemence of my passion for music was toned and restrained by the habits of my daily life, and when, after the dry routine of labor, I could feel myself free to indulge this passion, it was to me as love and fame, as home and wife and children are to other men. It was my solace, my rest and recreation.

"I came here. All the fashion of my life was changed. I no longer mingled with men, I no longer filled a place in the affairs of the world; the bonds that had for years held me to a positive duty, a defined position, were snapped at a blow. I had no longer hours, requirements, or responsibilities, save such as were self-imposed. My whole life was unhinged.

"Add to this a secret, a solemn mystery placed in my hands by a dying man, who bade me live here in this very room, where every handsbreadth of surface, every book, every mote floating in the air, the sea booming against its walls—yes, even my own organ—all know this secret, all taunt me with it, all whisper it forever in an unknown tongue, which I have wasted my life to learn, and yet do not know."

He looked slowly about the room, with a wild, hungry light in his sunken eyes, and Neria's heart thrilled with a strange fear. Gillies glanced sharply at her, and said, quietly,

"It would not be strange if my brain were unsettled, but it is not—as yet. Whether death or madness come first, Fate only knows."

"Fate!" said Neria, softly.

"Yes; or God, if you prefer. It is the same power by a different name. Do not talk of that.

"My nature is one slow to take impressions. For years the change wrought by this new life was almost imperceptible; as imperceptible and as unpausing as the hand of time. I gave myself up to music; I collected the works of the great masters in the art; I dreamed over them, and tried to find in myself the power to rival them; I brought from Germany this organ, the *chef-d'œuvre* of its artist; for he was a man who expressed Art in form, as the musician does in sound. I revelled in dreams and visions like those that break the hearts of poets, who can find in words no language to embody them. I lived a life of passion and excess with my beautiful Art, and she turned upon me, as these idols will, and slew me."

He rose and paced the dusky room in strong emotion, and presently sank back into his chair, pale and exhausted.

"I blaspheme," said he, in a choked voice. "It was not Art that slew me—it was I, who knew not that man is not as a God, and cannot live above the earth without sooner or later feeling earth's vengeance.

"Years of this life wrought their work upon me at last. My great passion had taken possession of my entire existence, forcing to unnatural development the impulses severely restrained by the rigor of my former life—awakening capacities and wants unknown to my earlier years. I was roused, restless, and unsatisfied. Then came the vengeance of earth—came in the old familiar form of—woman."

The bitter contortion of his mouth was not a smile, but matched well with the cruel self-contempt of his sudden glance.

"I know what you mean," said Neria, softly. "Do not speak of it, if it pains you."

"You know? Well, it spares me some pain, and so let it pass. Since then, my life has been the broken reed that has at last pierced to the heart. Aimless and discontented, it has no longer the pure purpose, the earnest faith, which Art demands of her favored lovers. The inspiration of those first years never comes now; I no longer create—I can only copy; and the masters whom I hoped to emulate no longer whisper their secrets to my heart. I profaned the pure worship of the divinity by conjoining a false idol with it, and now I am cast out, broken, forsaken, unworthy even to lie at the steps of the altar."

The wild gleam had returned to his eyes, and again he paced up and down the dim chamber, pausing in its midst, at last, to say:

"And this secret of the old man's: I have never found it out, and it haunts me day and night. You see now what it has done for me. Will you have it?"

Neria turned pale, and looked vaguely about the room, as she answered, reluctantly,

"I am afraid of secrets."

"But I cannot carry this one to haunt me in another world, as it has in this," said Gillies, nervously. "Besides, who knows whether that old man who gave it me may not demand a reckoning when we meet there beyond, and then it will be too late. And who is there but you?"

"Mr. Vaughn is far wiser than I—" began Neria, but Gillies impatiently moved his hand.

"It is to be told to none of the name or race of Vaughn," said he. "And if you will not have it, I must take it with me. But I hoped to leave it this side the grave."

Moved by his voice and manner, Neria took counsel with herself for a few moments, and then said,

"Can you trust me so far as to tell the secret, and then allow me choice in the matter of accepting the charge it contains? You cannot doubt that, at all events, I shall keep it inviolable!"

Gillies considered.

"Yes," said he, slowly, "I will trust you. Wait."

From a locked drawer of his desk he drew a sealed package, and, after attentively examining it, placed it in Neria's hands.

"There," said he, "is the letter the old man left for me, and it contains all the information I am able to give you. I have not advanced one step beyond. Keep the package carefully, and, when I am dead, read and act upon it as you think fit. You will then be mistress of Cragness, and may you escape the curse it has brought with it to me. Now go, for my gloomy mood is at hand, and you cannot help me."

Neria took the letter, and, as she touched it, a light shudder ran through her frame.

"After reading, I am free to accept or refuse the trust?" asked she, again.

"Yes; but, if you refuse, choose another agent, and give this house and the secret to him. It is your responsibility now—I have done with it."

"At all events, the trust is inviolable," said Neria, solemnly; but Gillies, who had thrown himself into his chair, with his face to the window, made no reply; and Neria, unwilling to disturb his reverie, silently left the room.

In the passage she met old Lazarus Graves, and, with a smile and kind word, passing on, presently found herself breathing more freely in the open air.

"How unfortunate," said she to herself, "am I, who dislike secrets so much, and have two of them given to me in one day."

CHAPTER V.
AND LAZARUS GRAVES OF HIS.

WITHOUT appearing to see Neria, to whose patient ear he was usually garrulous of the old days in which he lived, Lazarus Graves passed on into the library, and stood, with folded hands and smiling face, looking up and down the room with the humble fondness of a dog who watches his master's movements. But, of a sudden, a shade of bewilderment crossed the wrinkled face, and, turning his head rapidly from side to side, the old man, with his dim eyes, searched the room again, as does the dog who suddenly misses the beloved figure. With increasing perplexity he turned to look at the door behind him. It was close shut. Then he tottered across the room, and laid a hand upon the shoulder of the motionless figure in the arm-chair.

"Well?" demanded John Gillies, impatiently.

"Where is he gone?" asked Lazarus, in a voice as dim and hollow as a sound lost ages ago in the catacombs, and ever since trying to escape to the open air.

"Who?"

"Mr. Reginald. He passed me as I sat upon the doorstep in the sun, and smiled. He has a rare smile, has Mr. Reginald; and then he came in, and up the passage, and into this room. I hobbled after as fast as I could, for I wanted to hear him say I had kept all as he told me when he went away. And now, where is he?"

Gillies made no reply, but turned and looked attentively at the old man, who maundered on:

"He said he'd come back, and I knew he would; and I've been waiting this many a day just to hear him say I'd kept all as he wanted; and now he's come, and if he goes again I'll go, too; but—but where is he?"

Still, without answer to the pitiful appeal, Gillies watched the old man as he stood there in the sunshine, his bowed figure leaning on his staff, his thin, white hair floating over his shoulders, his mouth trembling with emotion, his dim, blue eyes always wandering about the room, while once more he piteously murmured,

"Where is he?"

"Where you and I will soon be with him, old man—and where is that?" said Gillies, at length; but Lazarus Graves did not hear him. Dropping his staff, he had clasped his hands and raised both them and his ashen face in a joyous ecstasy, while his eyes fixed themselves upon a point at the opposite side of the room.

"Why, there he is now," cried he, "with his hand upon that book he used to be so fond of. He's looking at you, sir. Why don't you speak to him. See!"

And the old man pointed impatiently, turning, as he spoke, to Gillies, whose fixed eyes never swerved from the seer-like face of the speaker.

"Ah, now he sees me; now he's going to speak," murmured Lazarus, taking

Drawn by Sol Eytinge

AGAIN HE SEEMED TO LISTEN, AND A BRIGHT JOY IRRADIATED HIS FACE.—

a step forward and smiling joyously, while he seemed to listen to a voice unheard save by himself.

"Yes, Mr. Reginald, you said you'd come, and I knew it," said he, at length. "And I've kept all as you'd wish it, so far as I was able; but I'm getting into years now, sir, and am pretty tired by spells. It's coming time for me to rest, as old folks must."

Again he seemed to listen, and a bright joy irradiated his face.

"Aye, that I will, sir," said he, "I carried you in my arms when you was a baby, and I've held to you ever since; and I'd have followed you long ago if I'd known where to find you. But now you've come for me, I'll ask no better than to go along with you. Let's be going, sir. Good-by, Mr. Gillies; you've been kind and good to me; but my old master's come back at last, and I'm going away with him. He's come for me."

"Say you so, old man?" muttered Gillies. "Then, by Heaven's grace, has he come for me, too."

Without heeding him, Lazarus turned, and moved a few steps toward the door, paused, tottered, threw up his arms with a stifled gasp, and fell forward upon his face. He had followed his master.

CHAPTER VI.

THE HOUSEKEEPER.

His family and guests dispersed to their several amusements or occupations, Mr. Vaughn sought his study, and, after an interval of anxious thought, summoned Mrs. Rhee to his presence.

She came, and, at a sign from her master, seated herself in the very chair where she had sat eighteen years before, while he told her of his intention to leave his home for an indefinite period. These years had, borne heavily upon the housekeeper, and her youth had departed with them, leaving but a pallid wreck of the beauty which had so impressed John Gillies on the evening of his first visit to Bonniemeer. In her dark eyes, larger from the attenuation of her face, still lay the old, unquiet mystery—still the hungry pain of an unsatisfied heart; and still they followed every movement of the master's stately figure, while he silently paced the room, as if they hoped and dreaded to read in his face an answer to their appeal.

At last, Vaughn stopped in front of her. His face was both stern and sad.

"You have not held to my directions with regard to Neria," said he, quietly.

The woman's face flushed, and her eyes drooped.

"How?" asked she.

"I desired that the knowledge of her birth might be kept from her. I desired that no difference should be made between her and Francia," said Vaughn.

"I have tried to obey, but you should have thought how hard a task you imposed upon me," faltered the housekeeper.

Vaughn impatiently waved his hand.

"There is the trouble," said he. "You will not forget, you will not put out of sight, what I have desired should be forgotten and put out of sight."

"You have found it very easy to do so; I am of a more faithful nature," said Mrs. Rhee, bitterly.

Vaughn frowned and resumed his restless promenade.

"At least," said he, harshly, "I might have expected you to comply with my directions that the child should not be informed of her origin."

"The secret escaped me in a moment of irritation at seeing her assume airs of superiority over Francia. You yourself could not give her the right to do that," said Mrs. Rhee, boldly.

"Yes, but I could," retorted Vaughn, again pausing and looking down at her. "I could give her the right to control every inmate of this house, simply by making her my wife."

The housekeeper turned frightfully pale, and uttered a stifled cry of rage and apprehension—a passion of sobs and tears, which shook her slender figure through and through.

Vaughn looked at her, while pity, pain and self-reproach swept by turns across his face.

"Forgive me, if I have been harsh, Anita," said he, at length. "I see how hard your life must have been; I cannot wonder at your present feelings. It was too much that I asked of you. Indeed, from the first, it was ill-judged of me to put you in your present position."

"It was my own wish, and I was content to abide the consequences," said the housekeeper, without looking up.

"I know, and I yielded to your solicitations, against my better judgment. It was a weak compliance, and, while it has made you no happier, has kept alive in my heart a painful secret that might long since have been put aside but for your presence."

Mrs. Rhee raised her head with dignity.

"It is better, then, that I should go, at any rate," said she.

"Perhaps it is, Anita," replied Vaughn, kindly, but with an unconcealed expression of relief upon his face.

"Do not think," added he, hastily, "that I am displeased with you, or that we part on other than the best of terms. I do not forget the tie that binds us together, and, though it can never be recognized, it shall always give you a claim to every care, every consideration, at my hands."

"*Every* consideration?" asked the housekeeper, with deliberate emphasis.

"Every consideration consistent with my own safety and my daughter's welfare," said Vaughn, impatiently.

Mrs. Rhee replied by a slow and bitter smile.

"You cannot expect me to sacrifice these, especially now, when I have guarded them, and forced you to guard them, for twenty years?" demanded Vaughn, sharply.

"I expect nothing but death, which must come, sooner or later, and to be forgotten," said the woman, bitterly, and glided from the room, leaving the master of Bonniemeer to ponder, through a weary hour, as many a man has done before, how best he might pluck out from his harvest-field the tares whose seeds had been sown with the wheat.

CHAPTER VII.
A MARRIAGE.

ALL through the day, John Gillies sat almost motionless in the embayed window, his dreamy eyes gazing far across the shining waters, his thoughts roaming beyond the limits of sea, or earth, or life itself.

Nancy Brume in vain invited him to eat of her choicest viands, in vain importuned him with questions as to the sudden death of Lazarus Graves, and the disposition to be made of his body. He answered everything with a briefly-expressed desire to be left alone, and the housekeeper, who had gradually acquired a profound respect for the wishes of her taciturn master, at last complied, and from the middle of that day to the morning of the next, did not venture in his presence.

The long summer day ended, and with the sunset came rolling up out of the the south great clouds which presently wrapped heaven and earth in a black and stifling mantle, through whose folds peered no light of moon or stars, although each sullen wave, as it rolled shoreward, was crested with the lurid light of its own phosphorescence, and, breaking upon the beach, tossed its fiery sparkles far up the level sands.

Dark and heavy as fell the night upon the beach, it fell darker and heavier yet in that close-mouthed and ghastly chamber, darkest and heaviest of all in the heart of the man sitting so rigidly in the old arm-chair, gazing, forever gazing over the phosphorescent sea, into the black void beyond, holding for him, not alone the secret he had so wearied to discover, but all secrets, the last great secret, the secret in whose utterance the lips of the Sphynx petrified forever, leaving the unspoken word to be guessed from her melancholy eyes.

Hour by hour the night stole on, until the rising tide lapped with its fiery tongues the foundations of the old house, and all the monsters that be beneath the sea rose, each in his place, to look in at the man who still sat waiting, always waiting until the hour should come. It came at last. A spirit moved upon the vast waters, entered at the open window and laid its shadowy pall upon that weary head and breathed upon those pallid lips; and before those wistful eyes opened a vision, a foreseeing, a promise such as no man who has seen has ever found tongue to tell.

Over the white and weary face came a smile such as had never rested there before, and the musician, softly rising, went through the gloomy room to place himself at the organ. His fingers fell upon the keys, and that sweet, strange smile passed through them, and embodied itself in sound. Such sounds! Such "long disquiet merged in rest!" Such full content and peace; such grand and solemn joy! And, ah! the glorious rending of the bonds and cerements that had cramped in earth's heavy atmosphere the spirit whose home was in the clouds! It was the song of the lark who sees the door of his cage thrown wide, and after weary months of pining, in one instant finds the prison far below, nothing but the subtle ether around, nothing but the sunbright heavens above, and who, thrilling upward to the sky, sends a joyful heralding of song before him, whose tones dropping back to earth, steal into men's hearts like the memories of their youth, like the faith of their childhood.

Such music it was that floated out upon the mirky air of the summer's night, until the listening monsters, catching its joyful meaning, lashed the waters into pools of fire with their ponderous glee, and sported together till the sliding waves broke in great shouts of laughter on the beach. Only the mermaids, the Undines, would not sport or laugh, but hiding their faces in their long hair, clung to each other trembling and sobbing, for they, whose merry lives are forever shadowed by the thought of the immortality denied them, knew that the joy of the musician's heart was a joy in which they had no share; they knew that from their golden harps no such notes should ever ring—through their soulless lives never thrill such ecstasy.

And as the dark night waned, and aged, and came to the dawning of another day, the musician gathered his life in his hands and inspired with it the tones that grew beneath his touch. It was no longer music, it was the soul of a man who had lived and died for music, and to whom the divine art had at the last granted its love and grace, and had entered into his form, and made itself one with his spirit, until soul and art together sang such a nuptial hymn, chanted their epithalamium in such a glory of triumphant harmony as never before has earth heard, never the heavens let fall to man.

And in that grand triumph of his life, in that glorious consummation of an eternal union, the soul of John Gillies emancipated itself from the broken body that had confined it, and soared upward until its broad vans were gilded by the rays of the rising sun.

CHAPTER VIII.

THE OLD MAN OF THE SEA UPON NEW SHOULDERS.

AMONG Mr. Gillies's few papers was found a will, bequeathing his entire property to Neria. This instrument was dated only the day before his death, and made no allusions to the peculiar conditions involved in the heirship. But to Neria's delicate conscience this silence only made her duties more onerous; and, on the day after the funeral, she went to Cragness, and locking herself into the library, opened and read the letter of instruction left by Reginald Vaughn for the guidance of his first heir.

Youth is brave, and Neria was too devout a worshipper of truth to be easily daunted by mystery. It seemed to her that, if one inquired earnestly after anything, he must be answered by flesh, or spirit, earth, air, or water. As an infant may, perchance, see in his first worldly surroundings and attendants the heaven and the angels he has just left behind, Neria fancied every man and woman an Ithuriel, armed with the diamond-pointed spear whose touch must extort truth from its most ingenious involvements.

So she doubted nothing of discovering at her pleasure this secret, whose responsibility had lain with such nightmare weight upon the musician's mind, and she only wished that he had sooner taken her into council, that, by seeing the mystery unravelled in his lifetime, he should have been relieved in death of the haunting anxiety and remorse so apparent in their last interview.

The names of Reuben and Nancy Brume were signed as witnesses to the will, but neither was aware of its contents; and the natural curiosity upon the subject burning in the mind of each was very pleasantly allayed by Neria's quiet information that she was now possessor of the estate, and should wish them to continue to fill their present position in the house.

"And will you come and stop here, miss?" asked the housekeeper, in some bewilderment.

"Not at present," replied her new mistress, with a smile. "My guardian, Mr. Vaughn, would hardly think me old enough or wise enough to manage a house of my own. But after a while, I dare say, I shall come and live here, and have you to take care of me, Mrs. Brume. Then it will be I who shall sit all day in the gloomy library, and play at night upon the great organ. It will be Mr. Gillies all over again. I always thought I should like it."

"That sort of a life ain't meant for young ladies," said the housekeeper, scornfully. "They'd ought to be going to balls and parties, and dressing up, and keeping company, and getting married. After that's time enough to settle down."

Neria smiled again, gently, but with such reserve that Mrs. Brume closed her lips upon the piece of advice just ready to issue from them, and asked, instead,

"Have you any d'rections to give, Miss Neria, about the way things are to go here, or shall we just keep on in the old way?"

"In the old way," said Neria, dreamily. "Let everything be just as it has always been, more as if the master were gone for a visit than for ever—as if he might return at any moment. I can hardly believe it otherwise, even yet."

With a gracious movement of leave-taking, the young mistress of Cragness descended the path to the beach and flitted away through the twilight, until, in the distance, she showed like some graceful vision fashioned of the rising mist, which, at the last, closed over it and reclaimed it.

Nancy Brume stood watching her from the cliff, with arms akimbo and brows drawn into the scowl universal among dwellers by the sea, whose eyes thus habitually seek to shelter themselves from the glare of sand and water, and so acquire a ferocious expression oddly at variance with the real kindliness of nature almost as universal.

Reuben, lying stretched upon the short, brown grass at her feet, amused himself with a solitary game of stick-knife.

"Reub," said his wife, "I ain't more notional than most folks, but something she said kind o' ha'nts me."

"'S that so?" asked Reuben, lazily, adding a slight "Phew!" as the knife, in its descent, caught him rather sharply upon the knuckles.

"Yes. Didn't you mind she said she wanted everything kept just as if Gillies had gone off for a little while, and might be back any time."

"Well, it's less work than to go to changing round, ain't it? What's the matter with that?"

"Yes, but, Reub, don't you mind how Lahsrus was always saying just the same thing?"

"Don't know as I do," returned Reuben, absently, his mind engrossed in the effort to catch the knife upon the back of his wrist.

"Well, he was. He was always telling that Mr. Reginald, as he called him, was coming back sure some day, and that everything had got to be kept ready for him. It used to make my flesh creep, odd times, to watch him going round and fixing things back when they'd got stirred a little. Don't you know the old boat he would keep chained to the rock down there till finally the boat rotted away, piece by piece, and left the chain hanging, just as they say men have done when they was chained up in dungeons and left to starve?"

"He was cracked, Lahsrus was," said Mr. Brume, with benevolent contempt.

"Mebbe he was, and then again mebbe he wa'n't," retorted his wife. "Any how, he see him, finally."

"Who—see who?" asked Reuben, leaning on one elbow and looking up in his wife's solemn face.

"Lahsrus see old Vaughn. It was the very day he died, and I was setting to my window sewing, and he was setting on the door-rock in the sun, kind of purring to himself, as he used to, when all to once I see him put his hand up, shading his eyes, and looking down the path. Then he kind o' lighted up all over, and looked more man-fashion than I'd seen him for many a day, and, says he, speaking up as clear and bright as you please, 'It's my dear Mr. Reginald—he always said he'd come.' Then he got up and stood o' one side, turning his head, just as if some one passed him and went up the entry-way, and then he followed right along to the libr'y. Mr. Gillies never told what he see or said when he got there, for he was struck with death himself at that very time; but I shall always believe that Lahsrus waited for his old master till he come, and that they both went off together.

"And now, don't you see, Neria kind o' sets it to us to stop here and wait just the same fashion for Mr. Gillies to come back; and, like enough, here we'll stick, year after year, and year after year, till we kind o' dry up and lose all our faculties, just as Lahsrus did, and finally they'll come back and carry us off. It's just like shipping aboard the Flying Dutchman—seems to me."

Reuben Brume sat upright and stared at his wife.

"Tell you what, Nance," said he, "you're getting cracked, too, I reckon; but, mind you, if it's so, I ain't going to stop here along with a loonytic. How would I know but you'd take the carving-knife to me some night? I guess, anyway, I'd best be looking out for a v'y'ge. It's dull work stopping here."

Mrs. Brume looked contemptuously down at her lord, again recumbent on the turf.

"'Fore you sign your name to any ship's books," said she, "you'd oughter tell the skipper that you're a sick man, and that your ailment's dreadful catching."

"What you driving at now, Nance?" inquired the husband, with an uneasy foreboding of an impending blow.

"Why there wa'n't never a clearer case of

> Fever-de-lurke,
> Two stomachs to eat,
> And none to work,

since time begun," said Mrs. Brume, dryly; "and I reckon your best course is to be off to sea as fast as you can. You'll get nussed with ropes' ends and b'laying pins there, and that's just the physic for your disorder."

Reuben turned upon his stomach and silently resumed his game of stick-knife, while Nancy, with a grim smile upon her lips, returned to the lonely house, where now, in the dim twilight, the shadows that all day lay hidden in the corners and corridors, in the height of the vaulted ceilings, or in the angles of the unlighted stair-case, came boldly out and flitted through the empty rooms, danced gleefully over the dead men's memories that lay beneath their feet, drew their clammy fingers over the keys of the great organ, crept into the chair where Reginald Vaughn and John Gillies had sat watching and waiting, until death came sailing across the sea and hailed them to take passage with him—hovered about the hearth and cowered above the blaze until it started up in wrath and flashed out such a sudden light and heat that the shadows fled gibbering to their corners, and the Knight in Golden Armor upon the wall stood boldly out, as if he were charging upon them with his black horse and his proud slogan: "*Dieu, le roy, et le foy du Vaughn!*"

CHAPTER IX.

A DROP-CURTAIN.

AND now, Mr. and Mrs. Livingstone, having completed their visit to Bonniemeer, were on the point of returning to the city, and Claudia insisted that Neria and Francia should accompany them, and make their *début* in society under her chaperonage. Francia was wild with delight at prospect of the gay life promised her by her cousin, while Neria looked and listened much after the fashion of a fawn, who, wandering to the edge of his native forest, sees suddenly before him a great plain with a city in its midst, its domes glittering, its many-windowed palaces flashing back the morning sun, shaded gardens nestling about it, and an army with plumes and pennons, fanfare of trumpets and flash of accoutrements, winding out of its gates, and stretching like a glittering serpent across the plain. So strange, so unlearned, so ominous, and so fascinating lay life before Neria, child of the sea and the sky, her feet set in the path worn deep by the steps of those who have trod it since first it led Eve away from paradise, her head still crowned with the glory lingering around every fresh work of the Divine Artist, her slender fingers folding close above her breast the shining robes of innocence and truth.

"Neria in a fashionable assembly!" said Mr. Vaughn, in reply to his brother-in-law's urgent advocacy of Claudia's plan. "Why it would be the Holy Grail upon the supper table of a *danseuse;* it would be both a desecration and an incongruity."

"As for the desecration, my dear fellow, we won't argue the point," said Mr. Murray, taking snuff. "And as for the incongruity, I must say that to be incongruous with the elements of a fashionable assembly, is, in my eyes, a very questionable virtue in a young lady."

"Neria's manners are above conventionality," said Mr. Vaughn, decisively.

"That is impossible. Conventionality is the religion, the *morale* of society —there is nothing above it; to be outside of it, is to be beneath it," retorted Murray, sublime in his faith.

But Vaughn, smiling, put the question by, and said,

"I suppose both Neria and Francia must mix in society at some time, but I confess I dread to see their country freshness wither in its atmosphere, and my violet and wild rose come back to me as hot-house flowers, all properly labelled and trained, but with neither perfume nor strength left in them."

"Come back to you? No, but I shall insist upon your taking up your quarters with me," said Mr. Murray, hospitably. "There are Fergus and I left by Claudia's marriage to keep bachelor's hall together, and we need just such an old traveller as yourself to come and show us how to manage. You should see me attempt to pour out tea, and Fergus boggle at cutting a pudding. Then you can keep watch over your daughter and your—ward, do you call her? and snatch them away from the naughty world at the precise moment when the polish is obtained, without the waste of a single particle of the gem. Will you come?"

"Thank you, yes," said Vaughn, heartily. "And I will confess that with Claudia as *chaperon*, and two utterly inexperienced girls as *débutantes*, I think it will be quite as well for me to be at hand."

"Claudia is a sensible young woman," said Mr. Murray, complacently, "and will, I dare say, before the season is over, marry Francia as handsomely as she has married herself."

"Heaven forbid!" ejaculated Vaughn, adding with a smile,

"But why only Francia, why is she not also to marry Neria?"

"Because, retorted Murray, quietly, "the very pith of your wish to come up to town is to see that she does not. You are resolved to marry Neria yourself."

'Vaughn started from his seat, and stood for several moments looking out of the window, then, resuming his chair, fixed his eyes upon those of his brother-in-law, saying, quietly,

"It is only now that I have resolved it."

"Consciously, yes. Unconsciously you resolved it long ago," insisted Murray; and Vaughn, searching his own heart for the truth of the assertion, forgot to answer it.

In another week, Bonniemeer was deserted, and left in charge of Mrs. Rhee, who, not having as yet determined upon her future course in life, was very willing to remain in her old home until she should do so.

CHAPTER X.
"BRONZE-COLOR: A GREYISH-YELLOW."—*Nicholson.*

"CARDS for a ball, a fancy ball, a masked ball, *mes filles!*" proclaimed Mrs. Livingstone, taking three envelopes from the table and tearing them open, as she and her guests entered the drawing-room, after their morning drive.

"How perfectly splendid! What a magnificent idea! O, Claudia, what shall I wear?" exclaimed Francia, bounding up from the sofa, where she had sunk, and quite forgetting her fatigue.

"The idea of disposing of such a question in a breath!" retorted Claudia. "Why, we shall discuss it all the rest of to-day and all to-morrow, and shall quarrel like the Three Furies before we are done with it. A proper costume for a fancy ball is a serious question, *petite*."

"The more reason why we should begin to discuss it at once," exclaimed Francia. "Neria, what are your most obvious sentiments upon the subject?"

"Of costume?" asked Neria, with her not unusual look of wistful perplexity; "I have none at all."

"As badly off as the old dominie, who pathetically remarked: 'Locke says the human mind is never entirely void of ideas; but I have been conscious of long intervals of time in which my mind contained absolutely no ideas whatever,'" suggested Claudia.

"I think I will be a gypsy," said Francia, dubiously.

"I think you will nothing of the sort," continued her cousin. "Wait till to-morrow, and I will think about you. At present, I have an idea with which to furnish poor Neria's empty mind. Neria, attention! You are Undine. You will be dressed in a robe of sea-green gossamer over green satin, which will sparkle through it just like the light in a wave. You will have your golden hair all down your back, and be crowned with water-lilies, and wear pearls upon your neck and arms. In your hand you will carry the chaplet of red and white coral that Undine drew from the depths of the river to give to Bertha."

"Beautiful! There couldn't be anything better suited to Neria. Your idea is an inspiration, Claudia," exclaimed Francia; but Neria shivered.

"Undine is an ominous character," said she.

"Don't be afraid. There is no Bertha in the case, dear," returned Claudia, with a significant smile.

"Nor any knight Huldbrand, either," added Francia.

"But to call myself Undine is to invite both," said Neria, smiling.

"And if they come, my dear, I hope you will prove the superiority of a woman over a mermaid by the manner in which you secure Huldbrand and circumvent Bertha. Undine behaved like a fool," remarked Claudia.

"And yet like a woman. It would be so much easier to quietly let one's heart break, than to plot and labor to retain a love that wished to escape," said Neria, softly.

"Love! That is as it may be," retorted Claudia; "But do you imagine any woman with the spirit of a canary-bird would stand by and see another woman steal away the man who had once vowed constancy to her, and never make an effort to reclaim him? Why, I would kill such a woman, though the man were one I never cared to see again."

"Dr. Lutrell," said the servant, opening the door of the drawing-room.

A gentleman upon the threshold bowed profoundly, and advanced into the room.

Claudia, on hearing the name, had half uttered an exclamation, and started from her chair. Instantly recovering herself, however, she restrained every symptom of emotion except the deep color that flushed her face, and, advancing a few steps toward her guest, extended her hand, saying, with a smile, courteous even if artificial:

"I am glad to see you again, Dr. Lutrell, and also to hear such pleasant things of you."

"Thank you. I did not know that my modest nuptials would make sufficient impression to be remembered after the brilliant wedding that made Mr. Livingstone the happiest of men and an object of envy to all the rest of us. Accept, in turn, my congratulations and good wishes."

A fine tone of sarcasm rang through the careful modulations of his voice, and was caught by Neria's sensitive ear. She turned to examine more particularly this new guest, of whom she had never heard.

A slight and elegant figure, small hands and feet, a perfect toilet—all this was well; but at the face Neria paused, and finally suspended judgment. Either it was very handsome or utterly repulsive, and for the moment she was unable to determine which. The clear-cut and regular features were almost faultless, the dark hair suited well with the *mat* complexion; the frequent smile displayed exquisite teeth, but the eyes—what was there in those furtive eyes that made Neria shrink from their passing glance and shiver as she felt them again resting upon her? The color was peculiar and indescribable, unless, perhaps, one named it yellowish-bronze; but the expression was something more than peculiar, and suggested to Neria vague ideas of hungry creatures lying ambushed for their prey, of serpents sleeping in deep jungle grass, of a Thug waiting patiently for hours behind his palm tree, while far down the valley the doomed victim comes riding on, his eyes filled with memories of home and love, a smile upon his lips, and hope whispering at his heart.

"Girls, let me present Dr. Lutrell. Miss Vaughn, Dr. Lutrell, and Miss Francia Vaughn."

Francia bowed with her usual smiling grace, and Neria, with an effort, raised her eyes once more to those so steadily bent upon her. She was glad when she had done so, for in this direct gaze she determined that, after all, there was nothing so peculiar about these eyes, except, perhaps, the color; and with a little feeling of self-reproach for her first impression, she exerted herself to answer, with sufficient courtesy, the enquiries and remarks addressed to her.

"We were talking of Mrs. Minturn's fancy ball," said Claudia, presently. "You will be there?"

"We have cards, but I had not thought of going," said Doctor Lutrell. "To select a character for a fancy ball you must commit either a stupidity or an indiscretion. Either you assume a disguise utterly incongruous with your personality, and so, utterly wearisome, or you select one which betrays to the whole world your own estimate of yourself, and so give Mrs. Grundy a rich opportunity for the good-natured little remarks in which she delights."

"I don't think people in general go so far as to measure the masker's own character against that which he assumes," said Claudia. "Most people don't think at all, and of those who do, the majority are persons who will, at any rate, be malicious. We are all fools or knaves."

The two young girls turned startled eyes upon their cousin, then Francia laughed, and even Neria's face swept a tide of color, showing that the deep fountain of her emotions was touched.

Dr. Lutrell's eyes flashed across the face of either, read them more than either knew, and came back to rest upon Claudia's with a meaning glance, which she read and recklessly answered.

"O, these girls have come to me to learn society; you would not have me turn out the pretty lambs to the wolves without warning them, as far as I may, of the style of creature they are going among."

Dr. Lutrell turned gaily toward the couch where Neria and Francia sat together.

"Don't believe a word she says, young ladies. Society, especially in this city, is an assemblage of all that is great, wise, good and beautiful in the world. Every one is amiable, every one is intelligent, every one speaks and lives the exact truth. Come among us and see! Mrs. Livingstone knows all this as well as I; but to-day she has the headache, or a dyspepsia, or was out too late last night."

He rose and bowed as he spoke, and passed down the long drawing-room. His hostess accompanied him a few steps, and said in a low voice,

"Why do you wish to deceive them in what they will so soon learn for themselves?"

"Why do you put your vase of wild flowers in the shade, instead of in the sun?" asked the guest, and went on his way with a smile in his tigerish eyes.

CHAPTER XI.

TRANSPARENT MASKS.

A KNOT of young men in various costume lounged in the hall of Mrs. Minturn's handsome house, and discussed the masquers who passed before them into the drawing-room, with a freedom characteristic of their condition. Three female figures descended the stairs, and were joined at the foot by a domino, who waited to escort them.

"A Cleopatra!" said a Charles II. among the *flaneurs*, in an audible voice, "and very well got up, too. See the golden asp upon her right arm, and the string of pearls upon her left. The crown, the starry veil, the royal robes—all correct, fair sister, but tell me, is it Marc Antony to-day, or another?"

The Cleopatra thus attacked threw an angry glance upon the questioner, and passed quickly on. Nothing daunted, the merry monarch continued his remarks.

"And a mermaid? No—Undine, by the string of coral, but," in a lower voice, "I had not supposed any woman in this city would have the effrontery to crown herself with water-lilies and wear pearls for her only ornament. She must be very new—or, very experienced. Probably the latter, for the innocence of a woman of the world is a great deal more natural than nature. *Mais voilà! la jolie petite marquise!* See the ravishing little waist displayed by the long points to her bodice, and the coquetry of that tiny patch just in the dimple of the chin, and the round white arms, and the turn of the neck! You may wait, my friends, for whom you will—I go to see if *la marquise* will not play Louise de Querouailles to my Charles II., for an hour, at least."

As the gay speaker separated himself from his comrades, and followed the object of his admiration into the drawing-room, he was joined by Mephistopheles, who had stood silently listening to his remarks, and who now said, as he passed his arm through that of the king,

"Your majesty and I are old friends, and should hunt in couples."

"The deuce we are!" retorted Charles, eyeing his companion askance.

"Just what I remarked, and a very pretty deuce we make; deuce-ace, if you will, for unlike most couples, we are two in one, or one in two, as you please."

"Go look for your Faust, I will none of you—my familiar never showed himself in company," said Charles, shaking off the grasp of his companion.

"That was because you were still running through your days of grace," retorted Mephistopheles. "But now you have come under authority, and are only out on leave to-night. It is I who am king, and—*vivat Rex*."

"*Tout bien!* Come, then, and advise me how to penetrate the incognito of the little *marquise*," said Charles, recklessly.

"I will advise you to let her alone, or at any rate to say nothing for which you will be sorry when you meet her unmasked," said his companion, significantly. "Try your gallantries on the Cleopatra if you will"—

"And leave *la marquise* to you! Thank you. *mon diable!* I am a worthier pupil than that. Compare notes with Cleopatra yourself, or see if a Becky Sharp does not lurk beneath those water-lilies; but 'leave my love to me.'"

The party had by this time reached the upper end of the long rooms, where stood the hostess in the dress of Dame Quickly, but without mask. As each guest bowed before her he presented a card bearing both his real and assumed title. After glancing at these, Mrs. Minturn dropped them into a vase zealously guarded by a roguish Cupid, who, with drawn bow and warning cry, menaced all who ventured to approach too near.

After a few words of compliment, the party moved on to make room for other guests, and the royal Stuart approached the Marquise with a low bow and a request that she would favor him with her hand for a valse-quadrille in the adjoining ball-room.

The Marquise hesitated, but after glancing at Cleopatra, who nodded assent, she silently accepted the proffered arm.

Mephistopheles, at the same moment, addressed to Undine a request to promenade through the rooms with him, offering to give her a lesson in reading disguises which she should find of use through all her future life.

Cleopatra motioned her to accept, and herself taking the arm of the domino who remained in attendance, slowly followed for a few steps, and then said, in a low voice:

"Go, now, and find some one else. I will take care of myself."

"All, right, my lady," replied Mr. Livingstone's thick voice; "only don't let the men be too free. They'll say things from behind their masks that they wouldn't dare to say without them."

"Not to me," said Cleopatra, haughtily, and each went a separate way.

CHAPTER XII.

A DEUX TEMPS.

In the ball-room the frenzy of the galop had subsided into the passionate tenderness of the waltz, and the band, led by a musician, rendered, with such fidelity and *abandon*, the wild heart-break of the Sophia waltzes, that one instinctively feared to see the whole place a necropolis of swooning and dying princesses.

Francia, in her charming costume, à *la Pompadour*, her supple waist encircled by the arm of the King Charles, his breath upon her cheek, her right hand pressed close to his heart, floated round and round the room in a strange ecstacy, wondering how she had lived so long and never before felt the joy of life ; wondering, too, at the passionate impulse of tears that almost suffocated her.

The music ceased with a long, piercing strain, that might have been the wail of the lover as his royal mistress fell dead at his feet, and Francia, blind and breathless, allowed her partner to support her for a moment longer in the embrace which we all consider so eminently proper while the motion of the dance continues—so very shocking a few minutes later.

"I never shall forget this waltz," murmured King Charles.

"Nor I, for I never enjoyed one half so much," said Francia, guilelessly; and behind his mask the merry monarch smiled a meaning smile.

"Let us promenade a little," said he, and led the way to the cool shadow of the conservatory.

"Do you believe in magnetism, Marquise?" asked he, seating his companion upon an ottoman and throwing himself upon a footstool at her side.

"I don't know anything about it," said Francia, wonderingly.

"Then take your first lesson of me, *ma belle*. It was a powerful magnetism that drew me to you the first moment my eyes rested upon you; it is that same magnetism that made our waltz to me the very culmination of my life; and, tell me, Marquise, may I be very frank, very bold?"

"Yes," murmured Francia.

"It was that same magnetism that wrought upon you when you said you never had enjoyed a dance so much."

He took in his the soft, white hand that Francia had nervously ungloved when she first sat down.

"I must see your face, I must hear your name, here and now," murmured he, half beseechingly, half imperiously.

The little hand grew cold, and trembled in his grasp, but it was not withdrawn, nor did the bewildered girl resist, as with a quick movement her companion untied the ribbon confining her mask, and suffered it to drop into her lap.

The face thus disclosed was indeed one worthy of a monarch's admiration; and just now, with cheeks and lips at their brightest, eyes at their bluest, and the perfect shape of the low white forehead displayed by the coquettish backward roll of the hair glittering with golden powder, Francia's fresh beauty was so bewildering that it hardly seemed an extravagance for her masked admirer to murmur,

"O, that I were indeed a king, that I might, with some faint hope of success, offer my throne to the Queen of Love and Beauty!"

Francia's head drooped lower and lower, while the carnation deepened on her cheeks, and even "the nape of her white neck flushed rosy red," but, alas! not "with indignation."

His bold eyes devouring her beauty, Charles grasped again the hand she had withdrawn, and murmured,

"Tell me what to call you, my queen."

A sharp step rang through the ante-room dividing the conservatory from the other apartments, and Francia, snatching away her hand, hurriedly replaced

Drawn by Sol Eytinge.

KING CHARLES AND THE MARQUISE.—

her mask. It was not yet tied when a knight in golden armor stood before her.

"Excuse me, sir," said he, haughtily, to King Charles, who had risen to his feet; "but this young lady is a relative of mine, and I am desired by her friends to conduct her to them."

"If the young lady desires to exchange my company for yours, I shall of course submit to her wishes, otherwise I shall claim my privilege of leaving her under charge of the lady from whose side I took her," retorted the *quasi* monarch, with right kingly imperiousness.

The knight hesitated an instant, then turned his back upon his rival, and said in a low voice,

"Francia, come with me."

The girl arose, but before she could accept the arm offered her by the knight, her late partner interposed,

"May I not have the usual privilege of a gentleman who has been honored with a lady's hand in the dance, and escort you to your *chaperone?*" asked he, in a voice so exceedingly guarded as to betray the irritation of his feelings.

Francia hesitated, half-turned toward the last speaker, then again to the knight, and whispered,

"I will go directly to Claudia, Fergus, and you can come, too."

"You will do as you choose," was the stern reply; and Francia, her eyes filled with tears, took the arm persistently offered by her other cavalier, and walked away in a very different mood from that of a few moments before.

"May I ask the name of that young man?" inquired King Charles, still in the tone of elaborate courtesy, so significant to a practised ear.

"He is my cousin," faltered Francia, instinctively answering the question her companion had not chosen to ask.

"Cousins have strange privileges, it appears to me," said the King. "Sweet ones, too, sometimes, if I am rightly informed."

"Fergus has always been like a brother to me," murmured Francia.

"Very like a brother, as I have found them behind the scenes," said her companion. "But may I not resume the inquiry you were about to answer when this peremptory cousin-brother of yours interrupted us?"

"My name? Mrs. Minturn can tell you. Ah, here is Neria."

"The Undine? But there is Cleopatra in the next room, with a crowd of courtiers about her. Will you go to her?"

"Yes, if you please."

And as she answered, the poor little *marquise* cast a timid look over her shoulder at the stately form of the golden knight who now stood in the doorway of the ball-room watching her movements.

"*Monsieur le cousin* appears to doubt either your word or my honor," said King Charles. bitterly, as he followed her eyes.

Francia made no reply, but hurried on, and in another moment stood beside Claudia, who received her with a little nod, and went on talking to the three gentlemen, who all claimed her attention at the same moment.

King Charles, with a low bow and a murmured word of thanks left her here, and went to look for Mrs. Minturn, with whom he was an especial favorite.

While Cleopatra and her courtiers flashed their javelins of wit and badinage over her head, Francia remained for some moments in a bewildered reverie, through which the waltz, the conservatory, the strange bold words of her late partner, and the displeasure of her cousin mingled confusedly. Recovering a little, she raised her eyes, and timidly explored the room for Fergus.

He was promenading with an elegant Diana upon his arm, and although he passed and repassed the spot where Francia stood, never by any chance turned his head toward her.

"How vexed he is, and how much I shall have to say before he will be kind again," thought Francia, and over the glitter of the ball-room and the flush of her innocent gayety came a dark mist, a chill, like that when upon a summer's afternoon, great white clouds of fog come rolling over the sea and wrap earth and sky in their mantle of bleak despondency.

She sighed heavily, and the domino who, although dismissed by Cleopatra in the first of the evening, had soon returned to hover near her, offered his arm.

"Tiresome, ain't it," said he, in a low voice to the drooping little *marquise* "Never mind, they'll have supper in a few minutes, and that will pay for all. If it was'n't for the suppers I couldn't stand this sort of life."

"I was not tired until just now," said Francia, accepting the proffered support.

Neria approached with Mephistopheles.

"And here we come," said he, "to a group whose disguises I will not venture to penetrate, and even could I do so, I shrewdly suspect you are better able to describe to me than I to you the graces and virtues adorning it."

"I hope you have been as correct in all your intimations as in this," said Neria, playfully.

"Do not doubt it, and I am glad to have been able to illustrate to you my remark of a previous occasion, that there are, after all, very few wolves in this so much maligned society of ours."

The latter part of the remark reached the ear of Cleopatra, who turned sharply round—

"Ah, it is you," said she, quickly.

"Great queen, who can withstand your penetration. It is the humblest of your slaves," said Mephistopheles.

"Malice avers that Lucifer was an ally of yours in the old times, and, according to his wont, deserted you at the last," suggested one of the courtiers.

"Malice was, then, as stupid as she generally is," said Mephistopheles, coolly; "for it was Cleopatra who deserted me."

A swift glance passed between the Queen and the speaker, and each turned to another companion. At this moment Mrs. Minturn approached on the arm of King Charles.

"Pardon the *mauvais goût* of an introduction *en masque*," said she, aside to Claudia; "and allow me to present my cousin, Rafe Chilton. He begs your permission to take Miss Vaughn down to supper."

"Certainly; I will let her understand that I sanction the movement, although your drawing-room is sufficient guarantee for any of your guests," replied Claudia, in the same tone, and Mrs. Minturn rejoined aloud,

"Will your majesty permit me to introduce a brother monarch, hight Charles of England."

Cleopatra, with a regal inclination of the head, extended her hand, which Charles made a feint of raising to his lips As he lifted his head their eyes met, and while Claudia remembered the saucy query, "Is it Marc Antony or another, to-day?" which had intercepted her entrance to the drawing-room, Charles saw that she remembered it.

"Generosity is a royal prerogative," said he, in a low voice.

"So your majesty found it when Louis Quatorze filled your exchequer with French gold," retorted Cleopatra, in the same voice.

Charles laughed.

"Let us forget all that we should blush for in our former lives," said he, "and begin our acquaintance from the present moment."

"Agreed; and unless we are better than most of the people about us, we shall, in the next hour, have accumulated a new stock of blushing matter, and shall have to begin over again," said the Queen.

"That can hardly be, for Cleopatra of to-day has preserved all the grace and none of the foibles of her prototype," said Charles, courteously.

"And the merry monarch of England has certainly freed himself from the reproach of having Never said a foolish thing, replied Cleopatra.

"Do not force him to believe, also, that he has 'never done a wise one' in seeking the honor of an introduction to your majesty," suggested Charles, with a royal audacity which did not injure him in the estimation of the lady he addressed.

"*Nous verrons*," said she, laughing.

"May I ask your majesty to present me to the young lady at your side, and allow me to escort her to the supper-room?" pursued the King, with easy grace.

"Mademoiselle, allow me to present King Charles the Second, of England, a monarch whose reputation is his best introduction," said Claudia, turning to Francia, who bowed without speaking.

"A breach of faith, royal sister. We had agreed to leave our former reputations out of the question," said Charles, meaningly; and Cleopatra, slightly abashed, made no retort.

CHAPTER XIII.

CHEZ MADAME LIVINGSTONE.

THE world had been informed that it would find Mrs. Livingstone "at home on Thursdays," and on the first recurrence of that day, after the fancy party, we shall see collected in her drawing-room nearly all the persons to whom this history has introduced us.

Mr. Vaughn had looked in, and without in the least meaning to do so, dwarfed the younger men by the polished ease of his manner, his dignity, and the knowledge of the world for which he was remarkable.

Fergus, seated near the elegant Miss Winchendon, was evoking that young lady's most gracious smiles, and rewarding them with a satirical dissection of their absent friends, mingled with covert compliments to herself.

Francia, who had not seen her cousin since the ball, watched this by-play from the corner of her eye, and grew more and more incoherent in her answers to the fashionable gossip with which Mrs. Minturn kindly tried to entertain her. But as that lady rose to go, the drawing-room door was thrown open to admit

Dr. Luttrell and Mr. Chilton; and as Francia noted the sudden frown clouding her cousin's face, a wicked impulse to brave the anger she despaired of softening, seized upon her, and she returned Mr. Chilton's bow with a smile that at once brought that young gentleman to her side.

Dr. Luttrell paused beside his hostess, who was, for the moment, disengaged.

"Where is Mrs. Luttrell?" asked Claudia.

"Where I am not," returned the husband, concisely.

"And always?"

"When it can be so arranged."

"Your honeymoon closed yesterday," said Claudia, with a bitter-sweet smile.

"A thing without beginning is also without end," retorted her guest, coldly.

"As, for example, the love a man professes to the woman he wishes to marry," suggested Mrs. Livingstone.

"I have, in my life, professed love to only one woman, and she—made a worthier choice," said Luttrell, suffering his eyes to rest, with quiet scorn, upon the stout figure of Mr. Livingstone, who stood, with his hands beneath his coat-tails, upon the hearth-rug, discussing politics with Mr. Murray.

Claudia winced a little, but recovered herself cleverly. "Ah!" said she, nonchalantly. "Who would suspect you of a *petite histoire?* You shall tell it to me some day. Just now I must go and talk to Mrs. Burton; and you, let me see?—you may bring Neria and the musician together, and get them into a conversation about art. They are counterparts and ought to find it out."

She glided away as she spoke, and seated herself to listen, with smiling interest, to Mrs. Burton's narrative of her struggles with her last cook, until she could adroitly contrive to entrap another matron into the conversation and herself withdraw imperceptibly to more congenial companionship.

Dr. Luttrell watched her, with a singular expression in his tawny eyes, not unlike a tiger, who, from the jungle, watches a stately doe surrounded by her courtiers, and says in his heart,

Theirs to-day, mine to-morrow, if I will.

Then he turned to look for Neria and the musician, who sat a little way from each other; she listening with grave attention to the chat between Fergus and the brilliant belle, he apparently absorbed in reverie.

Dr. Luttrell placed himself between them and began to talk opera.

CHAPTER XIV.

"RIXÆ, PAX, ET—"

THE last guest departed, and as the door closed behind her, Fergus turned to Neria, saying:

"Now, Neria, give me a little real music after the miserable tinkling of that —Percy do they call him? I am perfectly sick with it."

"Then I am quite sure I could not please you, monsieur," said Neria, gaily; "and I must go directly to my room and dress for our drive. Are you coming, Francia?"

"In a minute," replied that young lady, affecting to be busy in arranging some flowers upon the table. Neria left the room, and Fergus, with an abstracted look, was following her, when a timid voice recalled him.

"Did you see this rose-camelia, Fergus?"

"No, is it remarkable?" asked the young man, coming slowly toward the table.

"I don't know. It is very pretty."

"I see. Is that all you have to say?"

"Aren't you going to drive with us?"

"Not to-day."

"You have not been here lately."

"I am flattered that you should notice my movements so closely.'

Francia blushed scarlet, and bent lower over the flowers.

"You have not been without company, however," pursued her cousin, "I see that Mr. Chilton has established himself here upon a very familiar footing. You will be much improved by such association."

"O, Fergus, don't speak in that tone. How have I offended you?"

"Offended me? Not at all. I was speaking of Mr. Chilton in terms of the highest commendation, was I not?"

"Please, Fergus! Tell me what I have done, and let me say I am sorry, and then forgive me."

The clasped hands, tender blue eyes full of tears, quivering rosebud lips were very pathetic, and a half smile softened the stern lines of Fergus's mouth; but he said, coldly:

"I have no right to be offended; but I will own I was rather surprised at your conduct the other night."

"What conduct?" faltered Francia.

"In the first place, dancing round-dances half an hour with the same partner, and he one of the most notorious profligates about town; then wandering off into the conservatory with him, allowing him to unmask you, to take your hand, to say I don't know what to you. I did not try to listen, although I could not help seeing. Then, when I came to extricate you from your ridiculous and indecorous position, you absolutely refused to accept my guardianship, and clung to your new acquaintance as if he were a lover. Afterward you allowed him to take you down to supper, and danced with him again."

"Only a cotillion," interposed Francia.

"You danced with him—no matter what," pursued Fergus, severely. "And now, the next time I see you, this fellow is at your side, offering his insulting attentions in so conspicuous a manner that every person who goes away from here to-day will have a sneer for you the next time your name is mentioned in their company. You can do as you choose, or as my uncle chooses, I suppose, but you will excuse me if I say that I can give neither respect nor confidence to a young lady, who deliberately encourages the attentions of a libertine like Rafe Chilton."

"If Claudia and Mr. Livingston encourage his coming to the house, they cannot believe him so very bad," said Francia, with some spirit.

"I do not undertake to regulate my sister's affairs," said Fergus, coldly; "nor do I wish to discuss her movements—they do not concern either you or me. I was only explaining to you the reason of the change in my manner, which seemed to annoy you."

"I was not annoyed, Fergus, I was grieved."

The young man trifled a moment with the toys upon the table, and then said, reproachfully:

"You do not find Neria running into such follies, although she has the same opportunities."

"Neria isn't so gay—so—"

"So thoughtless as you. That is true enough; but to be thoughtless in these matters is something more then a foible, Francia. It is to estrange your friends, to injure your own prospects, to give foul tongues an opening to meddle with your name. Mr. Chilton's acquaintanceship is enough to ruin any woman's reputation; but if you choose to cultivate it, of course it is no affair of mine. Good morning."

"Good morning," said Francia, in a tone as cold as his own, and with sparkling eyes and heightened color, she walked toward the window. Fergus went to the door, but his gloves still lay upon the table where he had placed them while speaking. He returned for them, waited to put them on, and was again moving toward the door, when a soft voice whispered:

"Fergus!"

He silently turned and looked toward Francia. Fluttering, blushing, tearful, she glided to his side, and sweetly looked into his face. He took her hand, whispering:

"What is it, Franc?"

"I am so sorry. I won't if you don't want me to. Please, dear Fergus!"

He put his arm about her slender waist, he laid his hand beneath her rounded chin, and raising the rosy face that fain would droop, he looked deep, deep into the blue depths of her innocent eyes, and then—how does it go?

"*Rixæ, pax, et*"—what comes next?

Fergus stayed to dinner, and spent the evening. When Francia went to her room that night, she stood a long time looking from the window; and, as she turned away, murmured half aloud: "But he is my cousin, almost—just like a brother."

CHAPTER XV.

CHECK TO THE QUEEN.

THE winter went on, and went by. March had come, with its chilling winds and cheering sun, its raw certainty and its sweet promise—like a hoydenish girl of thirteen, whom we endure and even admire, in faith of the future.

It was evening, and Mrs. Livingstone's drawing-rooms were moonily lighted by hanging lamps with alabaster shades. In the boudoir at the end of the suite of apartments sat the lady herself, deep in a game of chess with Dr. Luttrell. In the next room, Francia, nervous, half-unwilling, and yet not quite unpleased, listened to the low-voiced conversation of Mr. Chilton, while the master of the house, dozing in an arm-chair near at hand, played propriety to the *tête-à-tête*.

In the drawing-room beyond, Neria, at the piano, softly played "O Bel Alma;" and Percy, standing beside her, improvised a dreamy accompaniment.

But the story that the musician told, the question that he asked, and the tender, mournful denial that Neria returned to his petition, are not now our concern. These are of the secrets that the angels keep and men do but guess. Let us rather watch the far from angelic game so skilfully played in the boudoir.

"Check!" said Dr. Luttrell; and Claudia, who had been dreaming over her game, suddenly found both king and queen menaced by an audacious knight, who had quietly approached, under cover of a manœuvre for the capture of a pawn.

"O, but I can't lose my queen!" exclaimed Mrs. Livingstone, examining the situation with dismay.

Dr. Luttrell silently leaned back in his chair and watched her. From between his half-closed eyelids gleamed strange green and yellow lights, flashing, sparkling, changing, like the great diamond on his breast. His thin lips smiled; but it was not a smile pleasant to look upon.

"Can you save her?" asked he, quietly, when Claudia had gone over every possible combination of her few pieces for the twentieth time, and at last placed a reluctant finger upon the king.

"No; but the game is lost. How could I have been so stupid?"

"'Whom the gods doom,' etc.—it was fated that I should conquer, and it would have been useless for you to resist, had you been ever so diligent in your efforts."

"You are a fatalist, then?"

"Are not you?"

"No, I will not give up my free will. In this case, if I had chosen to attend to my game, I should not have lost it."

"It was fated you should *not* choose to attend to it. It is very easy to reason after the event."

"But, warned by experience, the next game we play I will play with such care as to thwart fate, if she has decreed another stupidity on my part."

"Then you will again be the servant of fate, who will have decreed just the pains you take to thwart her."

"This is fearful," exclaimed Claudia, passionately; "this idea that, will as we may, struggle as we may, we are blindly hurried on by an unknown power, perhaps to good, perhaps to evil—at any rate toward a hidden end. What becomes of moral responsibility, of conscience, of any effort toward self-conquest?"

"They go down before the iron keel of destiny, who bears us on, resisting or unresisting, blind or open-eyed, to what you truly call the hidden end."

"Then why should men be punished for crime?"

"They should not. There is no crime. A man does that to which his temperament impels him—that which his destiny has pre-ordained from the beginning. He is no more accountable for the results than is this bit of ivory for your lost game."

He fillipped the captured queen as he spoke, and her head rolled across the board and dropped at his feet.

Claudia put aside his apology with a smile, and said:

"Like her mistress, she feels that in losing the game she loses all. She has escaped destiny now, at any rate."

"No, for destiny decreed that she should thus fall; also has decreed that, in spite of her attempt at self-destruction, she should be restored to all her former beauty and usefulness," said Dr. Luttrell, as he smilingly put the broken piece in his pocket.

Claudia looked at him with flushed cheeks and brilliant eyes.

"But this matter of destiny," said she. "Are you resigned to be thus blindly impelled hither and thither, and to feel all effort and resistance a useless struggle? Does not this belief deprive you of all interest in life?"

"Not at all. Life to me is an interesting novel, of which I am the hero. Fate turns the pages, and I read as fast as I am permitted. It is far less trouble and much more exciting than your idea of writing the book yourself. Authorship is not my *rôle*."

"At least you should never be angry with those who disappoint or thwart you," said Claudia, in a low voice.

"To the philosopher, disappointment is a word without value or meaning," returned the other. "It is folly to try to guess what is written on the other side of the page; but if you will do so, and find you have guessed wrong, why, there is an end of it—why be disappointed? What must be, will be; and why vex yourself by quarrelling with destiny? When you chose to marry Mr. Livingstone instead of me, you thought you decided for yourself; but you did not, and I knew you did not, and so felt neither anger nor sorrow; neither blamed you nor loved you the less, for I knew that you accepted this necessity of fate as unwillingly as I did. I knew, too, that this marriage ceremony would prove no solvent to the secret affinity which must forever bind our souls together, let our tongues belie it as they may."

He fixed his gleaming eyes on Claudia's face.

She returned the look defiantly.

"You have no right to say that," replied she. "Since I was married I have never spoken a word to you that should prove that I remembered—"

"Nor I to you; but have you not known it?"

"No," said Claudia, desperately.

Luttrell smiled.

"*Say* no, if you will, but do not try to think no," returned he, quietly, "for nothing is so weakening as self-deception."

"But I will not—you shall not—I, at least, am no fatalist, and will not have my free will thus quietly taken out of my hands," persisted Claudia. "I do not choose to remember or to know more than that Dr. Luttrell and his wife are pleasant acquaintances of Mr. and Mrs. Livingstone."

Dr. Luttrell smiled and bowed, hiding his shining eyes with their drooping lids.

Claudia waited for denial, for argument; but none came. She nervously replaced the chessmen in their box, and glanced toward her late adversary. His face wore an expression of regret, of mortification, perhaps, but he did not raise his eyes.

"I should have said friends, instead of acquaintances," said she, softly.

"The first is the better word," replied Luttrell, coldly.

"Then you do not wish me for a friend," said Claudia, wounded beyond her self-possession.

"I do not believe in friendship," returned Luttrell; "we have acquaintances more or less intimate; we have passions and affinities; but friendship is to me a word without meaning."

"You are cynical," said Claudia, bitterly.

"Not at all; I am philosophical, and it is one of my philosophies to talk as little as may be of myself, or of my own experiences. Do you notice how heavily the air of these rooms is charged with electricity?"

Claudia glanced at him inquiringly.

"I mean the moral atmosphere. There is enough passion, intrigue, hope, despair, restlessness circling about our heads to furnish matter for a score of romances."

Claudia slightly moved her position so as to command a view of the drawing-rooms.

It was the moment when Percy and Neria, standing hand in hand, looked farewell into each others' eyes. Rafe Chilton had drawn his chair close to Francia's side, and while toying with her fan, murmured behind it words to which she listened with blushing, half-averted face and down-dropped eyes.

Mr. Livingstone, aroused from his nap, studied the stock-list with frowning brow and muttering lips.

Unseen by all, Mr. Vaughn and Fergus Murray stood just within the doorway, the keen eyes of each taking in the *tout ensemble* of the scene, and each drawing from it his own conclusions.

"I see," said Claudia, in a low voice; and rising, she went to greet her guests, and to break up the too obvious *tête-a-tête* between Francia and a man whom she knew both her uncle and her brother disapproved.

CHAPTER XVI.

FRANCIA'S MISTAKE.

WITH slight notice of his sister or the rest, Fergus passed into the other room, and standing beside Neria, said impatiently,

"When are you going home, I wonder?"

"To Bonniemeer?"

"Yes, I am tired of stumbling over that mooning Percy every time I come here. As for Chilton, I am afraid that some day I shall take the trouble to impart to him my opinion of himself; and that might lead to unpleasant results."

Neria placed her cool hand upon his.

"Dear Fergus," said she, "cannot you make your circle of tolerance a little larger? One is so much happier in charity and love with all men. And it grieves us when you are ill-pleased."

"I cannot flatter myself that my words are so important," said Fergus, sullenly.

"You wrong yourself and us in saying so; us, by doubting our love and sympathy, and yourself in refusing to accept this love and sympathy, which would, admitted to your life, render it so much more peaceful and beautiful."

"Others are not like you, Neria," said the young man, in a softer tone.

"All here are like me in caring for you, Fergus."

"How much does Francia care, when she encourages that profligate fellow, after the expression of my disapprobation; after her own promise to give up his acquaintance?" asked Fergus, gloomily.

Neria looked troubled, but presently answered cheerily,

"Franc is so charming and so much admired, that we must be reconciled to seeing a good deal of homage offered at her shrine, and sometimes by unworthy worshippers. It does not harm her, and by-and-by she will be tired of her position as divinity. "We women have four seasons like the year," and it is spring-time with her yet."

"Some women's spring-time has all the freshness of her's without its crudeness," said Fergus, smiling into Neria's eyes.

"But not the rich and glowing promise," returned Neria, half sadly. "See, Mr. Chilton is going."

"That is a pity—for Francia."

"Now, Fergus, don't be cross with the poor child. You have not been kind to her for some weeks."

"Because she has allowed Chilton to haunt her like her shadow."

"To be unkind to her yourself, is only to make his courtesies seem the more agreeable. She is coming in here, and I shall go away and leave you to make friends. We go home next week, and it is quite time you were on good terms again. Be gentle and careful."

Francia approached with a nervous smile upon her flushed face.

"I thought Mr. Percy was here," said she to Neria, but glancing timidly at Fergus while she spoke.

"He went away a few moments ago. Sit down, dear, and sing us that little barcarolle, won't you? Fergus has not heard it."

Francia seated herself, played a simple prelude with faltering fingers, and tried to sing; but in the first notes her voice trembled, broke, and in a sudden burst of tears she ran away from the piano, and sought shelter in the deep bay-window.

With an expressive glance at Fergus, Neria went into the other room, and seated herself near Vaughn, who was carrying on a desultory conversation with Mr. Livingstone.

Fergus hesitated a moment, and then followed Francia, who crouched sobbing upon an ottoman.

"Franc!" said he, softly, as he seated himself beside her.

No answer.

"Don't cry, Francia. I'm not angry."

"But you will be."

"No, I won't. I suppose you couldn't help his coming."

"N-o-o."

"But you need not have let him whisper in your ear."

A fresh burst of sobs.

"O Franc, I wish you would be more womanly; show a little more dignity, or at least a little more regard for me."

"There, I knew you would."

"Would what, child?"

"Would scold. And you will be so angry."

"No, but I am not angry, and not going to be, only sorry. I love my little cousin too much to be really angry with her."

"I don't think you have loved me very much this last month," murmured Francia out of her handkerchief.

"It is because I love you so well that I have been sorry to see you—well, I won't say any more. So you thought I didn't love you, little girl?"

"Yes."

"Well, I never thought you didn't love me, so you see I was the wiser of the two. Now I will tell you what I shall do to prevent any such mistakes in future. I shall tell all the world that I love you and you love me, and that you are my own little Franc, and no one else is to come within six feet of you, or to speak to you any lower than they would to Mr. Livingstone. Then I shall send you back to Bonniemeer, and keep you safely there until I have a nice little cage all ready for you here or somewhere else; and then I shall come and bring you to live in it forever and a day, and—how do the story books end?

Lived happy all their lives,

Isn't it?"

He put his arm round her as he spoke, and drew her close to his side, but even in the dim light was startled to see the pale face and wild eyes she raised to his.

"O, Fergus, Fergus!" cried she. "Why did you not tell me sooner? How could I know—and—and I am engaged to Rafe Chilton."

Fergus started to his feet, and looked down with terrible eyes upon the fair young face, that seemed to wither beneath his gaze.

"I would not have believed," said he, at last, "that you could sink so low. Forget from this moment, as I do, that any other tie than our unfortunate relationship has ever drawn us together."

He left the room, the house, without another word; and Francia, sinking upon the floor, child-like, cried herself to sleep.

So Neria found her an hour later when Vaughn, the last of the guests, had departed, saying to his ward as he bade her good-night,

"I have something to say to you to-morrow. Will you ride with me at eleven?"

"Yes, Sieur."

CHAPTER XVII.

THE PERRY WOODS.

O, BLUE-EYED Katie Coleman, do you remember the summer days that you and I, two merry hoydens in our earliest teens, laughed or dreamed away among the joyous Perry Woods? Now it was a butterfly, a tiger-moth, a glittering dragon-fly which we chased, and left uncaptured at the last; now it was the white and yellow violets in the meadow beyond the wood that tempted us to the destruction of hose and shoon; now it was the nodding Solomon's seal, the purple orchis, the gay columbine, that we sought upon the hill-side, and though we lost each a shoe in the meadow, we found whole handfuls of lady's-slippers in the wood. And do you remember, Katie, when we pulled the farmer's radishes, and sitting under the edge of the wood, eat the stolen treasure with its clinging soil, and even while the acrid flavor brought tears to our eyes, assured each other that it was a feast. Ah, pretty Katie Coleman! Twenty years since then, my friend, twenty stages from that idyllian age of golden romance! But the sunshine that flecked the turf of Perry's Woods with sheen still glimmers duskily through my life, and shows me here and there around my feet a flower that, without it, I might never see.

And if this blue sky above my head arches also over yours, may it shed all balmy dews upon your path, all peace and love upon your life, for the sake of those blithe days bygone. And if, my Katie, you now dwell above, as I beneath the sky, I know right well that your pure heart and gentle nature will have led you to other woods and other flowers, fairer even than the sunny memories of youth.

So it was to Perry's Woods that Vaughn and Neria rode upon the breezy March morning when he spoke. The sky was a pure bright blue, islanded with great white cumuli. The south wind smelt of violets a-bloom whence it had come. The willow twigs made a wreath of rosy mist along the brook-side—the brook that warbled loud and warbled soft its spring-tide song. The earliest bluebird of the year praised God from the topmost branches of the elm. The exquisite tracery of twig and branch against the lucent sky was better than foliage, and the springing grass under foot was fairer to the winter-withered senses than all the flush of bloom that should bourgeon the summer.

Neria sat upon her white palfrey, and with her smiling eyes seemed to gather in and taken possession of the scene until its charm incorporated itself in her being, and shone forth again, adding a new and subtle beauty to what had seemed finished already.

Vaughn looked only at her, and the love of a man's strong nature made his face as that of a god. She turned suddenly, and met his eyes—met and read them, and her sweet face grew pale.

He took her hand.

"Neria, where are the words that I should say to you? How can I hope to tell you the reverence and love that has become my life? How dare I ask God to give to me, alone, the pure angel whom he has vouchsafed to mankind? You have so little of earth, dear Neria, that I cannot ask you to mate yourself with me, who, alas, am all of earth; but, sweet, if I may wear you on my heart as a blessed amulet, if I may stand between the world and you, and you shall stand between Heaven and me—if I may help you to make others happy, and you will help me to mend much that is amiss in my own life—Neria, if you will be the angel in my house and in my heart, then can I ask no more of Heaven than to give me life and grace to show continually how I prize its gift."

The sweet content of the spring-morning changed on Neria's face to doubt and alarm.

"Sieur, I have not thought of this," said she, simply.

"Think of it, now, dear child.

"I cannot. I must disarrange all the habit of my thought to place you in the position of—"

"Of a lover, you would say. I feared it would be so, dear. I am too far away from you—in years, in experience, in the circle of life—for you to find my love other than oppressive and unwelcome," said Vaughn, sadly.

"No, not that, Sieur, but it is so new. May I think about it a little, before I say any more?"

"Surely, dear, as long as you will, but you may not try to force upon your heart the belief that you can return this love of mine, and so offer yourself a sacrifice upon the altar of self-devotion. If you cannot give yourself to me frankly and fully, Neria, tell me so at once, and we will forget all this, and you shall be again to me a daughter, a trust; something to be loved, and guarded, and reverenced, as Arthur's knights guarded the San Grail, though no man among them dared lay finger upon it."

He turned his horse's head while he spoke, and they rode slowly home.

It was that very evening, as Vaughn sat alone in the twilight of the deserted drawing-room, that the faint perfume always enveloping Neria, suddenly floated around his head, although he had heard no step, and a slender hand crept within his own.

He looked up. Through the shadow of the twilight a fair face shone down upon him, saint-wise.

"Is it my angel, or the angel of mankind?" asked he, softly.

"O, Sieur, do not call me an angel; I am so weak, so ignorant! But if it is true that I can help you a little, let me do it in your own way."

It was not the loving confession he would have liked to hear, but it was acceptance; and the heart of the man was stirred as with strong wine, while for the first time he took his bride in his arms, and reverently kissed her lips.

CHAPTER XVIII.
COMING HOME.

THE great content of his new happiness disposed Vaughn to be more indulgent than even his wont to the wishes of his only child, and although he could not approve or sympathize in her choice, he would not absolutely refuse consent to it. He did not, however, refrain from expressing to Mr. Chilton his views with regard to some passages in that young man's life, and informing him most distinctly that his engagement to Francia must be a conditional one, to be broken at any time when her friends considered him to have failed in keeping the good resolutions that he now professed.

Chilton, quite seriously in love, and rather proud of bearing away the beauty of the season, as Francia had been styled, found himself very willing to subscribe to even harder conditions than these; and immediately removed his lodgings from a hotel to a quiet boarding-house; reduced his allowance of cigars to three *per diem;* confined himself in his convivialities to light wines; turned the cold shoulder to several of his former intimates; spent nearly an hour every day in the law-office, whose door-plate bore his name in conjunction with that of a partner who did all the work and assumed nearly all the profit of the concern; and, in brief, resolved, as he himself expressed the determination, to "try the Falstaffian lodge, 'eschew sack, and live cleanly.'"

Neria's consternation and regret upon first hearing of Francia's engagement were extreme. Her pure and true instincts had always negatived any feeling of admiration for Mr. Chilton's appearance or manners, and her sympathy with Fergus caused her painfully to appreciate the severe disappointment and sorrow underlying his silent displeasure. She, however, said but little upon the subject, especially to Francia, whom she treated with an added tenderness and delicacy, sufficiently expressed by Francia's playful wish, that she were a little girl instead of a great one, that she might call Neria mother.

Claudia was content with both engagements. Mr. Chilton was a man of wealth and fashion, and would, of course, immediately renounce the open offences against morality which had somewhat disturbed society in its wish to render him its highest consideration. As for the rest, Mrs. Livingstone's standard of life was not very high, and she held the tenet that every young man was either a sinner or a hypocrite.

Mr. Murray took snuff, and blandly congratulated Vaughn upon his own and his daughter's engagement.

Fergus almost deserted his sister's house, and professed himself absorbed in business.

It was arranged that Neria's quiet marriage should take place as soon as its preliminaries could be arranged, and that until then she and Francia should remain with Claudia, while Vaughn vacillated between the city and Bonniemeer, where he was pleasing his luxurious taste by some alterations and new furnishings in honor of the bride who was to be.

It was on a joyous April day that he finally brought her home, and, before entering the house, lingered a moment upon the terrace with her, to admire the capricious beauty of the landscape, where all earth seemed frolicking in her girlish glee, and afar upon the horizon line the bright blue ocean tossed its glittering foam against the bright blue sky.

Vaughn drew Neria close to his side.

"My wife," whispered he, "tell me that you are happy."

"O, so happy!" said Neria, brightly. "Such a heavenly day, and coming home to our own dear Bonniemeer, are enough for happiness."

"But to be with you in any weather, and at any place, is enough for happiness to me," urged the bridegroom, in a tone of half-playful reproach.

Neria looked at him a little wonderingly, and then raised her face heavenward with a smile of serene satisfaction; but whether evoked by his words or the joyous scene, Vaughn did not dare inquire.

"Come, spirit," said he, leading her toward the house, "I am afraid to let you stay here, lest you suddenly float away and leave me desolate. I will close you within walls, and only allow you to see the sky through non-conducting glass, until you are a little naturalized by sympathy with me. I anticipate that in course of time our natures will become equalized, to a certain extent, at least. You are to elevate and purify me, and I am to strengthen and practicalize you. So shall we both fill more perfectly our places in this world, and in each other's hearts."

Neria regarded him with a dreamy smile, and softly said,

"I cannot tell. It is all so new and strange to me as yet, but I am sure that you will be to me what you have always been."

"O no, dear child, but more and better," said Vaughn, eagerly. "Do you not feel the change that love has wrought in our relations to each other?"

"But I have always loved and reverenced you," returned Neria, with the pathetic intonation peculiar to her voice when she found herself perplexed or troubled.

Vaughn smiled a little dubiously, and led her into the house.

"See, now, my ocean waif, the bower I have been building for you," said he, leading the way through a richly-furnished bridal chamber and dressing-room, to the entrance of one of the apartments recently added to the house.

"Here is a boudoir, where you may, if you choose, fancy yourself still beneath the sea."

He threw open the door and Neria, standing upon the threshold, uttered a little cry of delight.

The arched ceiling, divided into four compartments by heavy mullions, represented in fresco, Venus rising from the sea, surrounded by rosy little Loves; Arion riding his dolphin, and drawing all the creatures of the deep to listen to his wonderful melodies; the nymph Tyro yielding half coy, half willing to the wooing of Neptune, who drew her toward his wave-borne chariot; and last, an exquisite design showing a fair child asleep in a great sea-shell floating upon a smiling sea, and rocked by the tiny hands of Nereids, whose sweet faces and shining hair floated above the waves, while their gleaming shapes showed fairly through the pure water.

From the cornice fell heavy folds of sea-green silk, draping the walls and lying upon a carpet of white velvet, embossed with groups of sea mosses and grasses, with sprigs of coral interspersed. Upon the mantle shelf, itself upheld by sculptured Tritons, lay two great sea-shells with flowers and trailing vines drooping over their rose-red lips, and between them an exquisite marble group, showing Andromeda chained half-lifeless to the rock, closing her eyes to shut out the sea monster, while Perseus stole to her side, and looked with admiring wonder upon her rare beauty.

Two or three paintings, gems of ocean scenery, hung upon the walls, and on the *étagère* lay some rare mosaics, cameos, shells, and sea pebbles. A little book-rack was filled with the poets Neria loved, the volumes bound in silk of the same tint as the hangings of the room. The furniture was of ebony inlaid with mother-of-pearl, the chairs and couches luxuriously cushioned with silk of the prevailing tint. A wide bay window let in a flood of morning sunshine, and commanded a wide view of the distant sea.

"Do you like it?" asked Vaughn, who had watched, with loving delight, the varying expression of Neria's face as she silently made the tour of the little chamber, gathering in all its beauty with her swift and comprehensive glances. As he spoke she came toward him and raised her lips to his with innocent grace.

"How can I ever do anything for you who are always doing so much for me?" asked she.

"Do anything for me, darling? By simply being, you do everything. My white angel, my pure saint, do you not know that it is by thus putting the smallest portion of my love into deeds, that I relieve my heart of this burden of joy which almost cleaves it in twain! Neria, you do not know, you do not faintly guess how much I love you. And you—ah, my love, my darling, be a little human—blush when I kiss your lips thus and thus; droop those pure eyes before the passion of my gaze; let those calm pulses beat, and pause, and beat again, as mine do when I clasp you in my arms. Neria, love me as I love you!"

And Neria, pale, passive, disturbed, answered in her plaintive voice,

"I do love you, Sieur—I love you very much."

Vaughn impatiently opened his lips, but left the words unsaid. Taking the slender hands of his girl-wife in one of his, he looked down into her troubled face for a moment, then smiled a little sadly, and tenderly smoothed her hair.

"You are tired, dear child," said he; "come into your chamber and rest a little. I will send up your trunks, and Mrs. Barlow, the housekeeper, to help you with your toilet."

Neria mutely obeyed, but when she was left alone could not rest for wondering why the love that had always seemed good and sufficient in Vaughn's eyes, had suddenly grown so inadequate to satisfy him.

*

CHAPTER XIX.

PUTTING THE BUTTERFLY INTO THE CHRYSALIS.

"WHO shall say that we are out of the reach of fashionable gayeties?" asked Vaughn, merrily, as he entered the boudoir where Neria, pale and pensive, sat reading aloud to Francia, who wrought at some embroidery secretly destined to adorn those "wedding clothes" over which the idlest-little maiden grows industrious.

"What is it?" asked Francia, eagerly, while Neria raised her languid eyes to her husband's face.

"I have been to Carrick," said he, "and in the post-office was addressed by Jones Merton, a young gentleman pursuing the profession of blacksmith in that place, but just now more interested in the management of a ball to be given to-morrow evening at the Mermaid's Cave, in honor of the fishermen who leave home upon the following day to be gone all summer. Mr. Merton, after giving these particulars, closed with a pressing invitation to me to be present myself, and 'bring my folks.' I told him I should be most happy to attend, but feared that the ladies of my family would be unable to accompany me. Did I do right?"

"No, indeed, papa, you did very wrong. I should like of all things to go," exclaimed Francia. "Shouldn't you, Neria?"

"I don't believe I should," said Neria, slightly smiling. "But I will go to chaperon you, if Sieur likes to take us."

"No, indeed, Neria; I shouldn't think of letting you make such a sacrifice; nor can I imagine any combination of person and place so incongruous as you in the ball-room of the Mermaid's Cave," said Vaughn. "If Franc likes to go, I will take her. The society of Carrick is not *exigeante*, in the matter of chaperons."

"Then *I* am not incongruous, papa," pouted Francia, so comically that her father kissed her ripe lips, as he answered,

"You are a little girl, and it is of small consequence what you do or leave undone."

"I am eighteen, and not so very little"—persisted Francia—"not so little but that I can put my arms about your neck, for all your six feet of dignity, *monsieur le père*."

She suited the action to the word, and suddenly found herself lifted from the floor and borne round the room in a very secure, if not a very dignified, position.

"There, now go and ask your mamma what you shall wear, and don't be too fine for the company," said her father, replacing her upon the ottoman where he had found her, and seating himself in such a position as to get Neria's profile against the green background of the hangings.

"My mamma, indeed!" exclaimed Francia, laying her bright head upon Neria's lap and looking up into her face. "Well, respected parent, what shall I wear?"

"Something that may be washed afterward, I should say," rejoined Neria.

"O, you fastidious child! I dare say the people will be just as nice as those we met last winter, only a little less cultivated."

"And a little more fishy," suggested her father.

"Well, Neria can bear to go to their houses and stay whole hours, seeing to sick people and babies and all ; so I think I may dance with them one evening!"

"Yes, indeed ; I was only jesting," said Neria. "I have no doubt you will enjoy yourself very much; but I wouldn't wear anything elaborate. White muslin, with a few blue ribbons, will be quite sufficient."

"And don't put on your pearls," suggested Vaughn, "or they will think you mean oysters."

"Or your coral, lest they should think you mean lobsters," added Neria.

"You horrid aristocrats!" cried Francia, indignantly. "And yet you both see more of these people than I do, or could bear to."

"Neria goes among them, not for her own pleasure, but for their good," suggested Vaughn, significantly.

Franc blushed a little, but put the lesson aside with a blithe laugh.

"And so do I," declared she. "I am going to give them a lesson in dancing."

"I beg your pardon, my dear ; here is a letter for you which I forgot until this moment," said Vaughn, suddenly, drawing from his pocket and handing to Francia a letter addressed in Mr. Chilton's handwriting.

"Thank you, papa," said she, shyly taking it from her father's hand and running away to read it.

Left alone with him, Neria glanced doubtfully at her husband, who was attentively regarding her, then, opening the book in her hand, asked,

"Shall I read to you from 'Aurora Leigh?'"

"Not just now, dear. I would rather have you talk. Neria, you grow paler and thinner every day; your cheerfulness is forced, and you are never joyous. All your occupations are matters of resolution, not of inclination. You are silent, thoughtful, and would always avoid me, did you not force yourself to endure me. You are totally changed from the Neria who married me two months ago, and I have seen the change working, day by day, from the very morning of our arrival here. Now, dear child, explain it to me, as you might to your own father. Forget, if you will, that I have ever claimed another relation to you, and may God and you forgive me if I judged wrong in assuming that relation."

He took her hand in his. It was cold as death, and every trace of color had left her face, while, in the large, luminous eyes, such a depth of sorrow, doubt, apprehension, expressed themselves, that Vaughn, covering his face with his hands, groaned aloud.

"O, Neria, Neria," cried he, "you will die, and it is my love that is killing you."

Neria softly laid her hand upon his head.

"Have a little patience, Sieur," said she. "It is all so new to me—I am so young. I did not know what love meant—other love than that I had always felt for you. I am very heartless, I think—I believe I cannot love in the way you would like me to, and I am afraid that, by trying so much, I have done harm to the love I should naturally have given you. I am afraid, Sieur, I never should have married any one, but have been your child, and loved you as I could."

"Miserable, selfish, coarse-natured creature that I am," muttered Vaughn. "What have I done? Because an angel hovered near me, I must grasp and bind her to my side, trying to make her as myself. Neria, I see it now—I see better than you can see yourself, the struggle that has almost killed you; I feel your sublime self-renunciation and my own blind selfishness far more acutely than you could ever feel them. Psyche and Silenus were as well matched—I see now, I see it all; and, if I had not been love-blinded, I had seen it sooner. I have watched you from day to day, and said, 'she is weary,' 'she is ill,' 'she is pre-occupied;' 'to-morrow, or the day after, it will be different, and in the end she will love me.' Now, I see that this will never be, and pray God that I see it in time. Neria, from this moment I am your father, your brother, your friend—what you will. I shall never again alarm you with a love that you cannot comprehend, and with which you have no sympathy, but show you only an affection that you can return in kind. We will forget the fatal error of our marriage, and go back to the sweet relations of the old time. You and Francia will be my children, and I will be a tender father to both. Does this please you?"

Through the forced calm of his tone pierced the sharp cry of a wounded and rejected love—the cry of a man's strong heart crushed back upon itself in all the vigor of its ardent life—the cry of a broken hope.

Dimly as the words of an unknown tongue, this voice reached Neria's heart, and, though she could not comprehend its suffering, she instinctively tried to solace it.

"But we loved each other very much in those days, Sieur," said she; "and so do I love you very much now. Why will you not be as happy to return to the old quiet way of loving? I shall ride and walk with you, and you will read and talk with me, and all will be well again. Do you not like it as well?"

"As well, and better, my Psyche, if you will be as happy as you were then," said Vaughn, raising to meet her gaze, his face pale, but resolutely calm.

"I will be as happy as you could wish," said Neria, joyously, as she lightly kissed his brow. "And you?"

"And I shall be happy," said Vaughn, not returning the caress.

So Neria, who would silently have broken her heart and died, rather than consciously embitter any existence that God had created, accepted the sacrifice of a man's life as simply as she would a flower; and Vaughn, devoting himself to a future of constant watchfulness, self-restraint, and feigned content, knew that his sacrifice must remain unappreciated, unthanked, forever—for not the most implacable coquette is so pitiless to the man who worships her as is the wife who knows not how to love.

With the rapid prescience of strong emotion, Vaughn, sitting calmly at his wife's feet, saw his future life outspread before him, and resolved upon even the minutiæ of his own conduct. Like Francia? No; she could never be like Francia, nor must he permit himself the caresses with her that he offered to his child. A guarded and undemonstrative affection was all that must be permitted to appear; a thoughtful attention to her wishes and comfort; the careful training of her intellect in study and conversation; a cautious enjoyment of her society; a great and constant care to hide every symptom of suffering or discontent. So far he had arranged the weary programme, when Neria's voice, blither than it had sounded for many a day, said,

"I am so glad you thought to say this to me, Sieur; and now let us forget it, and quietly return to our old ways. Don't you think I ought to go to the ball with Franc?"

Vaughn stared at her as might a man preparing himself for death, if asked whether he preferred his cravat tied in a bow or a knot.

Neria smiled merrily.

"A penny for your thoughts," said she. "I was speaking of the ball at Carrick."

"O, certainly, the ball. I promised to take Franc, I believe."

"Yes, but ought I not to go with her?"

"It is not at all necessary, so far as she is concerned; but if you fancy it on your own account, go, by all means," said Vaughn, quietly.

"I believe I will. I feel so gay, Sieur, now that I may be myself once more."

Vaughn smiled back her smile, and then abruptly left the room, feeling that he could bear no more just then.

CHAPTER XX.

THE BALL.

FRANCIA's letter, among more important items, contained the announcement that Mr. Chilton's only brother, a lad of sixteen years, and a midshipman in the United States Navy, had just arrived at home from a long cruise, and was about to set off upon another.

Between the two, he had so strong a desire to be introduced to his brother's *fiancée*, that Mr. Chilton had taken the liberty to invite him to Bonniemeer for a night, and they would arrive the day after the letter. Nothing could be more fortunately timed than this visit, as Francia immediately declared; for, besides providing her with an escort of her own, it would give the visitors an opportunity of seeing a phase of society to which they had probably never been introduced.

Her father and Neria acquiesced in what seemed to give her so much pleasure, although neither of them could feel any great delight in the prospect of seeing Ralfe Chilton, or extending their acquaintance with his family.

With careful hospitality, however, Vaughn sent his carriage to Carrick to meet the coach upon the ensuing afternoon, and the two young men arriving in time for tea, were informed of their prospective amusement, and then left in the library to be entertained by Mr. Vaughn, while the ladies went up to dress.

Chilton, whose boasted self-possession and *sang-froid* were always severely tried by the presence of his prospective father-in-law, fell into the mistake of many young men, in supplying the place of ease by audacity, and told stories, made jests, and asked questions, until Vaughn's glacial politeness froze him into sudden silence, and the host, turning to his other guest, kindly questioned him of his voyage, of his fancies for sea or land, and showed himself so thoroughly master of one of the most difficult arts in the world—that of conducting a conversation between a boy and a man—that Ned Chilton afterward declared to his brother that his "governor-to-be was just the jolliest old brick there was going."

The door opened to admit, first, Neria, looking like the spirit of the mist, in her dun-colored barege and green ribbons, then Francia, radiant in a diaphanous white tulle and coquettish little bows of violet ribbon that contrasted well with her clear complexion and sparkling eyes.

Chilton went to meet her, and his whispered admiration did not lessen the bloom he admired or soothe the flutter of spirits in little Francia's heart.

The midshipman stood afar off and gazed, his heart filled with a boy's admiration of beauty, his mind perturbed with a boy's wish to say something expressive of that admiration, and a boy's terror of making himself ridiculous by attempting it.

Neria did not know more of boys than she did of men, but a graceful instinct led her to his side.

"You are not surprised at your brother's choice?" asked she, smiling, as she followed his eyes.

"In his place, I shouldn't have been able to make a choice," said the midshipman, gallantly, although blushing scarlet while he spoke, and ready the next instant to bite his tongue through lest he had been too forward.

Neria was a little surprised, but smiled unaffectedly.

"You sailors learn flattery with navigation, I believe," said she. "Have you been long at sea?"

Ned, following this lead, launched into his nautical adventures, and by the time the carriage was announced, was quite at his ease, although suffering a slight relapse under the doubt whether he should offer his arm to Mrs. Vaughn, or leave that privilege to her husband. The question was solved by Neria herself, who, while still speaking to him, quietly slipped her hand under Vaughn's arm, and thus doubly attended, followed Francia, who was already seated in the carriage.

When the party from Bonniemeer reached the Mermaid's Cave, still kept by our friend Burroughs, now a widower, they found the festivities in full progress. Prisoned in a gallery at one end of the large, low ball-room, sat the orchestra, consisting of the two violins and a bass viol which, on Sundays, officiated in the village choir. The area of the hall was well filled with a joyous company, the ladies as smartly dressed as their wardrobes would allow, the swains varying in costume, from swallow-tailed dress-coats with brass buttons to the more becoming blue flannel shirt and belted trowsers—the fisherman's ordinary dress. A prevailing atmosphere of fish and good humor was very apparent, slightly vitiated in certain cases by the use of a perfume composed of musk and bergamot, popular, under various titles, among the less enlightened classes of the community.

"O-h!" crowed Francia, clasping her hands over Chilton's arm. "Isn't it charming? O, see that man shuffle, and oh, do look at that girl opposite him."

"Barnum ought to get hold of the whole affair and set it up in Broadway. It would draw immensely," replied the young gentleman, fixing his eye-glass upon his nose and coolly surveying the scene.

Mr. Vaughn turned round quickly.

"Francia!" said he in a sterner voice than she had often heard from him. "Let me beg you to make no more remarks of this sort. These people are our neighbors and well-wishers; they are in their own quarters and enjoying themselves in their own way. If we come among them at all, it must be as a civility, not as an insult."

A deliberate look into Mr. Chilton's face pointed the rebuke, and when Vaughn quietly led the way to the upper end of the hall, Francia and her lover mutely followed. Here the party was welcomed by Jonas Merton and Cephas Wild, the hearty master of the schooner Mary Ann, bound for the Banks upon the ensuing day, and acting meantime as second manager to the grand ball given in honor of the expedition.

These gentlemen Mr. Vaughn presented to his wife and daughter, and requested for himself an introduction to some of the young ladies who sat near. In these introductions Mr. Chilton and his brother shared, and the midshipman, resolved not to lose any of his opportunities, immediately led a partner to the foot of a country-dance already commenced.

"If you'll pick out a dance for next time, Miss Vaughn, I'll speak to the music about it. Anything you'd rather have, so's't we know it," suggested Captain Wild, who had engaged Neria as his partner.

"But your programme is arranged already, is it not?" asked she, in some surprise.

"That don't make no difference. We'll dance anything you'd rather."

Could the courtesy of the Tuileries go farther?

Neria expressed her appreciation of the politeness, but begged that the dance might go on in its regular order.

"Well, next comes Fisher's Hornpipe," said the captain, consulting a scrap of paper in his pocket-book. "How do you fancy that for a dance, ma'am?"

Neria was forced to acknowledge that she had never seen it, and begged to have the figure explained beforehand.

"Never see Fisher's Hornpipe! Why, don't they dance up to the city?" asked the mariner, in amazement.

"O yes, but seldom country dances. In those crowded rooms, cotillons and the round dances are more convenient," replied Neria, quite seriously.

"Round dances? Why, what sort 's that?"

"Polkas, waltzes, galops, and several others. Don't you dance the polka here?" asked Neria, almost as much surprised as the captain had been at her ignorance of Fisher's Hornpipe.

"I don't believe there's a feller here that knows polky by sight," said the captain, musingly. "Like enough, some of the gals do—they sort of pick up things, you know. But you said waltz, didn't you?"

"Yes."

"Like enough, now," pursued the manager, "Jim Todd can play a waltz, and you and the Square might dance it."

"O no," exclaimed Neria, alarmed. "I had much rather dance what the rest do. Please tell me about the Fisher's Hornpipe."

"That's easy enough. It's just down the outside, down the middle, cast off right and left, and four hands round. Stop, we'll try it on beforehand, if you and Miss Vaughn will stand up a minute 'long o' me and Jonas. Trypheny, you and Zeb stand up, too."

Trypheny, a tall, handsome brunette, who had just come in with the fine-looking young fisherman alluded to as Zeb, took her place in the impromptu set, and received Mr. Chilton's bold look of admiration with a conscious smile and toss of the head, which made Zeb's eyes travel wrathfully in the direction of her coquettish glance.

"There, that's all there is to it," said Captain Wild, after taking his partner twice through the figure. "Now we'll show 'em how it's done."

He led Neria to the top of the set already forming; Francia and young Merton came next, and next to them Chilton with Trypheny, whom he had quietly invited while she was leaning upon the arm of her lover, who had not considered it necessary to explicitly engage her for the first dance, supposing it an already conceded privilege. He now stood indignant and astonished just where the faithless fair one had deserted him, watching with wrathful eyes the movements of his rival, who, scorning the etiquette of the dance, chose to stand by his partner while the set was forming, talking in a style of careless flattery rather appalling, but utterly captivating to the rustic belle.

"Rafe is making a fool of that girl, and she doesn't know it," whispered Francia, laughingly, to Neria, who shook her head disapprovingly; while Vaughn, who did not dance, watched the movements of the young man with an uneasy eye.

The other set was ambitiously headed by Ned Chilton, who had secured the prettiest girl in the room as his partner, and left two others in the full conviction that he had rather have danced with them. The music began, and Neria, floating up and down the long lines, and through the intricacies of "cast-off" and right and left, with perfect grace and accuracy, seemed to shed upon the homely dance and dancers an atmosphere of fitness and refinement not always to be found among the dances and dancers of the *salons*.

"I was wrong," thought Vaughn. "This contact does not degrade her—it elevates them. I did injustice to the strength of her influence."

Next came Francia, who, commencing with the gravest propriety of bearing, found herself, before she reached the end, so carried away by the exhilarating motion, the sharp, quick time of the melody, and the half subdued impulse of her partner, that not Trypheny herself made the *chassé* down the middle so rapidly, or reached the foot in such a state of breathless mirth.

"Take care, little girl," whispered her father, as she returned to his side; "don't fall into the other extreme, and be too familiar instead of too supercilious. Watch Neria, and see how she bears herself."

Captain Wild had no sooner seated his partner than he sought the music gallery, and the result of his instructions to the band presently appeared in a lively strain from the first violin, greeted by Francia with the exclamation,

"A waltz! a waltz! How perfectly splendid, only I don't care to waltz with *all* these—gentlemen! Must I, papa, if they ask me?"

"I fancy there is small danger," said Vaughn, laughing. "Captain Wild just said there was not probably a man in the room who had ever seen a waltz, and this one is played entirely for our benefit. Mr. Chilton is coming for you."

"Will you waltz, Franc?" asked Chilton, approaching.

"Certainly; but tell them to play more slowly."

The message was transmitted, and Francia floated away upon the arm of her lover, who, however he might fail in certain traits of morality and honor, certainly possessed the cardinal virtue of dancing, to perfection, while Francia herself deserved the title of Terpsichore.

"Will you do me the honor, Mrs. Vaughan?" asked the midshipman, blushing and bowing.

"Thank you, but I only waltz with Mr. Vaughn," said Neria, in a low voice; and Ned went to look among his new friends for some one who knew how to waltz.

Vaughn hesitated whether he should accept the sweet intimation of a resolution he had never imagined, and then asking himself why he should be denied a privilege which, with most ladies, any stranger might claim, he smilingly took his wife's hand and said, "Come, then!"

Vaughn had waltzed in Vienna to the music of the elder Strauss, and the " gh born" frauleins and countesses who had been his partners were wont to assure him that he danced better than their own countrymen. With a difference, perhaps, he did, but the difference was on the side of stateliness, and a certain grandeur of motion, that never deserted him. The waltz is the only round dance in which it is possible for a man to look like a hero, and the waltz was the only round dance to which Vaughn ever committed himself. Neria's style had also its peculiarity. In dancing, especially in waltzing, she seemed to lose her slight affinity for earth altogether, and airily glided over the floor like a dream of beauty, visible but immaterial.

"Lean upon my arm a little, my mist-wreath," murmured Vaughn, drawing her closer to his breast. "You are too much of a fairy."

Neria glanced smiling up, and her warm, pure breath swept his cheek. Vaughn could hardly repress the wild desire to raise her in his arms, and cover those smiling lips with the kisses tingling on his own. With a terrible effort he paused, and released her from his embrace. "That is enough," said he, abruptly, and Neria looked wonderingly into his face for the cause of the harsh change in his tone.

"Are you dizzy?" asked she, kindly.

Vaughn recovered himself, and smiled. "It is some time since I waltzed," said he, "and I find it does not agree with me. I shall not try again, but if you like it, do not hesitate to accept such partners as your taste approves. You must not give it up because you are married."

Neria only answered with a smile, and the music ceased.

"Take partners for chorus jig," shouted Jonas Merton, and Captain Wild, after a whispered word with Mr. Vaughn, presented the young fisherman called Zeb to Francia as "Mr. Lewis," while an aspirant for Neria's hand appeared in the shape of an uncouth lobster-catcher, named Barrows, whose bandy legs, crooked fingers, and beady black eyes would of themselves have suggested his avocation. Neria, a little startled, and not a little repelled, replied to his invitation somewhat coldly.

"Thank you, but I am rather tired, and will sit still this dance."

A look of blank mortification displayed itself upon the lobster-catcher's face. "'xcuse me," said he, "for taking the liberty to ask you."

Neria's quick feelings were touched, and she made room upon the bench beside her. "I do not know this dance," said she. "Chorus jig they call it, do they not?"

"Yes'm. Like enough you'd find it kind o' rough. A body gets pritty well tuckered out by the time they're at the bottom on 't," said Barrows, glancing wistfully at the vacant seat, but not daring to take it.

"Do you go away with the fishermen to-morrow?" pursued Neria, smiling in spite of herself at the gaping look of admiration with which the lobster man regarded her.

"No'm. I'm a lobsterer, I am."

"Indeed? And how do you catch lobsters?"

The chorus jig was shorter than the answer of the delighted Barrows; and before it was over, Mrs. Vaughn, with no compromise of dignity or good taste, had secured a humble admirer for life.

Francia, meanwhile, was undergoing a somewhat startling experience. Zeb had placed her at the head of the dance, and briefly explained the figure, part of it, by the direction, "first lady turn second gentleman until the music is through." Pondering a little upon this curious phrase, Francia arrived at the designated point in the dance, and gave both hands to a stalwart young fellow, who, with a little smile of amazement, enveloped the dainty offering in his own hands, as brown and hard as a well-dried side of leather. Then they turned, and they turned again, and again, and again, and again, until Francia, dizzy, bewildered, and somewhat indignant, was very glad of the aid of the young fisherman's sturdy grasp in keeping her upon her feet. The next gentleman performed the same evolution, and, finding that this was the regular order of procedure, Francia entered into the spirit of it, and allowed herself to be twirled as rapidly and for as long a time as the music and her opponent's strength allowed. Arriving at the foot, she perceived, by looking up the dance, that she had been treated with the greatest circumspection, and that the *tours de force* in progress between the fishermen and their more usual partners were quite another affair from what she had experienced. In fact, the less agile and athletic young ladies were continually whirled off their feet, and fell either to their knees or into the arms of the whirler, who, to do justice, was generally ready to offer aid. One young lady, of rather diminutive stature, became so exasperated by repeated occurrences of this nature, that upon being whirled to the floor by a powerful young fellow, standing in relation of cousin to her, she sprang to her feet, and inflicted a box upon his ear so heartily as to affect him to tears, and every one else to laughter, while mademoiselle herself impartially indulged in both.

Four-hand reels followed, and Ned Chilton won the admiration of the company by his skill in "shuffling out the tune," and bringing down the final stamp on the exact turn of the measure. His only rival was his partner, Trypheny, who, with her hands upon her slender waist, head set saucily back, and lips and cheeks glowing scarlet, looked, as Rafe Chilton found an opportunity to whisper, "Quite too charming." So thought Zeb Lewis, who had given up dancing and devoted himself to communion with the green-eyed monster, who prompted him, as the reel finished, to seek his betrothed, and emphatically inform her that if she was ever going home with him again she had "got to go now." Trypheny, somewhat awed by the suppressed emotion in her lover's face, submitted to authority, and, with one sidelong look of farewell in Mr. Chilton's direction, allowed herself to be led away.

The party from Bonniemeer soon followed, leaving the majority of the revellers to dance until the day dawn summoned them to their hardy toil.

CHAPTER XXI.

THE GREAT ORGAN.

A FEW weeks after the ball, the post brought in a letter from Mrs. Livingstone to Neria, in which among other matters she mentioned that

Dr. Luttrell was looking for a quiet house upon the sea-shore where he might spend the summer with his wife, who was very much of an invalid, and suggested that Cragness would probably suit him exactly, and give some pleasant neighbors to Bonniemeer. In fact she acknowledged she had already mentioned the house to Dr. Luttrell, who was much pleased with her description of it, and only waited for her permission to formally apply for it.

This suggestion Neria referred at once to Vaughn, without even confessing a certain repugnance in her own mind, to seeing strangers installed in the shadowy rooms so associated in her mind with her old friend and teacher, Gillies. Vaughn, however, who had seldom been at Cragness, and regarded it simply as a piece of property, thought it very well to turn it to account, and in compliance with his advice, Neria answered Claudia's *quasi* application so favorably that in the course of a few days, Dr. Luttrell himself came down to look at the premises, previous to engaging them.

Mr. Vaughn drove over with him to Cragness, to the consternation of Mrs. Brume, who was, as she expressed the situation, "all in the suds"—a dilemma shared by her lord and master, who, as the gentlemen drove up, was to be seen at the back door, with rueful face and reluctant arms, splashing a heavy "pounder" up and down in a barrel half filled with dirty clothes and hot water.

Nancy, who, through the mists of her tub, had seen the approaching visitors, found time, before they fairly stopped at the door, to clutch off the uncomely cap adorning her grey hairs, to replace it with a smarter one, to put on a collar and stern brooch of Scotch pebble, and to tie a white apron about her waist as tightly as if, like a Hindoo devotee, she sought to cut herself in twain, by way of penance for her sins. Finally, she wiped her face so vigorously upon the discarded tow apron as to impart to her features a genial glow, not unlike that of the sun setting behind a fog-bank. Then she darted to the back door, and, catching Reuben by the arm, said, in a rapid undertone:

"Go round to the door—there's folks!"

And, after all this by-play, the daughter of Eve stood in her door, a minute later, the picture of innocent surprise, as she exclaimed:

"Well, I declare for it, Mr. Vaughn! I don't see how you got up 'thout some of us seeing you."

Vaughn returned her greeting with the debonair manner which made him the idol of his humble neighbors, introduced his companion, and mentioned their errand.

Mrs. Brune readily accompanied them through the house, not unwilling, perhaps, that her employer should see how faithful she had been to her duties, although left without supervision or control.

In the library all stood as it had done upon the night when its last master departed thence to voyage upon unknown seas, with an unknown pilot at the helm. Over the fireplace, the knight in golden armor, his face covered with his helmet bars, still guarded the secret of the place, and, from the scroll at his feet, still faintly glimmered the proud device, "*Dieu, le roy, et le foy du Vaughn.*"

"A somewhat gloomy chamber, this," said Dr. Luttrell, looking about him, with a slight shiver.

"Decidedly so," assented Vaughn, striding to the window.

"The last proprietor and one of the servants died here very suddenly, I understand," pursued Luttrell. "Was it in this room?"

"Yes, I believe so. Do such associations disturb you?" asked Vaughn.

"Certainly not. I am not superstitious by nature, and a medical education blunts one's mind to imaginative terrors very thoroughly. I was wondering whether there is anything unhealthy about the place. Mrs. Luttrell, as you know, is quite an invalid."

"Candidly speaking," returned Vaughn, "I should think the gloom and darkness of this room would be very depressing to an invalid; and what affects the spirits is apt to affect the body, especially when the latter is unsound."

"That is true in some cases," said Luttrell, reflectively; "but my wife is not in the least fanciful, and cares very little for the moral or imaginative atmosphere surrounding her, so that she does not miss the material luxuries to which she is accustomed."

Vaughn simply bowed, not choosing to enter into a discussion of Mrs. Luttrell's peculiarities, especially with Mrs. Luttrell's husband.

"What is this, an organ?" asked the doctor, penetrating, with his keen gaze, the dusky corner where poor Gillies's familiar was niched into a recess built to accommodate it.

"Yes, and a fine one, as I am informed. Mr. Gillies imported it, at a considerable cost, from Germany."

"Ah? I have done a little in this way myself. Indeed, there are few things I have not tried, and still fewer which I have not found wanting," said Dr. Luttrell, turning the key in the door of the organ and throwing it open. "Yes," continued he, "this looks like quite a grand affair. I should like to try it, if you will not be bored, Mr. Vaughn."

Of course Vaughn was delighted at the prospect, and courteously seated himself to listen.

"But the bellows—how is that managed? Does some one outside attend to it?" asked Luttrell, looking about him.

Vaughn did not know; but Mrs. Brume, on being summoned, explained that Mr. Gillies, not choosing to be dependent on human aid for his capricious minstrelsy, had invented a piece of mechanism, and had it attached to the organ in such manner that he could introduce air by his own action.

This machinery was set in motion by turning a crank, which she pointed out.

"Aha, that is easily done," said Luttrell, seizing the handle and attempting to move it; but the rusted wheels refused to turn, and when, applying more force, he jerked and pushed the handle violently, it suddenly gave way, and a loud whirring noise within the organ told that some fatal injury had been committed.

"The organ is faithful to its master. It will serve no other man," said Vaughn, lightly, as Luttrell, half angry, half mortified, began an apology for the mischief he had done.

"With your consent I will make it serve me, if I send to Germany for the man who built it to repair it," said Luttrell, eyeing, with grim determination, the thing that had foiled him.

"Pray do as you like with it, if you come here," said Vaughn, rising; "but the air of this gloomy room is chill as that of a tomb. Let us go."

"As chill as that of a tomb," repeated Doctor Luttrell, softly, as he followed his host from the room.

A few days later Vaughn received a letter announcing that his late guest engaged the house and domain of Cragness, upon terms already specified, and would take possession as soon as the summer weather should be fairly established.

CHAPTER XXII.

OBI.

WHEN Mrs. Rhee left Bonniemeer, just previous to Vaughn's marriage, she had gone no farther than Carrick, and still kept up a sort of left-handed connection with her old home through the negress, Chloe, who, in the fine summer days, would frequently creep over the two miles of road, staff in hand, peering sidelong at every creature she met, and muttering to herself, until all the children, and some of their elders, were quite sure that she was a witch. Through the old nurse, Mrs. Rhee constantly sent messages of regard and remembrance to Francia, with numerous humble petitions that she would come and visit her, if only for a few moments. Francia's kind heart would not allow her to neglect these petitions, and the consequence was that she often called upon the whilom housekeeper, until one day, her father passing Mrs. Rhee's cottage, and seeing his daughter's pony at the door, entered the little parlor, where he found the young lady seated in Mrs. Rhee's lap, while a refection of cake and currant wine upon the table showed how she had been amusing herself.

In a few decided words Vaughn informed his daughter that he was ready to escort her home, and, when she had gone out, he added to Mrs. Rhee:

"And I do not wish Francia to be upon these terms with you. It is not in woman's nature that you should keep our secret inviolable under such circumstances."

"I do not know that I shall always keep it," returned Mrs. Rhee, defiantly. "You have pleased yourself in marrying, why should I not please myself also?"

"Because you dare not brave my anger," said Vaughn, quietly.

Mrs. Rhee looked at his white face and steady eyes, and turned away her head.

Vaughn strode to the door, but returned and held out his hand.

"Let us be friends, Anita, for the sake of the dead, and of the past—a past which no future can undo; but remember that I am master."

The woman took his hand, and kissed it passionately.

"You are master," said she, and when he was gone gave way to a tropic storm of sobs and tears.

So Francia was informed that she was to go no more to see Mrs. Rhee, without especial leave; and soon lost all inclination to do so, in gathering anxieties and apprehensions caused by her lover's irregularities, reported to her by certain officious correspondents in the city; while his own letters grew every week briefer and more unsatisfactory.

Old Chloe's walks to Carrick remained undisturbed, as were indeed all her other movements; for Vaughn had advised his new housekeeper that the old nurse was a privileged person, not to be controlled or reproved by less authority than his own or Mrs. Vaughn's.

It was to Neria, then, that Mrs. Barlow came one day, and, after some preamble, inquired if Mrs. Vaughn knew that Chloe was in the occasional habit of leaving the house privately, in the middle of the night, and absenting herself for several hours. Where she went, or what she did during these periods, Mrs. Barlow could not pretend to say, nor had even inquired. If it were one of the maids she would not be long in finding out, continued the worthy woman, but Chloe was different, Mr. Vaughn had said she wasn't under any authority but his own, and perhaps he wouldn't even like to have her watched. She had hardly liked to speak, but concluded Mrs. Vaughn had better know.

Neria quietly assured her that she had done quite right in speaking, and promising to attend to the matter, dismissed the housekeeper, (a worthy, but commonplace woman, whose pride of office had been somewhat wounded by Mr. Vaughn's injunction), far better satisfied with her position and her mistress than she had been inclined to find herself.

"She's got a kind of a tact about her, Miss Vaughn has, that sets everything straight that she touches with so much as her finger-end," was the decision that evening confided by Mrs. Barlow to James, the English groom, whom Vaughn had long since promoted to the position of body-servant, and who had gradually assumed various other duties which, in an English establishment, would have belonged to the office of steward or major-domo.

"You're right, there, Mrs. Barlow," replied James, on the present occasion, "and the Squire's done a better thing this time than he did before, I can promise you."

"You knew the first Miss Vaughn, then?" asked the housekeeper, curiously.

"Yes, I knew her," replied close-mouthed James, picking up his cap and leaving the room.

It was on the ensuing night that Neria, unable to sleep, sat at her window, dreamily enjoying the beauty of the moonlight view, and listening to the distant beat of the rising tide upon the beach. The low sound of a closing door startled her from her reverie, for the hour was past midnight, and the orderly household had long since retired to rest. Suddenly the housekeeper's story returned to her mind, and she at once concluded that the untimely wanderer must be old Chloe. A sudden impulse to solve for herself the mystery of the nurse's nocturnal wanderings, took possession of her mind, and hastily wrapping herself in a dark cloak, with the hood drawn over her head, and protecting her feet from the heavy dew, she glided down the stairs and out at the garden-door, which, as she had correctly judged, was the one she had heard so cautiously closed. Outside, she paused a moment to look about her. Far down the garden path a distorted and crouching figure crept along between the roses, and reaching the end, passed through the little gate leading to the grove, beyond which lay the pine wood and the lake. Swift and silent as a shadow, Neria followed, bearing with her the perfume of the roses and the lilies, that opened wide their chalices to cast incense upon her path, for all Nature loved Neria, as Neria loved Nature.

Through the garden and through the dim oak wood they passed, until at its farther edge Neria paused, and, holding herself in the shadow, watched attentively the motions of the old negress, who, advancing to the foot of an oak tree, standing by itself in a little glade, busied herself in removing from its hollow interior an accumulation of brush and leaves. These she laid on one side, and then, thrusting her arm far into the cavity, groped for a few moments, and finally brought out an immense toad. Him she set upon the ground in the moonlight, and, prostrating herself before him, appeared to offer some prayer or supplication, to which the singular deity ungraciously replied by sparkling eyes and swelling throat. Rising to her feet, the negress described, with the sharp-pointed stick in her hand, a circle some three feet in diameter upon the sward, and, baring her head and feet, paced three times around it, chanting in a dim unearthly voice some barbarous rune, ending with a wild wail to which the screech-owl in the neighboring wood shrieked response. The circle complete, the negress placed the toad carefully in its centre, and describing another circle precisely similar, took her own position in its midst in an attitude as nearly resembling that of the toad as her form was capable of assuming. She now addressed to him some words, still in the unknown tongue of the chant; and after waiting a few moments, and finding that he remained motionless, took from her pocket a little vial and poured upon his head a few drops of liquid, which apparently put the poor creature into a state of frantic pain, causing him to writhe, leap, and contort himself into every possible shape. Without losing one of these motions, the negress applied herself to imitating them as exactly as possible, and the wondering spectator in the wood knew not whether to find the sight more grotesque or horrible, as the swollen reptile and the negress, deformed almost below humanity, vied with each other in such gruesome gambols as might fit the familiars of witch and warlock sporting in the moonlight upon some haunted heath.

Exhausted at last, the toad turned upon his back and lay apparently lifeless. Still Chloe imitated him, and lay like an ugly corpse upon the sparkling sward. Presently, however, she cautiously arose, and taking the toad in her hands, bathed his head with the abundant dew, and warmed him in her bosom. When he began to show signs of returning life she moistened her finger in his mouth, and signed herself upon the brow and breast, muttered another unintelligible charm, and finally replaced him in the tree, securely covering him with the *débris* under which she had found him.

Her next movement was to carefully pluck the grass from the spot where the toad had lain in his final exhaustion, and also that upon which her own head had rested at the same moment. This she carefully wrapped in the leaf of a plant which she had plucked as she came through the wood, and then turned her steps toward home, passing close beside Neria, whose slender figure was hidden by the trunk of a giant oak. As silently and as stealthily as they had come, the two shadowy figures returned toward the house, and the negress reaching it first, entered, and closed the door.

Neria, who was close behind, heard the heavy bolts shot into their places, and remained for a moment in doubt as to her own course, not wishing to let the negress know that she had been watched, and yet seeing no other way of effecting her own entrance. After a moment of hesitation, she glided along the terrace to the window of the little room used as Vaughn's private study. This room communicated with her own apartments by a winding stair, and Vaughn had of late converted it into a sleeping-room, averring that his late and uncertain hours of retiring made it more convenient. The maidenly instincts which Neria's brief and peculiar married life had not overcome, made her hesitate and tremble in tapping at this window, and when at last she did, it was so lightly that Vaughn, lying awake to indulge the bitter thoughts which in the daylight he was better able to withstand, hardly knew whether the sound were other than the pattering of the vine leaves against the glass. It was repeated, and drawing aside the curtain, he looked out. Neria, shrinking away from the window, stood motionless, draped in her dark cloak, her pale face dimly showing beneath the hood, the moonlight sparkling in the dew-drops that gemmed her drooping head.

Vaughn threw open the window.

"Neria!" said he, in a hushed voice. "Is this really you?"

"Yes, Sieur. Do you not know me?"

"You came so spirit-like it might have been your wraith. But where are you going—what is amiss?"

"Nothing, Sieur, but I want to come in."

"To come in! What, the queen of Bonniemeer and of its master, wandering forlorn through the night and begging shelter for her royal head!" exclaimed Vaughn, gay in the sudden revulsion from his first terror. "Will you come in at this window, or must I open the hall-door for your majesty?"

"Can I come in at the window?" asked Neria, dubiously.

"Surely. Give me your two hands, put your foot on the ledge in the stonework, and—so!"

He drew her in at the window with the word, and as she lay a moment in his arms, pressed his lips to hers.

She smiled, but struggled to her feet. He immediately released her, and asked, gravely,

"Why are you out so late, and so thinly dressed, dear child? See, your hair, your cloak, are drenched with dew. Your hands are cold and damp—you are as pale in the moonlight as a true ghost. Explain."

Neria sank into an arm-chair, for she was indeed almost exhausted, and told her story as briefly as she might. Her husband listened attentively.

"The poor old creature must be deranged in mind," said he. "She is very old, for she was already past middle life when I first saw her."

"She came here to take care of Francia and me, did she not?" asked Neria, a little surprised at his hesitation.

"No, dear, she was here before. I have always taken care of her on account of past services, and we must still protect her, although it may become necessary to restrain these wanderings. Can you imagine any object in the strange proceedings you saw to-night?"

"None," said Neria, hesitating. "None that I can mention with any show of reason, and yet I felt—O, Sieur, I felt like one who sees his scaffold built before his eyes. I cannot tell why. I know it is fanciful, perhaps unjust, and yet I feel sure that all these spells and charms were in some way directed against me."

She fell into a fit of aguish shivering as she spoke, and raised her face to Vaughn like a little child who seeks protection. He stooped and took her in his arms, gathering her to his broad breast with an impulse of yearning tenderness not to be withstood.

"My poor little dove, my timid nestling!" murmured he, "who would harm you? What creature so monstrous as to wish you ill? Do you not know that my life stands between you and hurt? My darling, my darling, may I never tell you how much I love you?"

Neria nestled into his arms and laid her head upon his breast, with a sigh of content. Vaughn's heart gave a great throb. Had the happiness for which he no longer hoped, come to him now of its own sweet will? Did Neria love him at last, wife-like? He tried to deny the hope, he tried to doubt, he tried to reason, and in the end, with a terrible shock, the great love that he had bound down within his heart burst its bonds, and rising in its might, took possession of the man who had striven to deny its God-given life. He pressed her to his heart, he covered her lips, her eyes, her brow, her hair with kisses; he murmured in her ear every caressing name, every passionate endearment which he had been wont in half-bitter, half-plaintive mockery to lavish upon her picture, her glove, her airy image. But with an unmistakable movement of repugnance, Neria repulsed him, and extricating herself from his embrace, hurried to the door of the staircase leading to her own apartments.

Vaughn followed, and, seizing her by the hand, demanded passionately,

"Why do you leave me thus? Why do you refuse my caresses? Do you, then, absolutely loathe me?"

"No; O, no!" said Neria, faintly. "But do not touch me, do not kiss me again! O let me go, I am faint."

She snatched away her hand, and groped for the handle of the door, swayed heavily forward, and fell swooning upon the stairs.

With a sharp revulsion of feeling, Vaughn raised her again in his arms, bore her reverently up the stairs, and laid her upon a couch near the open window.

A *flaçon* of cologne-water stood upon the dressing-table. He applied it to her temples and poured some drops into her mouth. In a few moments she revived, opened her eyes, turned them upon Vaughn, shrank away and closed them again. He took her hand. It was withdrawn.

"I have broken our pact," said he, with stern sadness; "but it was because I deceived myself. I fancied for a moment that you returned my love, might return my caresses. Even now I will have no doubt remaining between us. Speak plainly and as frankly as you would pray to God. Do you love me; do you think you will ever love me other than as a child loves its father, a sister her brother? Will my caresses ever be other than repugnant to your feelings?"

Neria sat upright, her white face, gleaming eyes, and cloudy hair, giving her the look of the angel of tears and sorrow. She raised her hands in unconscious deprecation of her own words as she said,

"O, Sieur, how can I bear to tell it you, but I fear I never can; I fear that if we are to be happy at all, if even I am to live at all, you must never again forget what you have promised. Sieur, I pray God that I may die soon, and leave you free to love and marry soon one who will love you as I cannot. O, I pray that I may die and leave you free."

The plaintive tone in her voice deepened to a heart-break, and as she finished speaking, she fell into a passion of tears and sobs, shaking her slender form to its centre. It was the first time in all her life that Vaughn had seen her weep, and he was more terrified than he had been when she swooned.

"May God be merciful to us both!" cried he, bowing his face upon his hands, while through his heart thrilled the fierce pang of which a man's tears are born.

Presently he took Neria's hand. It lay cold and lifeless in his own.

"My wife," said he, solemnly, "for you are still my wife, to cherish and to guard, if not to love, all this shall be set right for you, if not for me. You will forgive what I have made you suffer, and not blame my broken faith too harshly; for, O, child, a man is not as a God, and my strength was taxed heavily, heavily. Forgive me, Neria, and show that you forgive, by never in your inmost heart again wishing me the terrible punishment of your death."

He waited for no reply, but was gone; and presently stepping from the window where Neria had entered, he sought the wood, and wandered there until the night was done, the summer night of moon, and stars, and richest balm of dewy flowers, and dreamy chirrup of half-awakened birds, and wooing whispers of the warm west wind, and solemn diapason of the distant sea; and yet, the night than which no night was ever blacker, or fiercer, or more blankly starless in the life of Frederic Vaughn.

CHAPTER XXIII.

THE GREAT BANNER.

THE days had come when the "blood-red blossom of war" bloomed upon our fields, and the tocsin was loudly summoning her laborers to reap the harvest which, sown by anarchy and oppression, is in the divine order of events to be gathered into the garners of peace and widest liberty.

The stern echo of this cry had jarred discordantly upon Vaughn's bridal joy and he had answered it with his wealth, his influence, his earnest wishes. Himself he had withheld, for he had said he was no more his own, but Neria's. Now, however, as devotees will give to God the heart that earth has broken, Vaughn was ready to offer to his country the life that love had wrecked.

The next day after his decisive interview with Neria he applied for a commission as colonel, volunteering to raise and equip the color company of a new regiment at his own expense.

Pending the answer to this application, Vaughn busied himself in setting his affairs in order, with the same solemn tenderness with which a man who feels his death at hand, will care for the welfare of those he loves and must leave behind. Heedful even of Neria's fantasy, as he deemed it, he sent for Chloe to his study, and closely questioned her touching her nocturnal rambles; without, however, telling her how he had heard of them.

The old negress appeared at first utterly stolid, but when pressed for the motive to her curious pantomime with the toad, she mumbled some broken sentences implying that she had been working a charm for the benefit of her own health, and that to preserve its efficacy this charm must remain a secret.

The explanation seemed to Vaughn very consistent with the superstition and secretiveness of the negro character, and he contented himself with warning Chloe that such exposure to night air and damps was far more likely to injure than to benefit her health, and desiring that she should in future omit them. He further informed her that he was about to leave home for some time, and inquired if she would prefer remaining at Bonniemeer, subject, of course, to Mrs. Vaughn's pleasure, or be placed with Mrs. Rhee at Carrick. Whichever home she selected, however, Vaughn decisively forbade any private communication between the two, and sternly desired the old woman to understand that no messages from Mrs. Rhee to Miss Vaughn were to be delivered, whatever might be the urgency of the housekeeper's entreaties.

Chloe turned up her head, and gave Vaughn one of her wicked sidelong looks. So forcibly did the action remind him of some ill-omened bird, some crafty raven who had learned a secret of sin and shame, and only waits the fitting moment to prate it in the ears that last should hear it, that he could not restrain a smile.

"'Pears nat'ral 'nough, arter all, dat Miss 'Nita like to hab missy Franc come see her odd times," began she; but Vaughn, no longer smiling, raised a finger.

"Hush, woman!" said he, sternly. "If you speak of what is forbidden, I shall know that you are crazy, and send you to a mad-house."

"Lors, mas'r, it be you dat's mad, not me," replied the old woman, with such simplicity that Vaughn remained uncertain whether she had understood him or not, and after ascertaining that she preferred remaining at Bonniemeer, contented himself with placing a considerable present in her hand, and charging her, in a kind but authoritative manner, to remember his injunctions.

Chloe mumbled thanks; and with a promise of compliance, shuffled away, pausing with the door in her hand to once more glance sidelong at her master, and mutter in her own barbarous dialect some unintelligible phrase.

"I wish she had chosen to go, but I cannot turn her out, and I believe she is harmless," said Vaughn, as the door closed; and then, dismissing the unpleasing subject from his mind, he turned to more important matters. The management of his large property he continued in the hands of Jones, Brown, and Robinson, the hereditary advisers of his house; but for a personal and confidential adviser in any difficulty, Vaughn recommended Neria to apply to Mr. Murray, whose talents as a business man were undeniable, and whose interest in the concerns of his kinsman's family was not to be doubted, although occasionally shown in a somewhat unadvised manner.

Neria acquiesced in everything, listened patiently to her husband's minute directions and council, and opposed none of his arrangements, not even the primary one of leaving home. Indeed, since the hour when the decisive though involuntary expression of her distaste for his love had so wounded Vaughn's heart, Neria had grown timid, silent, and pre-occupied; brooding, not as her husband bitterly told himself, over the untoward fate that had bound her, past release, to his side, but perplexing herself afresh over the yet unsolved mysteries of love, of her own life, and of man's nature.

So the days went on, all flowers and sunshine and song of summer birds upon the surface, while dead men's bones, and crawling worms, and cold, and dark, lay beneath the surface. So with the great earth herself, so with many a smaller sphere swinging in a smaller orbit, and yet indissoluble from the finely graduated scheme of the universe. No Thalberg, no Gottschalk, no Listz can so endlessly vary his theme as can nature, and yet the foundation of each variation is the theme itself.

Vaughn received his commission, and was busied day after day in the city with regimental affairs.

At home, Neria and Francia wrought silently at the great silken banner destined to be borne by the men of Carrick, who had answered to Vaughn's spirited appeal for their support and assistance so unanimously that the *corps d'honneur* which he proposed to raise, was almost entirely composed of men who had either grown up with him, or who had from boyhood looked upon him as their natural leader and adviser.

So Vaughn led forth the men of Carrick, and Vaughn's wife and their wives remained in their lonely homes.

CHAPTER XXIV.

MRS. LUTTRELL.

THE Luttrells were settled at Cragness after several delays on account of weather and the health of the invalid; and Neria, with Francia, drove over to call upon them.

Shown into the library by Nancy Brume, they found Mrs. Luttrell lying upon a couch near the window, alone. She half rose to meet them, but sank back with a murmured apology for her weakness, and looked indeed so fragile that no apology was needed. While Francia, always fluent and at ease, made talk upon the weather and the debilitating influence of the first hot days, Neria looked at the invalid with a painful and perplexed interest.

It had so chanced that they had never met in the city, and Neria found it impossible to account for the impulse of tenderness and sympathy now possessing her. She could not even decide whether the face of the invalid was more prepossessing or painful in its wan loveliness.

Tall and slender in figure and handsome in feature, Mrs. Luttrell had, at the time of her marriage, been considered a beauty; but now, her abundant fair hair seemed to have lost its light and gloss; her complexion, from delicate, had become transparently pallid; her white teeth shone ghastly between lips almost as white, while her large blue eyes had acquired a singular expression of anxiety and terror, a dreamy watchfulness, a weary foreboding, never lost, as she listened or as she talked. Her slender hands, too, Neria noticed had assumed an unnatural pearly whiteness and a stiff and laborious motion, while beneath the nails appeared a violet tinge instead of the rose-red hue of health.

Her manner, too, was changed. Naturally serene and undemonstrative, it now was marked by uncertain flutter, a rapid alternation from animation to abstraction, with frequent lapses into reverie. In a pause of the chat, which even Francia found it hard to sustain, Neria kindly inquired if Mrs. Luttrell found benefit from the sea air.

"The sea air?" repeated the invalid, vaguely. "Oh, it makes no difference about that." She stopped with a frightened start, and presently continued, in a tone of forced gayety:

"O, I am doing very well—quite as well as I could expect. The doctor says it is only that I am nervous."

"How long have you been so ill?" asked Francia.

"I don't know when it began—I can't think," replied Mrs. Luttrell, in a low voice; and from the last word she seemed to drop into an abyss of reverie, so profound that neither of her guests liked to interrupt it.

Through the half-open door glided the figure of Dr. Luttrell, and, although noiselessly, his wife, who had lain with her back to him, raised her head and moved, so that she could see him; nor from that moment to the end of the call did her eyes ever wander from his face for more than a moment. This fixed and anxious gaze did not, however, seem to embarrass its object, who never, by any chance, returned it, although he occasionally addressed his wife. The ladies of Bonniemeer he professed himself delighted to welcome, and hoped they would often take compassion upon Mrs. Luttrell, who was too much of an invalid to move about much.

The conversation no longer lagged. Inquiring if Neria had seen the sunset of the preceding night, Luttrell launched into some new theories of atmospheric effects, solar rays, and the aurora; had some new discoveries in the moon to narrate; and, with a turning toward Francia, closed with a droll story of a farmer who must cut his salt hay in apogee, and, because his work pressed, sent to Cambridge to request that apogee might be put off a week or two, offering to pay "anything in reason" for the accommodation. Then he spoke of Vaughn's devotion to his country's cause, and, with a half glance toward his wife, said that "had he not a paramount duty at home, nothing should deter him from following so fine an example."

A sudden impulse drew Neria's eyes to Mrs. Luttrell's face as these words were spoken, in time to see the doubt, the terror, the torturing uncertainty, deepening and deepening in the great blue eyes, while they dwelt as earnestly upon the speaker's face as might those of a child on the page where is written a fascinating tale in an unknown tongue.

Luttrell felt the gaze—felt its expression, too, as the sudden knitting of the brows and compression of the lips sufficiently proved; but still he never looked toward his wife, never paused in his conversation, but presently, as if unconsciously, took a fire-screen from the table, and, playing with it while he talked, held it between his wife and himself.

The face of the invalid grew clouded. She moved uneasily upon her couch, closed her eyes for a moment, and lay quite still, as if gathering strength for a struggle, and then opening them wide, while all the power of her body seemed gathered in their luminous rays, she fixed upon Luttrell a gaze which pierced through every defence, every subterfuge—a gaze which, though it might drain the vital energy of that delicate organization, could not fail of its object. Luttrell paused suddenly in what he was saying, threw down the fire-screen, and walked to the window. His wife moved slightly, that she might still keep her eyes upon him.

Neria found herself oppressed and agitated with the mystery floating around her, and blending with the old mystery of the place, which had of late begun to haunt her with a sense of duty unfulfilled. She glanced at Francia and rose to go. Mrs. Luttrell half rose, made an adieu as brief as courtesy would admit, and sank back. Her husband, visibly anxious to escape the room, seized his hat and escorted the ladies to their carriage. As they drove down the hill they saw him turn toward the beach and stroll away with the air of a man who has several hours to dispose of, and is in no hurry.

"He won't go home very soon, by his looks," said Francia, laughing, as she touched her ponies with the whip.

"No."

"How do you like Mrs. Luttrell?"

"She is very interesting—I pity her.

"Well, I don't know. She didn't seem interesting to me; I thought her too much taken up with herself, and dull, like all sick people. I like Doctor Luttrell ever so much," returned Francia, positively; and Neria said, pointing to the headland before them,

"See the Lion's Head against the evening sky. Isn't it grand?"

CHAPTER XXV.

THE weather became oppressively hot, and Mr. Chilton, forsaking his usual summer orbit, came quietly down to Carrick and took lodgings at tne Mermaid's Cave, Colonel Vaughn's absence preventing his receiving an invitation to stay at Bonniemeer.

Neria watched the effect of this movement upon Francia with much interest, for it had been too obvious during the last few weeks that some great anxiety or doubt had taken possession of the child's mind, and was exerting a morbid influence on her character. Neria, fastidiously delicate in her fear of intrusion upon the personality of others, asked no questions—refrained, even, from that n.ute sympathy which sometimes is more intrusive than a direct appeal; and

Francia, for the first time in her life, seemed inclined for meditation rather than speech, so that, whatever lay beneath the surface, life at Bonniemeer went on as usual. Mr. Chilton was there much of his time, of course, and seemed quite sufficiently devoted to his beautiful *fiancée*—all the more so, perhaps, that she no longer beamed full moon upon him, but had her hours of depression, abstraction, even of pettishness. Also, she occasionally appeared with red eyes and feverish lips—new symptoms in her sunny life. The lover was not slow to perceive these changes, but, question he never so tenderly, could get no satisfactory explanation of them, and occasionally departed for Carrick in an undignified state of mind, characterized among children as "the sulks."

Two or three weeks had passed after this fashion, when, one morning, as Neria was about sending to Cragness to inquire for Mrs. Luttrell, Francia offered to ride over herself.

"Mr. Chilton will be here soon, I suppose," suggested Neria, glancing at her watch. "You might wait and have his escort."

"It's not worth while to delay," returned Francia, hastily. "He may not come before dinner, and it will soon be too hot to ride. I will just go over alone."

"Very well, dear," said Neria, a little puzzled, for she knew that Francia had once minded neither heat nor cold, and would have thought it little to wait hours for her lover's company.

The black pony was brought round, and as Francia, settling herself in the saddle, glanced toward the window with a nod and smile, Neria was struck with the change a few weeks had wrought in her face. From very pretty she had become lovely. The eyes that had been but roadside violets, smiling frankly up at every passer, were of a sudden violets shyly blooming in the deep recesses of a forest, where never penetrates the sun to drink the dew that trembles on their lips—never comes ruder step or harsher voice than the fawn's and the nightingale's.

The night of a year ago, when—she crowning him with water-lilies—Fergus had called Francia Undine, floated into Neria's memory, and while she thought, "It is the soul slowly crystallizing in the midst of her life that I see in her eyes to-day," she sighed.

> "Sighed for the grief and the pain
> For the reed that grows nevermore again
> As a reed with the reeds in the river."

Francia did her errand, and heard from Mrs. Brume that the invalid was no better—in fact, grew daily worse; and, to the inquiry if Mrs. Vaughn could send her anything, or offer any service, Nancy replied, with some hesitation,

"Well, if you or Miss Vaughn could come and set up a night with her, I should be dreadful glad, for there's no one but the doctor and me, and we're pretty near tuckered out. She's so notional she won't have a nuss, though I've heerd him offer to send to the city for the best that's to be got."

"Certainly we will come," replied Francia, readily. "That is, I will; and I have no doubt Mrs. Vaughn will, although she is not so strong as I. One of us will come to-night."

"That's real clever of you, now, I do say. I didn't expect both on you, though the more the merrier; and you've got sickness to home, too."

"Yes, poor Chloe does not grow any better; but Aunt Sally takes good care of her, and Mrs. Vaughn sees about it. Good morning."

"Good day, Miss Franc," said the housekeeper, and stood in the door, one skinny hand shading her eyes, while the other gathered together an apron not absolutely clean, watching the graceful figure of the young girl as she rode slowly down the beach.

"'Pears like there's something on her mind," soliloquized she, at length. "Wonder if she's heerd—"

Nancy went back to her work, and Francia rode pensively along the sands, where now the noonday heat began to quiver in a shimmering cloud, while the dunes heading the beach seemed parching and bleaching to a ghastlier white, and the scattered tufts of beach-grass lay prostrate and wilting. The round spot of shade at the foot of each ragged mound crawled slowly nearer to its base, and following, inch by inch, the fierce sunlight drank up the dew that the night had pityingly let fall upon the scorching traces of yesterday's heat.

A mile from Cragness the road to Bonniemeer wound in between two of these dunes, and Francia had already drawn her pony's rein toward it, when eye and hand were arrested by the sight of two figures, at some distance up the beach, seated under the shadow of a great rock, against which the female figure leaned, while her companion, stretched upon the sand, rested upon an elbow, with his head so near her shoulder that, in that drowsy atmosphere, a speedy contact seemed inevitable.

Francia's eyes were good, and her perceptions keen. Also she was Colonel Vaughn's daughter, and with a sharp turn of the bit she guided her pony back to the sands, put him to a canter, reduced, as she approached the rock, to a walk, at which pace she passed, glancing across the two figures as she glanced across the sands, across the gulls, as Lady Clara Vere de Vere glances across the face of young Lawrence, when she no longer cares to remember him.

As she approached, Chilton sprang to his feet and advanced a step toward her; then, catching the expression of her face, paused, and stood in all the awkward embarrassment inevitable to the most polished dissembler at some points of his career. His companion turned her face seaward and giggled nervously. Leaving them thus, Francia paced slowly on, sitting her horse with the nonchalant grace of an accomplished horsewoman, who feels herself free from the restraint of spectators.

Surely, a throne is not such vantage ground as a horse's back. Mounted, the rider who understands his horse, duplicates all the highest attributes of humanity. He is braver, he is nobler, he is more decisive, apter to attempt redress of the wrongs about him. Had Arthur's knights been foot-soldiers would there ever have been a Round Table? Had the horse refused co-operation would chivalry ever have glorified the earth, would the noble madness of the Crusades have done its mighty work upon the civilization of the middle ages? "When I am the king and you are the queen" we will apportion to every new-born child a steady horse, upon whose back he shall be cradled, shall learn to sit upright, shall find his home by day, his rest by night.

That evening, when Mr. Chilton appeared at Bonniemeer, very ill at ease, and as doubtful of his reception as he had a right to be, he found Francia seated with Neria in the drawing-room.

She bade him a courteous good-evening, but made no movement to meet him, asked no questions as to his occupations through the day, showed neither displeasure nor pique toward him, or indeed evinced any emotion whatever; and the slight shade of reserve pervading her demeanor was so delicately drawn as to give no ground for comment, or warrant any appeal for explanation.

Chilton made his adieu at an early hour, and walked slowly back to Carrick, wondering whether he was most pleased or annoyed at the course his *fiancée* had chosen. When he was gone, Francia rose, and, flitting restlessly about the room for a few moments, came and threw herself upon the floor at Neria's feet, laying her head upon her lap. It had been a favorite attitude of hers till lately, and Neria fondly smoothed the bright brown hair that rippled beneath her fingers like the tiny waves of a sunlit sea.

"Neria, darling, what shall I do?" whispered Francia.

"Ask your own heart, dear, not me," said Neria, sadly.

"But, if my heart has misled me once?"

"Was it your heart or your fancy, your vanity, that misled you, Franc?"

"But, if I have done something and think I should not have done it, is it worse to try to undo it, or to go on, hoping time will mend it?" asked the girl, earnestly, while she raised a pale face to the mournful one bent over her, and Neria said:

"O, Franc, how dare I advise you? I, who have guided my own life so ill. I am afraid, dear, I cannot help you, and yet I will not refuse. Think of it to-night, question your own heart, question the Father who, sooner or later, heals all wounds, soothes all sorrows. Take council with the night, and if, to-morrow, you still wish for such help as I can give, come and you shall have it."

They kissed and bade good-night, each taking for her companion through the sleepless hours, the Gordian knot which life presents to every one of us, and which most of us spend our years in the effort to unravel, finally perhaps borrowing of despair a sword to sever, not the knot, but the life entangled in it.

With the morning came Fergus, an unexpected envoy from his father to Neria. upon some matter of business. The ladies were together when he arrived, and from Neria he turned to Francia, who found beneath the courteousness of his greeting, a formality and constraint that she, sighing, told herself had been unknown to the old time. She sat while he talked with Neria, and listened, not to his words but to his tones, firm, deep, and resolute. She looked through her long lashes at his face; it was perhaps a little thinned, but full of energy and determination.

"Very little effect could such a girl as I have on a nature like that," thought Francia sadly, and sighed.

At sound of the sigh Fergus glanced toward her, but directly averted his eyes, and continued his conversation with Neria. So Francia took her sick heart to the solitude of her chamber, and there listening to its moanings, determined upon an experiment for its relief, in the heroic style of treatment.

When Mr. Chilton called, he was told that Miss Vaughn was not well and could not see him. He came in, and encountered Fergus, and although Neria exerted herself to fulfil every hospitable obligation to even an unwelcome guest, Mr. Chilton found the atmosphere of Bonniemeer so oppressive that he declined an invitation to dinner, and departed, to return in the evening.

Francia did not show herself until tea-time, when she came down stairs, pale, but with such an expression on her face that Neria looking at her, thought "she has resolved." Fergus glanced once, and then away. Perhaps his own eyes were for the next few moments more thoughtful than their wont, and certainly he did not speak, but what Fergus thought on this, as on many points, it was only Fergus who knew.

Tea over, Neria was called from the room a moment, and Francia, trembling very much but still, with the heroic mood uppermost, said, quietly:

"Fergus, I should like to speak to you. Will you walk toward the lake with me?" Her cousin looked at her with ill-concealed suspense, but replied:

"Certainly, I shall be very happy to do so. Will you go now?"

"Yes, if you please."

"If Mr. Chilton calls, please say I am out," added Francia, to the servant, as she and her cousin passed through the hall.

Down the garden path, and through the dim oak wood to the pine grove where the brown needles spread carpet-like under foot, and the heavy odor in the air told where the sun had lain hottest, and still Francia had not spoken, save in brief replies to the commonplace remarks of Fergus. They reached the mere, whose placid waters lay sleeping in the twilight, with fairy palaces all of gold and mother-of-pearl, showing fairly in their depths as the evening sky bent down to kiss them. The boat lay there, the very boat where, twelve months before, they all had sat—the memory brought so sharp a pang to the poor wounded heart that from its very suffering it gained courage, and Francia desperately began, "Fergus, you are my cousin, and I have no brother. I need a brother's help and council to-night—will you give them to me?"

It was quite a moment before the answer came, and then it was,

"If you ask them in a matter where I may properly give them."

"O, Fergus, do not be cold, do not be cautious; what concerns me, concerns you; what I may properly confide to you, you may as properly discuss."

"Go on, if you please, Francia."

"You don't call me Franc now."

Fergus glanced at her in surprise. The inconsequence of the reproach in the midst of so much earnest feeling was so purely feminine a trait that his virile nature failed to comprehend its consistency.

Francia as little comprehended his glance of surprise.

"Did you not mean to change?" asked she; "I am glad of that, but indeed everything seems changed about us both. Last year, Fergus—do you remember?"

"What was it you wished to consult me upon, Francia?" asked Fergus, gravely. Francia paused, collected herself, and said at last,

"It is this. If you have done a thing—made a promise, perhaps, and find you were wrong—feel sure indeed that you should never have done it—what then? Is it worse to break your promise, or to keep it, knowing it to be a bad one?"

"You are too indefinite. I cannot answer so general a question," said Fergus, turning a little away from her, and looking far across the shining water to where, over the eastern hill, hung a crescent moon with a great white star beneath.

Francia tried to speak, but the throbbing of her heart choked her voice. She glanced at her cousin. Pale and stern, his eyes still bent upon the wan moon, he gave no answer to the look. She tried again.

"It is about myself and Mr. Chilton," said she, desperately. "I am afraid I never ought to have been engaged to him. I am afraid I never really cared for him. I think it was only my fancy, my vanity, that he appealed to. I never have been quite happy, and lately, since I know what sort of a man he is—" She waited, but Fergus remained silent and immovable.

"Ought I to break the engagement, Fergus, or to keep it? Which is more dishonorable?"

At last he turned toward her, and in his brooding eyes she read the answer before he slowly spoke it.

"Four months ago, Francia, when I, with every reason to suppose my love returned, asked you to be my wife, you told me of this engagement. I gave you then my opinion of it; I mentally foresaw that this very moment must arrive; this, the beginning of a train of disgust, mortification, disgrace, should you become Rafe Chilton's wife; of unceasing regret for a solemn promise broken, a degrading experience undergone, if you do not. Choose between these alternatives for yourself; I am the last adviser you should have sought. It is a cardinal principle of my life to interfere in no affairs not connected with my own. This certainly is not, and I must decline to express any opinion upon it.'

All the spirit of the Vaughns flashed in Francia's eyes, mantled in her cheeks, and curved her lips.

"You will excuse me," said she, coldly, "for intruding upon you affairs, which, as you say, are certainly none of yours. I had been so foolish as to imagine that being mine they might have an interest for you. The mistake will never be repeated, and I hope, in the improbable event of your requiring sympathy in some trouble of your own, you may meet a friend as nearly like yourself as possible."

She walked quickly up the path with feet that scarcely seemed to touch the earth, and head haughtily uplifted to the evening sky. Fergus followed, saying quietly,

"You are angry, and unjust, as angry people always are. When you think calmly of what I have said, you will see that I am right."

Francia did not reply, but hastened on toward the house, nor did her cousin make any further attempt to conciliate her. In the hall they parted coldly, and the next morning Fergus returned to the city.

CHAPTER XXVI.

THE VENETIAN GLASS.

NOTHING is so selfish as love-sorrow. Not the maelstrom itself is so absorbent, and, from Huldy Ann, whose mother complains that she is no longer "wuth her salt," to Rosa Matilda, whose canary bird would starve but for the parlor-maid's attentions, you shall find its victims self-absorbed, dreamy, and forgetful of the life about them. So Francia never thought again of her promise to Nancy Brume, until that worthy woman sent to Bonniemeer an explicit inquiry, whether she was to count upon either of the ladies there as "a watcher" for Mrs. Luttrell.

Francia, vehemently remorseful for her negligence, insisted upon going the first night, and returned in the morning with a melancholy account of the condition of the invalid, whose prostration of body had become excessive, while her mind alternated constantly from gloomy depression to excited fancies and hallucinations, hysterical emotion and frightful mirth.

"You told them I would come to-night, didn't you, dear?" asked Neria, when Francia had given the experiences of her arduous watch.

"Yes, but I don't think you ought to stay alone with her. She seemed out of her head part of the time, and was so excited she quite frightened me. Then she is so weak that she cannot stir without help. It will be too much for you, Neria."

"O no, dear. I will ask Mrs. Brume to sleep within call in case any help is needed, and I am not at all timid."

"You are nothing that would prevent your doing good to other people," said

Francia, fondly, and sighed at her own deficiencies, while Neria's heart contracted with a sharp pain as she thought of Vaughn and the good she had wrought in his life.

When Neria arrived at Cragness she was received by Dr. Luttrell, who announced that he should share her watch, as the condition of the patient was so critical that the end might be expected at almost any moment.

They stood together in the library while he said this, and Neria raised her eyes to his face with some expression of sympathy and concern upon her lips, but the words died in an incoherent murmur as she looked. Always pale, Dr. Luttrell's face was to-night of a ghastly yellowish tinge, scarcely changed even in the dry lips at which he gnawed incessantly. His eyelids drooped as if to conceal the tawny eyes, alive with electricity, gleaming and sparkling in their lurid depths as they wandered impatiently hither and thither, with a watchful, expectant look—a look of desperation and yet of terror—a look like that of the baited tiger, who knows the jungle closely environed by the hunters, and with his haunches gathered for the spring, watches every point at once for the first assailant.

The vigilant eyes did not fail to perceive and interpret Neria's gaze. They flashed upon her and away, then back, with a steady daring, and held hers, while the dry lips said:

"You find me changed, Mrs. Vaughn. It is now two weeks that I have spent every day and nearly every night at my wife's bedside. Remember, I am her physician as well as husband and nurse."

"You must be very much fatigued," said Neria, slowly, as she tried to analyze the ominous echo of these words in her mind. "I beg," continued she, earnestly, "that you will trust me with the sole charge to-night, and try to rest yourself thoroughly for to-morrow."

"No; O, no!" returned the doctor, hurriedly. "That is impossible. To-night is, I believe, a crisis in the disorder, and I must be present. It is my duty, and, at any rate, I could not rest." Nancy Brume opened the door.

"If you're ready to go up stairs, Miss Vaughn, I guess I'll be off to bed. Like enough I shan't more'n get my forty winks 'fore I'm called up," said she; and Neria followed, without reply, to a large and gloomy chamber upon the second floor, where lay the sick woman, a pale spectre, shadowed and surrounded by dark bed-hangings and furniture, that seemed to oppress the air of the room with their funereal atmosphere. The two windows looked upon the sea, which now came booming up beneath them, each wave smiting the foundations of the old house with the sullen roar of a cannonade. A half-open door showed a dressing-room, with a handsome toilet-table and apparatus, among which stood a shaded lamp, and an arm-chair beside it. Nancy pointed toward the door.

"The doctor 'll set in there and read, so's he'll be handy in case anything goes wrong. He'll give her the medicine when the time comes."

With these words she departed, and Neria, approaching the bed, looked compassionately down at the patient, who had altered sensibly for the worse since she had last seen her. Her eyes, showing supernaturally large in her ghastly and emaciated face, were wide open and glazed. Beneath them a circle of violet stained the otherwise colorless skin, and the same tinge had deepened under the transparent nails of the hands folded languidly upon the counterpane. The parted lips were parched and blackened, and Neria tenderly moistened them with some water in a goblet upon the little stand beside the bed. The patient looked up and smiled.

"You are Michael, the angel who fights with the devil," said she, quietly. "He was here a moment ago, and I suppose is hiding from you. He poured some fire down my throat while I was asleep one night, and it burns—O, how it burns!"

She laid her hand upon her chest, and looked piteously into Neria's face, bending above her with a divine compassion in its every line.

"He keeps his imps in the next room, all in bottles," pursued the sufferer, in a mysterious whisper; "and sometimes he brings them out and shakes them up before my eyes. Then they dance—the imps do—dance just like the fire down in that old library—did you ever see how that dances in the twilight?—and when it flashes into the dark corners you can see—ugh, I've seen them time and again! That was before he caught them and put them in bottles, I suppose. And then that old man who sits and plays on the organ in the dark—did you ever see him? He never makes any sound, but he plays and plays till the ghost of the music fills the whole room—only the ghost, you know; you can't hear it, but you feel it. It comes creeping, creeping through your blood, till it chills it to ice. I believe that's the way I first came to be so cold; and now I never am warm. Good Michael, can't you take the ghost out of my blood? It freezes me even while the devil's fire scorches."

Neria took the thin, white hands in hers. They were indeed ice cold, and had the stiff, hard feel of flesh no longer instinct with vitality. She pressed and chafed them in her own. The patient smiled gratefully.

"Ah, that is comfortable," said she. "I feel the little spears of life going out of your hands into mine. If you had come sooner you might have saved me; but now I have drank too much of that fire. Wait—I want you to do something for me—will you?"

"What is it?"

"You see that wardrobe over there?"

"Yes."

"Well, open it and I will tell you.—Ah, there he comes! Now, where's your sword! Now you will fight him! Now you can make him take away the fire out of me!"

She rose in her bed, and, with a long, white finger, pointed past Neria, while in her eyes the look of terror and foreboding dawning there when she first came to Cragness shone full-moon. Neria glanced quickly over her shoulder. In the door of the dressing-room, holding by the lintel, stood Doctor Luttrell, his ghastly face and brilliant eyes thrown out from the dark space behind him, into which his figure seemed to melt.

"He's got a head, you see, but no body—that is bad," said the sick woman, anxiously. "But you might crush his head. Don't the Bible tell about putting your heel on his head?"

"Neria did not answer. She was held by the glittering eyes that seemed imperiously to demand of her her inmost thought. For a moment she quailed and grew confused, but then a great wave of divine strength and power seemed to swell through her soul, filling it with a serene assurance. The wild words of the dying woman bore of a sudden a strange significance. She had called her by the name of the Warrior Angel, and something of his sublime courage and ardor raised her to a level above that of ordinary moods. She lifted her head, and looked back the look of these opalescent eyes, while her own quickened with lambent fire, and deepened to their darkest hue. The color rose lightly to her cheeks, her lips parted, and her golden hair seemed touched with a glory like that of sudden sunshine, or the aureola of a saint.

The white face in the doorway writhed with a bitter sneer, but retreated into the darkness.

"There, he's gone! But he'll be back in a moment," gasped the sick woman, who still sat upright, clinging to Neria, while her staring eyes and pointing finger seemed plunging into the darkness in pursuit of the object of her terror.

As Neria turned to answer and soothe her, a stealthy foot crept over the carpet, and before she knew that he was near, Dr. Luttrell's voice said, significantly, "You see that my wife is very ill, quite out of her senses, in fact, and as frequently is the case in mania, her fancies are the direct opposite of her impressions when sane. For instance, she was but now, I believe, describing me as a fiend, and you, the most feminine of women, if I may say it, as a warrior. My poor Beatrice!"

He laid his hand upon his wife's brow and smiled pityingly down upon her. Neria made no answer but watched him attentively. So did his wife, who lay now perfectly quiet, her whole consciousness apparently absorbed in the wary questioning look she fixed upon him. Luttrell drew a little nearer to her, and, still pressing his hand upon her brow, seem to plunge the concentrated rays of his burning eyes into hers, which soon began to waver, to droop, and finally closed altogether, while from beneath the long fair lashes, great tears stole out, and ran down the pallid cheeks.

"She is asleep," said Dr. Luttrell, turning toward Neria, but not meeting her eyes. "It will do her good if anything now can. You had best go into the dressing-room and read, or rest on the arm-chair you will find there. You need not try to keep awake. I will call you if anything is needed."

"On the contrary," said Neria, quickly. "It is I who will stay here, and you who had better go and rest. I am in no need of sleep myself, and should prefer to stay with Mrs. Luttrell."

He glanced swiftly at her, and said, carelessly,

"As you please, of course. I think she will sleep until midnight, when I will give her a draught."

He glided away as he spoke, and presently Neria saw him light the shaded lamp and seat himself to read, in such a position that his eyes commanded both the bed and the chair in which she sat beside it.

The night wore on, as slowly as it always wears for those who wake while others sleep; and Neria, who had laid her watch upon the little table at her side, could hardly believe that its slender hands moved at all, so reluctantly did they creep over the dial.

For the first two hours she was painfully conscious that the eyes of the motionless figure in the other room were fixed upon herself, and her own gaze wandered perpetually from the pallid sleeper at her side, to the circle of light beneath the reading lamp, showing a book, two white hands, a dark-clad figure as high as the breast, and nothing more, except the occasional gleam of two bright points a little higher, flashing out of the darkness toward her.

But no mind, however active, however subtile, can absolutely control the body, and as midnight approached, Doctor Luttrell slept, at first lightly, but finally with the heavy exhaustion of overtaxed nature.

As he dropped to sleep, the corpse-like figure in the bed stirred slightly, and Neria turning, found the eyes of her charge fixed upon her face in a dumb appeal for help, not to be misunderstood or denied.

"What can I do for you?" asked she, softly.

"I don't know. I think nobody can do anything now," said the sufferer, sadly, and with no appearance of excitement or hallucination. She paused, still looking with anxious entreaty into the heavenly face above her.

"I do not know," said she, slowly. "But I think there is something wrong about this illness. I was always well until a few months since, and my symptoms are so strange. My husband calls this a decline, but—well, it would do no good to know. A few more hours will end all; and I love him, yes, I do love him dearly, and shall die loving him. If he had asked me for my life, I would have given it freely—he need not have taken such pains to steal it. It was long ago. O so long, that this dreadful suspicion, this great shapeless doubt came into my mind, and then I began to watch him, to see if I could find out from his eyes— they are such strange eyes—did you ever notice them? But I never could, and I don't know now. There is one thing you can do—not that it means anything, you know, but just to amuse me. Open that wardrobe, please, the door is in the middle, and on a shelf with some trinkets you will see a ruby-colored wine-glass in a gold stand. Will you bring it to me?"

"Certainly," said Neria, a little surprised at the request, and taking the night-lamp from the fireplace she opened the wardrobe, found the glass without difficulty, and, as she brought it toward the bed, curiously examined its singular and admirable workmanship. A golden serpent resting on his coil, reared aloft his swelling throat and evil head, between whose wide distended jaws was fixed a bubble-like bowl of ruby glass, capable of holding, perhaps, a spoonful of some priceless nectar—nectar such as that with which la Borgia stilled the too urgent reproaches of her injured lovers; and as Neria slightly turned it in her hand, the faint lamplight striking through the ruby bowl flashed down upon the scaly folds of the serpent, and glanced off with a gleam like trickling blood. She held it before the weary eyes, that momently grew heavier and duller.

"Yes, that is it! It is a Venetian glass—one of those that they used to make in the old time; the art is forgotten now. My mother was an Italian and this was in her family for generations. Will you have it—or, rather, wait; perhaps it will not be worth giving. You see that vial on the table—that tiny one. Now, please pour some of its contents into the glass."

Neria took the vial—a very small one, without label, and about half filled with a colorless, odorless liquid—uncorked it, and was inclining it toward the glass, when Mrs. Luttrell said, hastily, "Put the glass on the table first, for fear."

Neria, without question, did as desired, and, setting the cup upon the table, filled it half full.

"That will do; wait, now," whispered the sick woman, eagerly fixing her eyes upon the glass, whose contents were already in a state of strange ebullition, foaming, flashing, and sparkling through and through, as if interpenetrated with tiny shafts of flame, while a dark wave of color, as if it were the breath of the serpent, came creeping up the sides of the ruby bowl, changing its pure tint to a turbid stain. The boiling contents reached the lips of the glass, the turbid stain sullied the last line of color, and, with a clear, sharp explosion, the glass flew into a million pieces.

Dr. Luttrell, startled from his sleep, sprang hastily to his feet, approached the table, saw all, understood all, and turned to Neria with the look upon his face of Satan summoned to answer for his conspiracy. She confronted him as did Michael confront that Satan. He turned to his wife, who had sunk back upon her pillows, pale and breathless. As he approached she suddenly aroused, and grasped his hands in both of hers, while in her eyes, the weary question answered at last, gave place to a tender and fathomless love, unmingled with reproach

"It was not needed," said she. "I would have died if you had told me it was necessary to your happiness that I should. I knew you loved her better than me always, but you might have told me, and let me go away somewhere out of your sight, and die of my broken heart as surely, and less painfully. I have suffered so much. It was hard to feel my life torn out of me inch by inch—it was such a brave young life when you began. But don't be sorry—not too sorry —I am willing now, although when I began to know, I was not—and I fought against it, fought hard, and tried not to believe. It was to find out that I watched you always, and I read it at last. It began far down in your eyes, so far that it only showed like the great dim creatures that live under the sea, and then it came up slowly, slowly, and every day I read it plainer, until now it is written there so that a child might read, *D, e, a, t, h*—that's the way it goes. Don't look at any one—don't let that angel see, who was here just now—he might write it with his finger on your forehead, just as God did on Cain's, you know— I am so tired now—so—tired. Good-by—don't be too sorry—when—"

The next breath that crossed the white lips was inarticulate, then came a long sigh that seemed to strike a chill through all the air of the chamber, and then the pale, sad face dropped of a sudden into the sharp outlines, the marble rigidity, unmistakably distinguishing the most sleep-like death from the most death-like sleep. The eyelids drooped, but again slowly opened, and with the last instinct of vitality the eyes turned to those of Luttrell, while from their blue depths arose once more the solemn question, whose answer was Death, and stood there patiently—stood, even when Neria, with trembling hands, had closed over it the lids that could not hide it, stood there when the pale form lay encoffined, when the earth was laid upon it; and when he, the mourner, came back to his lonely home, the question was there before him, always, everywhere, waiting, waiting, always waiting, till it forced the answer to his own eyes, and he shrank away from men lest they should read it there—shrank most of all from Neria, of whom the dying woman had bid him beware, as the angel whom God had sent to write the secret upon his brow.

CHAPTER XXVII.

CHLOE'S SECRET.

"So disasters come not singly," murmured Neria, as she rose from the couch, upon which she had thrown herself on returning from Cragness, and prepared to obey a summons to the bedside of Chloe, the negress, whose health had been rapidly failing ever since her nocturnal excursion, and who now, as she felt her last moments approach, sent an urgent message to her young mistress, imploring an interview without delay. Wan and trembling from her late vigils and the terrible doubts filling her mind with regard to Mrs. Luttrell's death, Neria came, and seated herself beside Chloe's pillow, looking like a waiting spirit sent to conduct the almost enfranchised soul to its eternal home. The violence of the disease was past, as was its suffering; and death, in his grisliest, most unrelenting form, had laid his hand upon the poor distorted body, soon to be all his own. "You do not suffer now, Chloe?" asked Neria, finding that the sufferer did not speak.

"No, mist'ss, I's struck wid def," said Chloe, simply. "But I's got suffin to tell you fust, mist'ss. I's hated you awful bad, fust and last, but 'pears like, now I's goin' to die, as if I see things diff'ent. Miss 'Nita was de one dat put 'im in my head. Mas'r's fust wife was her darter, you see, missy—"

"Mrs. Vaughn was Mrs. Rhee's daughter!" exclaimed Neria, in amazement.

"Yes, missy, and dey was bof slaves, jes' like me," replied the negress, with a diabolic grin on her pinched features.

Neria looked at her in silent dismay.

"You see, missy, w'en mas'r was a young fellow, he went travellin' down Souf, an' one day he see Miss 'Nita put up for sell on de auction block cause our ole mas'r was dead berry sudden, and his wife was mad wid 'Nita, cause ole mas'r like her de bes'. So Mas'r Vaughn buy her an' gib her her freedom, an' den he bought me 'cause I'd alluz nussed Miss 'Nita, an' she was drefful fond ob me. Well, we stayed long a' Mas'r Vaughn, an' went trabellin in Europe a while. You see, mist'ss, he was so kin' he couldn' say no w'en she axed to go; an' she couldn' bear to part from him nohow, she was dat fon' ob him. Den we come home, and Miss 'Nita's darter, dat had been at de Norf at a boardin'-school, was growed up, an' Mas'r Vaughn bought her, so's not to let her young mas'r get holt of her, as he meant to, an' den she was dat pooty, an' arter a w'ile he married her, an' den lily Missy Franc was borned, but as pooty as she is, she got de black drop in her, same as ole Clo'. An' 'twor Miss 'Nita put me up to pizonin' you in de choc'late, an' now I's tole all. Not quite dough—hol' on a minute, Miss Neria. W'en your mammy was fotch in here dat night dat Miss Gabrielle died, I was tole to lay her out, 'cause she was stone dead w'en dey foun' her, an' so I did. She'd got on a braceret dat I gib to Miss 'Nita, an' she gib it to mas'r, but 'sides dat, dere was a book full ob writin,' wid shiny hooks to it, an' a picter of a gen'l'man inside ob it, in her pocket, an' a ring on her finger, an' dem I kep' for mysef."

"The book with writing in it! O, Chloe, where is that?" asked Neria, breathlessly.

A capricious gleam of the hunchback's constitutional malice shot from her eyes. "I didn' t'out, missy, dat I'd eber tell you dat," said she.

"But you will, Chloe—O, Chloe, I do not know my father's name. I never saw my mother's face."

"Dere's lots ob pooty gals down Souf just as bad off as dat, an' wusser, too, cause dey is sold roun' from one mas'r to anodder just as it happens," said Chloe, sullenly.

"Chloe, the Lord is waiting for your soul. Will you go to him and say, 'I might have made one of your creatures happy, and I would not, I did not?'" asked Neria, with solemn earnestness. A spasm of sudden pain contorted the whole body of the negress, and she threw herself into a horrible grotesque attitude.

"Obi's a comin' arter me ag'in," shrieked she, writhing to and fro upon her bed.

Neria laid a firm cool hand upon her forehead. "It is the truth that tortures you thus," said she. "Speak it out, for your own sake."

But a fiercer convulsion of pain seized upon the unhappy wretch, even as she spoke. She grasped at Neria's hands, and wrenched them within her own until the pain forced a deep flush over the pale face of the young woman, who yet made no effort to release them, who even forgot to pity the suffering before her in the devouring anxiety that had seized upon her. A sudden and terrible strength surged through her will, and inspired her whole soul. Fixing her dilated eyes upon the dying woman, bending her face until her pure breath mingled with Chloe's expiring sigh, she issued her irresistible mandate.

"Speak; speak out! Where is this paper? Tell me, or you shall not die!"

"The tree—the old oak tree"—a horrible sound closed the sentence; it was the death-rattle, and with it the stiffening fingers slid from their grasp of Neria's hands, the painful struggle ceased, and the sufferings of the unfortunate creature were at an end. . . . . . .

It was not till night, and in the seclusion of her own chamber, that Neria unfolded the little canvas-covered package she had found in the cavity of the oak, where it had lain for months guarded by Chloe's loathsome familiar. A small, thick note-book, clasped with silver, lay within, and as Neria carefully opened it, the pages, glued together by mould and time, tore apart as reluctantly as if they knew that the secret of a lifetime was about to be snatched from out their keeping. Within the cover lay a miniature, painted on ivory, the picture of a young man, handsome, proud, noble; the face not of a stranger, but as familiar to Neria as her own, and yet she knew that she had never seen it in the flesh. Where then? Her mind wandered to Mrs. Luttrell and her death-chamber, and chiding itself for the wandering, came back to study every lineament of the face already beloved, for nature told her that it was her father's. And still the vision of that great gloomy chamber, with its mournful bed, and the pale figure lying so motionless upon it, came floating between her and the picture, enveloped, blurred, effaced it, clamored, "turn to me, I am the solution, this the puzzle."

Beneath the picture lay a bit of folded paper. Neria opened it, and found a little plain ring, small enough for her own slender finger, and engraved with the initials G. de V. from E! V. This, Neria laid aside with the picture, and turned impatiently to the little book which was, she hoped, to explain everything. It was a journal, and the first date was that of twenty-two years before:

Here am I at Venice, and here I will stay for a while, at least, for in truth I am tired of rambling. Besides, where are eyes like those of Giovanna Vascetti, and where such clustering locks of gold? The real Venetian style so rare out of Titian. Heigho! What more is there of life? I believe I have seen it all, and *une vie réchauffée* must be the tamest of all feasts. Love! Bah, I have loved a hundred women, and twenty of them had hair as bright and eyes as blue as those of Donna Giovanna. What do I care? I wonder if one mightn't drop lazily to the bottom of these canals and lie there very comfortably. It would save such a deal of bore, as they say in England. England? Well, home I may as well call it, for I believe I was born there. Stop, I will begin by registering myself duly at the commencement of this my journal, that the Austrian *mouchard* who, doubtless, will read it, may find no trouble in identifying its writer, and bringing him to justice for whatever treasonable expressions he may see fit to insert. First, then, I am Edward Vaughn, five-and-twenty years of age, six feet high, with brown curled hair, hazel eyes, etc., etc. My father was Alfred Vaughn, a gentleman of America, State and town unknown, to me at least. He left home on account of fami y differences, and not as an emissary of the American Government to spy out the secrets of that of Austria—(that's for you, *mon mouchard*.) My mother was a Spanish gypsy, with whom my father chose to fall in love, and I suppose, to marry. I never saw her, or heard much more than is here set down. I have lived at English schools and college until three years ago, when my father appeared, from the Lord only knows where, said to me, "Come, my friend, let us be comrades. Forget that there is a tie of blood between us, as I shall; otherwise we shall hate each other." I saw that he had reason in his decree, and I assented. We lived in Paris, Petersburg, in Vienna, at Baden, Rome, London, wherever the world lives. We saw it, and Vaughn *père* showed its secrets to Vaughn *fils;* until when, a year ago,

Vaughn *père* went to *flaneur* in another world, Vaughn *fils* was quite competent to protect himself in this. *Voila tout!*

So finished the first entry. Those that followed it were more fragmentary and interrupted, giving little information beyond memoranda of the writer's engagements, and occasional aphorisms in the same spirit as the first page. But under a date of two months later, came an entry, more carefully written, which Neria devoured as fast as her eyes could decipher the blurred and faded script.

Giovanna is an angel, and I—well I am ashamed of my audacity in loving her. Here is her little note before me—"my heart, my soul, my noble lord, my king and law," so she calls me—and I? When I look back through my life and count its stains—stains of which the smallest and faintest puts me beyond the pale of her most daring conception of wickedness, I feel such torture as Satan might, if bound at the foot of the Throne. And she loves me! Yes, all her pure bright life is placed between my hands to cherish or to crush. If I bid her forth, she will leave her father's palazzo to-night, and join me in wanderings as wild as those from which my father rescued his gypsy bride. Ah, ha! I wonder, after all, if that gypsy mother does not rule my blood, and if I might not be happier as king of a tribe, with a bold-browed, black-eyed queen at my right hand, than with this golden-haired maiden, who shrinks, if I do but bend my brow a little earnestly. Pshaw! Heaven sends an angel to draw me out of the slough, when I sink deeper every day of my life, and I hesitate to yield myself to her guidance. Let me not believe that my taste is already too vitiated to appreciate a pure love, that caviare and not bread is my staff of life. No, rather I will hope that it is conscience, which withholds me from too eagerly accepting this affection; that it is because I feel too keenly the vast gulf between this pure child and myself, which life—my life has set. If I marry her, can I assure myself of her happiness, and without such assurance, should I not be the basest of mankind to join her to my capricious life and uncertain fortunes? Have I the strength to make myself what Giovanna's husband should be, and, failing in the effort, would not the humiliation of failure sink me lower than I already am? Bah! It is too late to make Egbert Vaughn into a saint, and he is yet too much of a man of honor to pretend to be other than he is, or to sully the innocent life of the purest woman he ever knew by bringing it into contact with his own. It is better, my Giovanna, that your blue eyes should weep a few idle tears now, at what you will fancy my unkindness than that by-and-by your heart should weep tears of blood at the certainty of my unworthiness. Go you your way, and I mine—the one leads up, the other down.

Neria paused, and taking the picture from the table, looked at it long and earnestly, seeking, in the noble cast of the features, the lofty bearing of the head, a contradiction of the characteristics which the journal made no attempt to disguise. But still the haunting remembrance of the chamber at Cragness, and Mrs. Luttrell's death-bed swept between her and the pictured face. She kissed it sadly, and laid it down, murmuring, "My father still! I know that you were my father."

The next date was three weeks later, and under it was written:

"*L'homme propose, mais le Dieu dispose*," is as true a saying to-day as when it was first spoken. Giovanna is my wife, and here we are hidden in the little village of Fieschi, as happy and as loving as the ringdoves that coo all about our cottage. And it has all come about in such an irresistible sort of fashion, that I take no shame to myself for inconsistency, even when I read the last two or three pages of this journal. It was just after writing them that I got Giovanna's little, teary, heart-broken note, saying that the old dragon of a marchesa had discovered her daughter's *tendresse* for my unworthy self, a foreigner, a heretic, and above all a *mauvais sujet*; and, that at the end of a terrible scolding, had come the decree that my poor little girl was to return forthwith to her convent, and there await the movements of her parents, who were already arranging a match between their daughter and Count Montaldi, the ugliest, oldest, and richest man in Venice. She did not say, this little Giovanna of mine, "Come and rescue me, for I love you." but she did say, "Good-by forever—unless I see you for a moment on the road to the convent."

Of course I was on the road to the convent, and with the aid of one servant personated so successfully a whole troop of banditti, that coachman and guard fled in terror from the first glimpse of our excellent get-up, and the hideous old duenna, hiding herself in the bottom of the carriage, shrieked dismally,

"O, Donna Giovanna, we are but lost maidens. These banditti respect neither youth nor beauty."

We left the ancient dame uncomforted, for her mistake was precisely the idea we wished to inculcate; and, diving into the mountains, soon found the three horses hidden there since morning, mounted, and in a few hours were safely housed at this place, recommended by my valet, who was, I believe, born here. Before night we were married, and already my wife has nearly done blushing when Paolo addresses her as signora.

The last words were nearly unintelligible, and Neria vainly tried to separate the few succeeding leaves; the mould and damp had so firmly united them that she found it impossible, and it was only with great difficulty that she was able to decipher the following brief entry, under the date of nearly a year later:

The child is gone, stolen I have no doubt, Giovanna is inconsolable, and I am more affected than I would have believed possible. Paolo must have played traitor and sold the secret of our hiding place to the Vascetti, who, considering Giovanna irredeemably lost, have snatched her infant as a brand from the burning, and will educate it to take its mother's place in their house. I suspect all this, but cannot know, at least, not at present. My immediate concern is to hide Giovanna where they will not get hold of her also. We must leave the country I think. The old dragon would not flinch at poisoning her, if she fancied it would wipe out the stain upon their name.

After this, for many pages, Neria could distinguish only an occasional word or sentence from which to infer that the writer, with his wife, had removed from Italy to Switzerland, and that he had satisfied himself that his child was actually in the hands of the family of his wife, from which he found it impossible to rescue her. The next decipherable page was dated in England somewhat more than a year after the last entry, and ran thus :

I have decided at last to go to America and look for my father's family. Giovanna wishes it. She is haunted with terror lest this child should be stolen from her as was the first. It is a pretty little creature and we call her Neria, because she was born upon the sea. We shall take passage in a sailing vessel bound for Boston, in Massachusetts, within a few weeks, our means not allowing us to indulge in the luxury of a steam-passage. Indeed we have been obliged to sell some of our valuables already, to raise the necessary funds. Giovanna has insisted upon disposing of her most important jewels, and would even have sold the serpent-bracelet, the hereditary ornament of the daughters of her house, would I have permitted it, but this must be kept, at any rate, to deck the arm of little Neria, when it shall have attained mature proportions. I am sorry Giovanna could not have possessed the goblet also. She says an ancestress, a second Lucretia as it would seem, had these two golden serpents fashioned in precise similitude, except that between the jaws of the one was set a tiny Venetian goblet, and in the head of the other, intended to be worn as a bracelet, was placed a small quantity of a deadly poison, which may be ejected by pressing the finger upon the jewel forming his crest, when a slender spear shoots forward, pierces the finger and leaves death in the wound. Thus the possessor of this brace of serpents commands, through them, both the lives of others and his own safety. My gentle Giovanna will never be likely to use the weapon or need the defence, but I like the idea of these hereditary jewels, and thank the sanguinary ancestress for her idea, and also for leaving us her name, graven upon both serpents beneath the crest of her house. Fiamma Vasetti, thou wast a woman of rare fancy and had a very pretty idea of assassination! Well, well, what is all this to the present. I must set myself to making the necessary arrangements for our passage. I wonder if any of the Vaughns survive, and if they will own their errant kinsman. Not that I will ask more than a welcome of them : I mean to earn my living for myself somehow, but just how I cannot now say. Since I am husband of Giovanna, I dare not pursue the little occupations by which my honored father accumulated the property his son has just spent. I detest the sight of a green table and a pack of cards, and would as soon play with the bones of my ancestors as with those my father so often tossed, and so invariably to his own advantage. *Eh bien!* I find by my father's papers that his family lived near a little town called Carrick, and thither we first will betake us on arriving in America. If these Vaughns repudiate me they cannot fail to welcome my lovely Giovanna, my innocent little Neria, and if they will make them happy I ask nothing for myself.

This was the last. A few more pages had been partially written over, but the disconnected words still legible gave no clue to the meaning of the whole, and Neria was fain to finish the sad story for herself. She readily conceived that the voyage had been accomplished, that her father had died either upon the passage or soon after his arrival in America, and that the hapless wife thus widowed had attempted to reach, with her infant, the unknown friends, of whom her husband had doubtless told her. Reduced to absolute penury, she had probably been obliged to perform the last part of her journey on foot, and before reaching Carrick had sunk upon the spot where Mr. Vaughn had found her. Neria covered her eyes and shuddered, as fancy, or it may be something which is not fancy, pictured before her the black bitter night, the angry sea, the desolate shore, and the poor young mother struggling on, her baby in her arms, shrinking before the piercing blast which froze the tears upon her cheeks before they had time to fall, while close behind her stalked Death's grim form, his fleshless jaws grinning, his bony hand already outstretched to seize his unconscious prey.

"My mother, my mother!" moaned Neria, and in the bitterness of her pain felt a momentary resentment at Vaughn, that he had not arrived in time to save mother as well as child.

She took up the journal again and strained her sight in the effort to distinguish something more in the blurred pages at the end of the book. Here and there a word was easily to be read, but nothing connected or intelligible, until in the middle of the last page appeared the words : "secret cipher of the Vaughns, formed by using our motto as an alphabet, it has been—" Neria dropped the book, as a sudden conviction flashed across her mind. "The secret! Poor Gillies's secret!" murmured she, and flying to her desk she found and opened upon the table the letter of Reginald Vaughn confided to her keeping by the musician. Her eyes ran hastily over the familiar sentences until she came to the cipher, upon which she had so often and so vainly pondered :

EDAOLU OE OLUDLUV.

The motto of the Vaughns was as familiar to her as her own name, and hastily writing upon a bit of paper the words : "*Dieu le roy et le foy du Vaug!n,*" she placed the letters of the alphabet beneath the letters of those words, and by assuming the upper letter as the name of the lower one, found herself possessed of a new alphabet, by whose aid she translated the three words of cipher into the phrase : "Father of Heralds."

Here, however, was a fresh enigma ; and Neria, utterly exhausted in body and mind, put it aside for the consideration of a calmer moment, and locking the journal, the picture, and letter in her desk, threw herself upon the bed with eyes already closed, just as the earliest bird uttered his warning note of the coming morn.

CHAPTER XXVIII.

THE GOBLET FRAME.

WHEN Neria awoke from a brief and disturbed sleep, it was some time before she found it possible to understand what change had come upon her life. And as one after another of the strange revelations which Fate, after withholding them from her most urgent researches, had capriciously piled before her in a single day, rose to her mind, she set it aside to turn to another, which for the moment seemed more important. She was herself a Vaughn then! She had the same right by birth to his proud name, as the husband who had bestowed it upon her. She might name her mother with tears, perhaps, but without a blush. And her sister? Did not that dying woman say that the Venetian goblet was an inheritance from her own family, and was it not in exact similitude with the bracelet which Vaughn had, soon after their marriage, given her as her sole inheritance, the only relic of her parents? And was it not thus—and as this thought flashed into Neria's mind she caught her breath sharply as if the poisoned tongue of the golden serpent had pierced her own flesh—was it not the resemblance in her father's picture, to the face of that most unhappy and foully-wronged of women which had haunted her when she first beheld it? Had she not sufficient ground for the conviction that Doctor Luttrell's wife had been her own and only sister? And he? With what emotions must she henceforth meet him? And what was her duty, in regard to communicating her suspicions to those who would sharply investigate their foundation? And even were they verified, what satisfaction could the result bring to the life already broken upon the dark and cruel purpose of this insatiable man?

And Francia! Brilliant, careless, beautiful Francia! whose life had yet known no darker shadow than a lover's quarrel, how could she bear the shame and misery of the story the old nurse had told of Vaughn's first wife, and her mother? But at this point Neria once more paused aghast. Vaughn! Her husband, the man whom if she had not wholly loved she had revered and trusted, and accepted, in his every deed and thought, as worthy to be her law! What was this story of his early life, almost his present life indeed? Mrs. Rhee had lived at Bonniemeer until Vaughn's marriage with herself, and Chloe had distinctly said that the housekeeper had loved her master with an idolatrous passion, and had jealously sought the life of the woman to whom he had given the love for which she had pined through so many years. How had this woman dared to love him thus, and how had he received her love?

Neria hid her face in her hands, and a hot blush tingled over her face and neck, and even to her fingers' ends. O, if Vaughn was not pure and good, what hope was there that she should ever love him better than she had done? And the hereditary secret of the Vaughns, whose solution became more binding upon her than even before, now that she was herself a party to it, and now that a certain clue had been placed in her hands—what was she to do in this matter?

A sudden resolution formed itself in her mind, and seating herself at the table, she hastily wrote a few lines to Fergus, merely saying that she needed his help and counsel, and begging him to come to her without delay. The address was hardly written, when, after a gentle tap, the door was opened by Francia, who entered so quietly that Neria, looking up in surprise, was startled to see how pale and haggard she looked, and how large her eyes had grown in a single night of watching and weeping.

"I have come to see if you are ill, dear," said the girl, gliding behind Neria's chair to avoid her questioning eyes.

"No, Franc, but I can see that you are," and Neria, rising, took Francia's hands in hers, and looked into her fair face, while the malign assertion of the old negress rushed back upon her memory—"She got de brack drop in her veins for all her pooty looks."

With a sudden and womanly impulse, Neria opened her arms, and taking her adopted sister close to her heart, kissed her tenderly, and with a warmth very unusual to her ordinarily reticent temperament. Francia, whose heavy eyes needed but this invitation to overflow, hid her face upon the other's neck, and wept unrestrainedly, while Neria, gently smoothing the ripples of her hair, found something terrible in the thought that this poor child had come for shelter and comfort to her of all others—to her, who had become the recipient and possible betrayer of a secret, before which these tears should dry as morning dew before the terror of a devouring flame. The very idea that she must hide so much, even while appearing to receive and repay the mute confidence of these tears, made Francia's presence distasteful to Neria's sensitive truthfulness, and after a few moments she gently withdrew from the embrace, and said, with an attempt at cheerfulness,

"I fancy we are neither of us very well or bright this morning, darling. Will you please tell them to send me some coffee up-stairs, and then take something yourself? I will not come down just now."

"Yes, Neria," and Franc, wiping her eyes, and a little hurt at feeling her confidence repelled, was turning away, when her eye caught the direction of the letter upon the table. A quick wave of color swept into her wan face; and as she hurried away, a second burst of tears gave a significant clue to the origin of the first.

Neria looked after her thoughtfully, and from the door her eyes turned to the letter upon the table. "Yes," said she, aloud, "it is right that I should tell Fergus all—everything. He has as much right to know these matters as I."

An hour later, Mrs. Vaughn ordered her pony-carriage, and drove herself along the beach to Cragness, at which place Doctor Luttrell still lingered. Inquiring for him, she was shown at once to the library where he was sitting. Surprised, and yet relieved that she should come to see him, Doctor Luttrell advanced to meet his guest with outstretched hand. Neria looked at him quietly, and the hand sunk as if palsy-smitten.

"I supposed by your coming to see me that you were my friend," said he, sullenly; "or is this a business call? I am aware that my lease has expired."

"It is a business call, but not connected with your lease," said Neria, calmly disregarding the sneer. "I wish to ask you some questions with regard to the late Mrs. Luttrell." She fixed her eyes upon him as she spoke, and he, resisting the impulse to evade or quail before that straightforward glance, held his feline eyes unwaveringly upon hers, although in the effort his lips grew white, and contracting slightly upon themselves gave a cold gleam of his glittering teeth between. To speak was impossible, but a haughty bow signified his assent to the proposed inquiry. "Will you tell me Mrs. Luttrell's maiden name?" asked Neria, presently. An expression of relief crossed Doctor Luttrell's face. "I thought all the world knew her to have been Miss Davenport," said he, with a sneer.

"I knew that she was so called, but I have reason to suppose that she had the right to another name by birth," pursued Neria, undauntedly.

Dr. Luttrell considered for a moment, but seeing no sufficient reason for attempting to conceal facts with which Neria appeared, at least, partially acquainted, he assumed an appearance of candor, and said, "Certainly. You have very probably heard that Mrs. Luttrell was actually the daughter of an Italian noble, the Count or Marquis Vascetti, who, like many of his countrymen, retained nothing of the ancient splendor of his house, except its haughtiness and its traditions. Mr. and Mrs. Davenport, spending a summer in Venice, hired the palazzo of the Marquis, who retained a modest corner for himself, his daughter, and one old servant, the last survivor of the hereditary retainers of the family. The Davenports became much interested in the daughter, whose name was Beatrice, and when, one fine morning, the old marquis was found dead in his bed, and it seemed probable that the bed itself must be sold to pay for burying him, they stepped in, as the *Deus ex machina*, put the old man decently under ground, or under water, (as it is of Venice that we speak), pensioned the servant, left the palazzo to the Jew who had foreclosed his mortgage upon it, and taking the poor little orphan under their paternal and maternal wings, brought her home as their adopted daughter. *Voila tout!* And if you find this bit of family history a bore and out of taste, remember, madam, that it is you who have asked it of me."

In the course of his long address he had recovered his native coolness, and in speaking the last words, looked into Neria's face with an assured smile, mingled with something of supercilious inquiry, as to her motive in thus questioning upon matters which, as he intimated, were not her own.

To this unspoken taunt Neria quietly replied. "You will excuse the apparent intrusiveness of my inquiries when I tell you that Mrs. Luttrell was my only sister. I will not trouble you with particulars; but of the fact, your late account of her parentage has enabled me to speak with certainty. With this explanation I think you will no longer wonder that I should feel a more than common interest in her life, or in her death." And with this last, she fixed upon him such clear bright eyes that he shrunk as from the pitiless gaze of the noonday sun, and could only stammer with averted eyes,

"Your sister?"

"Yes, my sister; and it is of you—of you, her husband—the sworn protector and defender of the life and happiness of that unfortunate girl, that homeless orphan—poor in the midst of wealth, because denied the ties and the love that make the humblest home a happy one—it is of you, Wyvern Luttrell, that I ask a reckoning of my sister's year of married life—the year which has closed, in pain and terror, the story of her young life. Why is she dead at two-and-twenty, she who should have lived to see the glory of maturity—the peaceful joy of age? Why is she dead?"

As her regard had pierced his heart, so did her thrilling voice strike through his brain. He shrunk together, and, with sidelong, sullen look, that dared not rise above her feet, muttered, "How am I to tell? Her time had come?" Neria paused a moment, while her soul gathered its strength, and the solemn light of prophecy made her face awful in its angelic beauty. Then she said: "And God's time will come at last for you and for me. Dare not approach me until that hour." Livid and shrunken with terror and impotent rage, he made no reply, offered no response to her gesture of farewell, but stood, with down-dropped head and hanging arms, like Eugene Aram, when, in the clear morning light, he saw, in all its hideous meaning, the vision of his sleeping hours.

At the door she turned and said, coldly: "My sister, in her last moments, gave me the remnant of that ancient jewel of our house, whose Venetian glass was shattered by the draught you were about to administer to her. It is a sacred relic to me, but can hardly be so to you. Will you give it to me?"

He looked toward but not at her, muttered something in his throat which his white lips refused to articulate, then left the room, and presently returning with the goblet frame in his hand, offered it, without a word, to Neria.

She took it as silently, hastily sought and found the minutely engraved initials and crest which completed the chain of evidence establishing her own and Mrs. Luttrell's parentage, and then, with no pretence of leave-taking to the guilty man who stood watching her with doubt and terror struggling in his feline eyes, she withdrew, leaving him alone with the shadows and the memories of that ghostly chamber.

The next morning brought Fergus again to Bonniemeer. Neria welcomed him joyfully, and at first felt as if half her perplexities were removed, now that she had so efficient a counsellor and assistant to whom she might confide them. But, when seated with him in the library, she began to consider at what point of the story she should commence, she found herself restrained by delicacy toward Francia, by honor toward Vaughn, from repeating the details given her by Chloe, while a reluctance to show her suspicions of Doctor Luttrell with any one whomsoever, deterred her from giving more than a vague outline of her sister's life and death.

But the finding of her father's journal and its contents, the proof obtained from it of her own and Mrs. Luttrell's parentage, as well as the identity of the bracelet and Venetian goblet with the hereditary jewels of the Vascetti, all these she related fully, as also the story of the secret trust bequeathed by Reginald Vaughn to John Gillies, and by him to herself; all this she repeated clearly and without reserve, ending by placing before the young man the letter of his granduncle, the few lines left with it by Gillies to her, and the journal containing the key to the cipher.

Fergus listened attentively, read minutely, and then asked:

"Is Doctor Luttrell still at Cragness?"

"Yes, but leaves to-day."

"Then to-morrow we will go over there, and I shall try to prove the correctness of a theory which suggests itself to me in connection with this story of the cipher. Meantime, allow me to congratulate myself upon the relationship newly discovered between us. I had rather consider you as my own cousin than as my uncle's wife." He took her hand and kissed her cheek as he spoke, and Neria felt a strange thrill in this her first recognition by her kindred. "Now show me, if you please, your father's journal and picture, with the bracelet and goblet frame," continued Fergus.

Neria laid them upon the table, and the young man took first the picture, which he examined minutely.

"Yes, this is a Vaughn," said he, at length, "there is no mistaking either the family likeness or the likeness to yourself. You show no trace of your Italian blood, unless in your golden hair, which is truly Venetian and like that of Titian's women."

Neria looked up in surprise, for a compliment from the truthful and exact Fergus was a circumstance; but he, not noticing the look, was now curiously examining the bracelet and goblet frame.

"Yes," said he, "here is the name on each, 'F. V.,' for Fiamma Vascetti. And the fact of Mrs. Luttrell's inheriting this goblet is certainly proof of the strongest in support of your consanguinity. Do you imagine the bracelet still to possess its death-dealing powers, or has time destroyed them?"

"I have never been able to move the spring which should project the little shaft mentioned in father's description," said Neria. "Perhaps he or my mother had it destroyed, and sacrificed the romance of the thing to the safety of its wearer."

"Probably," replied Fergus, after some futile efforts to move the emerald in the head of the serpent, who seemed to writhe and coil beneath the torture of the attempt. "That would have been the common-sense course to adopt with regard to so dangerous a plaything, and I presume you are correct. Now, if you please, I will take this journal to my own room, and see what I can make of it."

Neria signified assent, and, when Fergus was gone, sat for some time indulging the pleasant consciousness that she might safely rely upon his clear head and decisive judgment for important aid in her various perplexities. Unconsciously, she compared him with Vaughn, and found herself better content with the uncompromising integrity, commanding will, and stern self-control of the one, than with the other's more suave, more polished and finely graduated characteristics.

Francia did not appear until teatime, and then scarcely looked at Fergus, who treated her politely, but with indifference. Neria watched both uneasily.

"She loves him only too well," thought she; "but he—how does he regard her? and, even if their love should be mutual, what would Fergus think of Chloe's story?" With these questions perplexing her mind, Neria became more silent than her wont. Francia scarcely spoke at all, and Fergus evidently only talked to avoid silence.

CHAPTER XXIX.

Under these circumstances, the time could not but pass heavily, and Neria had several times sought a private interview with her watch, hoping to find the proper hour for retiring arrived, when the sound of a carriage driving rapidly up the avenue was heard, and the next moment it passed the front of the terrace, where the cousins were seated.

"Whom have we here, I wonder?" inquired Fergus, rather superciliously, as a common covered wagon stopped at the foot of the steps, and a man in fisherman's costume leaped out.

"Some one on business, probably," said Neria. "Will you see him, Fergus, and, if I am right, send him round to the housekeeper?"

"I shall suggest, also, that this house has a less conspicuous entrance than the front door," muttered Fergus, slowly walking down the terrace. But he had not yet reached the steps when the visitor ran lightly up them, and with a civil, but not deferential bow, inquired:

"Can you tell me where to find Miss Vaughn, if ye please, sir?"

"Miss Vaughn? Do you wish to speak with her personally?" inquired Fergus, in surprise.

"Yes. I've got something for her."

"Oh, a parcel. You may leave it at the top of the steps, and I will see to it."

"No; that won't do," returned the man, in a voice less rude than determined. "I have a word to give along with the parcel, and I must see Miss Vaughn herself. Is that her down there?"

Fergus looked rather indignantly at the speaker, but found something in his bronzed face and manly bearing which so modified his first impression, that he only said, quietly:

"You are very decided in your tone, my man; but I will ask Miss Vaughn if she will see you."

"That's right," replied the intruder, briefly; and, running down the steps, he rolled up the back curtain of his wagon, and began to handle a heavy mass of something lying in the bottom of it.

Fergus watched him for a moment, and then went to summon Francia, who, accompanied by Neria and himself, approached the steps just as the man, ascending them with some difficulty on account of the bulky nature of his burden, arrived at the top, and deposited it at their feet.

"Mr. Lewis!" exclaimed Neria, as she recognized the young fisherman, and saw the nature of his burden.

"What is this? who is this man?"

She stooped as she spoke, and examined, by the light of the failing moon, the features of the body which, pinioned, helpless, but convulsed with rage and shame, lay writhing at her feet.

"Which is Miss Vaughn?" asked Lewis, recovering his breath by a painful effort, and, looking from one lady to the other.

Francia stepped a little forward. The young man bowed and removed his hat.

"This fellow, I believe, ma'am," said he, putting one foot lightly upon the parcel lying between them, "is a friend of yours, or, perhaps, you only think he is. I've brought him here to-night to tell you what he is, and leave it for you to say what shall be done with him." Francia made no reply, and he continued: " I come home unexpected last night, partly because I'd had such luck with my fishing I thought I might as well be married before I got another v'y'ge, and partly because I was sort of anxious—just why I couldn't tell. I hadn't been in town ten minutes when I went to see the girl I've been a year expecting to marry. Her mother looked scared when I asked for the gal, and said she didn't know where she was. I told her if she didn't she'd ought to, and I was going to look for her. I asked round a little at the neighbors, and, finally, one fellow told me, with a sarcy grin, that he reckoned I'd find her somewhere up the beach, along with this fellow."

The fisherman's foot emphasized the last word by a slight motion, beneath which the "fellow" writhed like a wounded snake.

"I knocked down the man that said it, of course," continued Zeb, quietly. "But I went up the beach, and just as I was going to turn back I heard Trypheny's voice talking to some one. They were sitting under the lee of a big rock, and I walked up to the other side and hearkened a bit to what they were saying. Just what it was I ain't going to tell you, for it wasn't talk fit for you, or any woman who thinks much of herself, to listen to; but among the rest I found he was planning to take her off to the city when he went, and she was in a hurry to go. That was enough; and I stepped round the rock, picked up the mean rascal who wasn't even man enough to hit back when I struck him, and gave him as much of a thrashing as it was in me to give to such a white-livered sneak; and then I tied him up this fashion, put a cobble-stone in his mouth to keep him quiet, and left him propped up against the rock while I took Trypheny home to her mother. I didn't say much, nor I didn't feel mad as she thought I did. If it had been something that could have been got over, I might have tried to put it into words, and, after a while, be done with it. But nothing that any human being could say will ever undo the ten minutes I spent listening behind that rock, nor can ever put the girl I had thought so much of in the place she's fell from. So I said nothing to her and to her mother, no more than that if she didn't know where her daughter had been, I did now, and that I bid her good-by, once for all. Then I went and got a horse and wagon, drove up the beach to where my young man was waiting very patient for me, loaded him in, and brought him here. Now, ma'am, it's for you to say what I shall do with him next."

"It is not for Miss Vaughn, it is for me to decide that question," said Fergus, in a voice of suppressed rage. "Untie him, Lewis, if you please."

"Wait. It is for me to say, I think," interposed Neria, with quiet dignity. "That no violence shall be committed in my presence, or within my grounds. Fergus, you will not touch this man in any manner."

Fergus turned impatiently toward her; but when he had met her steady look and fixedly returned it, he bowed his head—that head so seldom bowed in deference or submission to any one—and murmured,

"*Pardonnez moi. Votre volonté est ma loi.*"

Neria slightly bent her head, still more slightly smiled her thanks, but before she could again speak, Francia laid a hand upon her arm.

"No one has my right to act in this matter," said she, in a voice whose suppressed emotion tingled through its every tone, and made her low accents as thrilling as the trumpet pealing the onward charge of an army. All paused and turned to look at the slender girl who stood beneath the moon, transformed in an instant, as it were, to a stern Dian pronouncing judgment on Actæon, a Boadicea rehearsing wrongs which no blood could ever drown. The pride of her father's house, the brooding sense of injury, the life-deep passion of her mother's race shone together in her eyes, throned themselves upon her lips, as presently she spoke, looking at Lewis.

"The insult this man has offered me, the bitter wrong he has done to you, are not to be in the lightest measure undone or satisfied by any insult, any penalty that could be inflicted upon him. What you said with regard to that unhappy girl, holds good for him. Any words that could be framed by mortal lips would but insult the feelings they could never express. Any attempt at retribution would, while it gave us only an angry disappointment, comfort him with the idea that his crimes were expiated. What I will have you do is simply this. Remove his bonds and leave him to slink away into the night, alone and unnoticed, like a faithless hound whom one scorns to beat, but turns from the doors, as no longer worthy of so much as a hound's place in the regard of man or woman.

"Untie him, Lewis, and let us see that he departs. One would be sure such a thing did not lurk about the house."

No one offered reply or opposition to the haughty words and gesture. The fisherman silently cast off the lashings, and removed the gag which had held his captive quiet, but ostentatiously refrained from any roughness or insult. When he had done he stood aside, and beneath the scornful eyes, the more scornful silence of those whom he had so foully wronged that he could never do them right again, Rafe Chilton, the exquisite, the debonair, the curled darling of many a boudoir, the successful rival of Fergus Murray, the chosen husband of Francia Vaughn, slowly rose from the dust where he had grovelled, and stood before them shaking with rage and agitation. He turned to Francia.

"You've had your say, my beauty," began he, in a voice thick with passion, "now hear me!"

Fergus uttered an angry exclamation, and would have interfered; but Francia with a hand upon his arm, while her eyes never wandered from the face of the speaker, silently asserted her right to control the moment.

"It is all very natural that you should feel a little mortified at being jilted for a common fisherman's daughter, and that between the disappointment and the cursed pride which is a part of you, that you should be somewhat bitter in your remarks, but for all that I know you love me still, and would at a word follow me over the world—"

"Francia! you shall not restrain me!" exclaimed Fergus, shaking off her hand indignantly, but still with her eyes upon the face of the man whose words could no longer be held of so much value as to be an insult, she again grasped her cousin's arm and said below her breath.

"Hush! let him speak!"

"Yes, Francia Vaughn," continued Chilton, in a tone of concentrated bitterness, "you love me now as you loved me when you let me steal you from that proud fool of a cousin who dared not then, and dares not now resent either my deeds or my words, and I want no better revenge for this night's work than the chance of telling you that I never cared for you so much as for your father's money, and that just by your own outrages and your own insolence you have driven me to a determination that with all your pride and all your pretended anger you will not hear unmoved. I will marry the girl whom I love better than ever I loved you—a girl whose pride and whose honor and whose very existence begin and end in my love; and when I give her to the world as my wife, if that world says that pretty Francia Vaughn wears the willow wreath that Trypheny Markham may wear the bridal roses, who shall contradict it?"

He finished and stood staring malignantly into her face, hoping to find there some trace of the anger or chagrin he had hoped to arouse. But no marble was ever colder or more changeless in its scorn and pity than the face of Frederic Vaughn's daughter, as she looked and listened until his own eyes wavered and he half turned away. Then Francia, still with her hand upon her cousin's arm, led him toward the house, saying softly to herself in a tone of bitterest self-contempt,

"And I fancied that I loved him!"

Fergus made no reply, but as Neria entered the door after Francia, he quietly drew back, and would have returned to the spot where Chilton still stood, had not Neria lingered beside him, saying quietly,

"Remember, Fergus, that you are under the roof of my husband and Francia's father, and must respect our wishes."

"But it is too much—too much that you require," muttered Fergus hoarsely, as he half threw off her grasp.

"If it is much, so much the deeper the gratitude your forbearance merits. Fergus, for Francia's sake!"

"For Neria's sake!" whispered Fergus, as he suffered her to lead him into the house.

Lewis slowly mounting his cart was already driving away, and as the heavy hall door closed upon him, and he felt himself alone, an outcast and a social outlaw where he had been an honored guest, the bitterness of defeat writhed serpentlike about the heart of the libertine, and stung to its black centre.

CHAPTER XXX.

THE RIDDLE READ.

THE next morning, after a *tête-à-tête* breakfast, for Francia kept her room, Fergus and Neria drove to Cragness.

Nancy Brume opened the door to them, and in answer to Mrs. Vaughn's inquiry, said that Doctor Luttrell had left upon the previous evening.

"And though the old place ain't the delightsomest of housen at the best," pursued the worthy woman, as she opened the door to the library passage, "it's perked up wonderful since he took his black favoret fiz-omy and his cat's eyes out'n it."

In the library, with closed doors, and with the solemn mystery ever brooding more or less tangibly over the house and its inmates, boldly confronting and as it were daring her to its solution, Neria sank into the arm-chair of the bay window, her sensitive organization succumbing, even while her spirit rose to the crisis which instinctively she felt approaching.

Before her dazed eyes the dim room seemed to reel and shimmer like objects seen through mirage; the black books crowding the shelves on every side seemed gathering momentum for a forward plunge, which should bury the intruders beneath an avalanche of dead men's thoughts and fancies—thoughts and fancies which, instead of peacefully perishing with the brains where they were bred, had been condemned to some such life-in-death as befell the maiden chilled to sleep for a hundred years, in company with the bear, the crocodile and the serpent. Above the fireplace the knight in his golden armor seemed stirring in his saddle, and fixing, through his visor, eyes of gloomy menace upon the irreverent descendants of his house who dared attempt to pluck from his hand the secret of a lifetime. From the dusty corner, where stood the organ, shadowy forms seemed to wave hands of ominous warning, to sigh and moan in a voiceless lamentation that their realm was to be invaded, their unnamed charge to be snatched from their guardianship.

Doubt, mystery and menace embodied themselves on every hand, expressed themselves in every form the place contained, except in the figure of the man who stood upright in their midst, strong, hard, unimpressible, and regnant.

Upon his thoughtful face Neria's eyes at last rested, and there found support and reliance. Fergus was the first to speak.

"This secret, Neria," said he, slowly, "is one that must now be known. If Reginald Vaughn had been a man of decision and character he would never have left it for us to settle the quarrel between himself and his conscience, which seems to have tormented him into his grave. Certainly the absurd compromise of half concealing and half revealing it to Gillies, a perfect stranger to him and to the family, could have given him little comfort in his perplexity, and was the occasion of infinite annoyance to the unfortunate monomaniac, upon whose shoulders he, in dying, foisted it. He should either have carried it to his grave or revealed it at once."

"Do not judge harshly of the dead, Fergus," said Neria, softly.

"Every man, dead or living, must consent to be judged by his life, and those of Reginald Vaughn and his legatee seem to me to have been miserable failures," replied Fergus, coldly. "Vaughn, as I have said, showed a pitiable weakness in neglecting to either keep or tell his secret; Gillies, an unpardonable want of determination in neglecting to unravel it—"

"He could not, interposed Neria, "and his anxiety to conquer the impossibility hurried him to his grave."

"Impossibility is merely an arbitrary sign representing an unknown quantity," returned Fergus, with a slight smile. "I do not think it need be used in this instance at all. I already have a theory upon the subject, and shall be somewhat surprised if we do not, by its aid, spell out this wonderful secret before we leave the room.

"We already know, through the key contained in your father's note book, that the words Edaolu oe Oludluv may be translated Father of Heralds, and it is easy to infer that this sentence, meaningless in itself, contains a reference to something more important."

"The oldest English herald of note is Guillim, and in fact I have seen him referred to by this very title of Father of Heralds. Now, do you know, Neria, of a copy of his work in this library?"

"No," replied Neria, doubtfully, "I don't think I have ever heard of him."

"Then let us look," returned her cousin briefly, and immediately commenced the search, while Neria forgot other occupation in watching his energetic movements and the rare emotion betrayed by his glittering eyes and flushed cheek. An hour passed thus, and an impatient frown was beginning to darken Fergus's face, when from the depths of one of the sunken book-cases he drew a black, moth-eaten quarto volume, evidently of great age. Opening at the title page, the young man inhaled his breath with a quick sound of joyful surprise, exclaiming, "The very thing! Old Guillim himself, venerable Father of Heralds. Now let us see."

He seated himself, the book upon his knee, and Neria looked anxiously over his shoulder. With deliberate hand Fergus began to turn the leaves one by one, searching for some loose paper laid between them, but the end of the volume was reached in this tedious manner, with no result. Blank leaves at the beginning and end there were none, and Fergus remained staring a moment at the quaint colophon in a sort of angry disappointment at the result of his well-laid calculations.

"Perhaps there is a false cover," suggested Neria, quietly.

"Of course not. The outside is leather," replied Fergus, somewhat impatiently closing the book. "And yet," continued he, examining it more minutely, "I don't know but you may be right, Neria. This outside leather slips a little—yes, I think it has been placed over the original cover and glued down upon the inside. Let us see."

A sharp penknife soon established the correctness of this theory, and after a breathless moment of expectation Fergus drew from between the two covers a sheet of thin paper, yellow with age and covered with the crabbed and peculiar manuscript of Reginald Vaughn. It was written in cipher, but with the key before them the cousins readily translated it to this effect:

"The sins of the fathers shall be visited upon the children," says the Book whence Christendom receives its law. The Book is to me no more than the earliest historical record of mankind; but in this axiom is closed a great law of human nature. The destiny of my house has pursued and overtaken me unawares, and I know not how to deal with it, other than by leaving it to its own fulfilment.

Many years ago the weakness of my own and another's nature, crushed beneath my father's iron prejudices, led to certain results; chief of which was the birth of an unfortunate child, whose mother died in the same moment, whose father never will, never can recognize him as his own. Nor yet has he been utterly abandoned.

It was a heavy bribe from me which induced the Scotchman Gillies to select from among the inmates of the asylum, where I had placed him, the child whom he as little knew to be my son, as the child of his own lost sister, and consequently his own nephew. Could I have done better for the miserable little creature than to place him under guardianship of his maternal uncle? As he grew to man's estate I found him amply able to care for himself, and consequently dropped from my fingers the invisible thread which had so far bound his life to mine. Now I am about to resume it, and under peculiar circumstances.

My earliest recollections are of the stormy scenes constantly occurring between my two elder brothers, or between one or both of them, and my father, and I still remember the relief I experienced when after a violent quarrel, in which all three had taken part, it was announced that Alfred, the younger, had left home, as he professed, forever. Not that he was to me the most disagreeable of my two brothers, for his storms and freaks of rage were as temporary as violent, while Egbert's temper was of the sullen and vindictive turn far more dangerous as well as unpleasant to encounter.

I was, at this period, about twelve years old and, when soon after Alfred's departure, Egbert married and settled at Bonniemeer, I became my father's companion and friend. This was the happiest period of my own life; and, as I think, of his also. Our amusements, our studies, our interests were identical; he treated me as an equal, even while he adapted himself to my youth and inexperience, and, within certain limits, I was allowed to treat him with a familiarity upon which his elder sons had never presumed.

Upon certain points, however, he was inflexible, and I, cowardly and secretive by nature, never dreamed of opposing him openly, however I might secretly disobey him. The most positive of these restrictions was one never distinctly expressed, but most distinctly understood, debarring me, as I grew to manhood, from seeking the society of the other sex. Lazarus Graves was our only attendant, and no woman's face ever brightened the dim chambers of our home. My father never visited, even at Bonniemeer; and I should as soon have ventured upon the grossest insult toward him, as to have noticed by more than a distant salutation the pretty daughters and wives of the fishermen who occasionally met us in our walks or rides. But strong passions and weak principles are the distinctive brand of the Vaughn character from the earliest record, as the story of Marion Gillies and her luckless boy would prove were it here set down, as it most certainly will not be.

Absorbed in my own secret and the precautions with which I surrounded it, I hardly noticed my father's failing health and increasing gloom. He preferred to be much alone, and when in my company fell often into profound reverie, from which he aroused himself with a scrutinizing glance at me that more than once sent the guilty blood to my heart with the conviction that I was discovered. Now, I do not doubt that my father was considering the safety of intrusting me with a mystery which weighed even more heavily upon his mind than the disease already leading him to the grave.

He died, and in his last moments struggled piteously to speak to me. I do not doubt it was the secret, the shameful secret which even then tortured him with its demand for an utterance denied to it by death. I could not guess at his Nemesis, nor did I care to do so, for my own had overtaken me. Marion had died the day before.

I laid my father in the ground and returned to Cragness, the lonely, loveless man I have remained ever since. The years since then are so nearly a blank that I pass them over in silence until a day, now years ago, when, in some curious examination of the carved woodwork above the fireplace of the library at Cragness, I hit accidentally upon a secret spring, distant six inches in a right line from the spear-head of the knight in heraldic device there blazoned. Within the crypt, disclosed by the movement of this spring, I found the secret which, having driven my father to his grave, then turned back to fasten upon me, and will, as I am certain, never release me until I lie beside him. How to dispose of it is to me a question as unsettled as my own existence beyond the grave; and after tormenting myself with it for years I have at last resolved to make this plain statement of my own personal interest in the affair, to hide the statement as securely as possible, and then to fly from this accursed house forever. Once abroad I shall die to the world, soon, as I doubt not, to earth also, and in my legal death I shall bequeath this place, the secret, and the knowledge of his own, his mother's, and his father's shame, to my son, John Gillies. I shall place a blind clue in his hand at starting, and after that I leave him to Destiny, and to the slow and terrible justice of Destiny, which will sooner or later ordain that through the wrong done by me to him and his, the wrong done by another to the proud name of Vaughn shall be exposed.

The manuscript closed thus abruptly; and, at the last word, Fergus and Neria, raising their eyes to each other's face, withdrew them suddenly, while the frown upon his brow, the burning blush on her's, already verified Reginald Vaughn's bitter application of the curse ordaining that the shame and suffering of the father's sin shall be surely visited upon the innocent children so long as the world endures.

Then, without a word, Fergus folded the yellow sheets together, and hiding them in a desk upon the table, went to the fireplace, and stood for a moment minutely examining the carved scroll-work surrounding, like a frame, the dim blazonry of the shield. From its midst the golden horseman looked sullenly through his closed visor at his opponent; and, to Neria's strained fancy, the lance in his grasp seemed quivering with the rage of an approaching onset.

"Six inches in a right line from the spear point," muttered Fergus, measuring the distance with quiet exactitude. "And this," pursued he, after an instant, as he pressed his finger upon a slight projection half hidden beneath a rib-like scroll—"this must be the spring."

As he spoke, the spring yielded to the pressure, and, with noiseless motion, the shield, with its baffled knight, its solemn crest and haughty motto, slid away, revealing a small closet or crypt constructed in the thickness of the massive chimney. From its interior Fergus silently took a folded parchment and an old-fashioned pistol, primed and loaded.

"These are all," said he, returning to the table, where Neria sat watching his movements with dilated eyes and pallid cheeks. The panel, released from the pressure of the spring, slid noiselessly back to its former position, and from its face the effigy of the baffled and impotent guardian of old Egbert Vaughn's secret, looked down with ghastly rage upon its audacious heirs.

Beneath the lock of the pistol was closed a strip of paper with these words written upon it:

If one of my sons shall discover the secret place where is hidden this pistol and the confession of his father's follies and crimes, I counsel him to lay the latter upon the fire, and to discharge the first into his own head. So best shall he shield the memory of his ancestors, and spare himself their inheritance.

These ominous words read Fergus; and withholding them from Neria's outstretched hand, said, softly:

"No, my cousin. It was not meant for us, and will only shock you. Let us look at the parchment."

Laying the parchment upon the table, Fergus carefully laid open its stiff and yellow folds, and seated himself beside his cousin, that they might together learn the mystery which for a century had hung over the fortunes of their house, and for more than one of its members had mingled its dusky shadows with those of the grave itself. A gleam of sunshine, piercing of a sudden the stormy sky, flashed across Neria's pallid face and wildly lighted her sombre eyes, glanced over the bent head and dusky face of her cousin, and touched, as with the finger of Fate, the secret lying before them. Then, flickering upward, it lighted to a flame the golden blazonry upon the wall, lingered yet a moment upon the closed visor of the knight, and was gone, leaving a darkness and chill behind which struck upon Neria's sensitive nerves like a breath from the tomb, whence, as it seemed to her, they were about to pluck its sacred mysteries.

"O Fergus," whispered she, pressing closer to his side, "let us leave it as we find it. It is not good to meddle with the secrets of the dead. Put this paper back, leave it for another to find, and let us begone. This place is killing me."

"Hush, child. Do not yield to womanish fancies now, when all is accomplished. Give up the secret when it is within our grasp? What folly! Remember, Neria, we are performing a solemn duty."

He placed his arm about her as he spoke, and Neria sheltered within its fold as quietly as on her mother's breast. So together they read:

When I, Egbert Vaughn, was but a boy, I loved my Cousin Maud, and she, in the pride of wit and beauty, sneered at my passion. I left her with the silent oath that we would yet change places, and that it should be my turn some day to triumph and hers to plead.

Three years after, when I returned from my distant voyage, I forgot my oath in wonder at her beauty and the sweetness of her welcome. I loved her more than I had ever done, and she confessed to an equal passion. I pleaded for an immediate marriage, and she and her cunning mother opposed me only so much as to excite my ardor and give impetus to my wishes.

We married; and I waked from my fool's elysium to find myself the dupe of an infamous plot.

My cousin, true to the violent passions, the rampant pride and easy principles of her race, had chosen to secretly marry, during my absence, a fellow so low, so debased, so disgraceful in every manner that even she dared not acknowledge him before the world, or even to her own family. He was a sailor—a common foremast hand—and some weeks after their marriage, had been induced, during a drunken frolic, to ship with some comrades on board a whaler just ready for sea, and when he recovered his senses found himself out of sight of land, with a three-years' voyage before him.

This was only a month previous to my return, and Maud Vaughn, remembering that her marriage was without witness or proof, and under a feigned name, and, moreover, already weary of her folly, at once resolved to forget the secret chain binding her to it, secure that, even in case of her husband's return, he would never dare to claim her without proof or even probability to adduce in support of a pretension which she should indignantly deny.

In the first moment of my return she spread her lures, and baited her cunning snare with the smiles and sighs, the blushes and half-uttered regrets for former misconduct, which might have led a sounder judgment, a colder heart captive. She had not intended to reveal the secret even when her object was effected; but, cunning and resolute though she was, she had found in me her master, and I forced the confession from her lips, word by word, without her finding the power to resist.

When she had done, she cast herself at my feet and implored me to shield her, to aid her in ridding herself of her disgraceful connection, for the sake of the love I had borne her, for the sake of the life she would lead in the future—for the sake of her unborn child. I laughed in her face.

Then she stood up, her eyes all ablaze with the haughty fire of her blood, and bade me, if I dared, to tarnish the name we both were proud to bear, to cast dishonor on the time-honored race whence we both were sprung. When she was willing to lay a woman's nature in the dust, to deliberately break the laws of God and man rather than live degraded in her father's house, where the proofless marriage would never be credited, was I, she said, was I—a man—to be less brave, less daring in shielding the honor of our house?

"O noble house!" sneered I, "as all its daughters are '*sans reproche*,' so should its sons show themselves '*sans peur*.' I do not wonder, fair cousin, that you exhort me to be brave."

I left her without any promise as to the future; and, day by day, and week by week, and month by month, I watched the gnawing terror consuming her heart as I dallied with the secret, half-revealing it to some chance visitor, or pretending solemn confidences with her own relatives, whom I encouraged to frequent the house. Many a time, as, after a stern and warning look at her, I have beckoned her grey-haired father or her fiery brother from the room, have I seen her eyes darken, her lips blanch with the anguish she could not quite conceal. I never went farther. I did not wish to spoil my own sport; but chose rather, at times, to quiet the sufferer by periods of cool kindness, or even indifference. Then, when a feeling of security had nursed her to a little strength, a new blow fell, waking in an instant all the old terrors.

Was this amusement a little cruel? Does it remind one of the Inquisition or its archetype and patron down below? Perhaps; but remember that this woman had deliberately plotted to injure me as never man was injured yet and forgave the injury. I had loved her with all the trust and strength of my ardent nature ; and now I hated her ; yes, hated her with the rancor of a love poisoned at its spring, and I took my revenge after my own fashion.

Her child was born. The old serpent, her mother, her only confidante, had not yet discovered that I made a third in the pleasant little family secret, and so came to me the day after the child's birth with her honeyed congratulations, and an inquiry if my son should be christened by my own name.

"Give the boy his father's name by all means, my dear madam," said I, looking her in the eye until her cheeks grew white beneath her rouge, and her false mouth quivered with rage and fear. But she mastered herself as only so well-drilled a votary of Satan could have done, and, looking back my look, said, defiantly:

"Certainly; we will name him Egbert."

"Ah ! I do not wish to be inquisitive ; but it is a curious coincidence if it is so," said I.

She did not ask what I meant, but left the room and the house. They named the boy Egbert—and I allowed it ; for I had resolved to suffer him to grow to manhood before I should reveal his true birth, and turn him, as an impostor, from my doors. Through the son, too, lay a new road to the mother's heart, a new weapon in the life-long punishment I had ordained for her.

It was about a year after this that a returning whaler brought tidings that the ship on which my cousin's husband had embarked was lost at sea, with all hands on board.

This news I hastened to communicate to the widow, adding the suggestion that, as she was now free, she might marry whom she would, and that I advised her to make the whole story public at once, to withdraw from my protection, and make arrangements for a more reputable life.

I could have pitied her then, if pity had not died out of my heart in the first year of our quasi-marriage. She implored me not to cast her off, not to compel her to reveal her early folly and subsequent crime. She confessed, with sobs and groans, her sins toward me ; but she protested that, through all my harshness, she had learned to love me, and that now no new misery could equal the parting from me, and she ended by a passionate petition that I should privately marry her again, and, accepting her for the future such as she would make it, should forget the past and suffer her to forget it.

I have never, even among the beautiful daughters of my race, seen a woman so gorgeously beautiful as Maud Vaughn ; I have never heard so sweet a voice, never felt the witchery of so seductive a manner, so tender or so winning an appeal. As I stood and looked at her, kneeling at my feet, every nerve in her graceful body trembling with the passion of the entreaty she had made, I felt the hard determination which had cased my heart tremble and crumble beneath the magic of her presence. The old love rose up like a mighty sea, and swept over all that had come between, burying it fathoms deep. Already I stooped to gather her to my heart, when the door opened and the old mother entered with the child in her arms ; the child whom they had impudently named by my name and imposed upon my bounty.

The sight sent back that mighty flood of love and forgiveness with as mighty an ebb. I spurned the woman at my feet with such words as I never before had spoken to her. I fiercely bade the wrinkled hypocrite at her side begone, and never darken my doors again. I snatched the screaming child from her arms and would have tossed it through the window to the roaring waves below ; but its mother caught it from my arms, and stood before me, defiant and beautiful as a Judith, braving me to my cruel worst.

I rushed from the house and wandered the whole night upon the beach. At daylight my determination was reached. I would put all future relentings out of my own power, destroy at a blow all hope for the future in the heart of my temptress, and in so doing prepare a new torment for her in revenge for the weakness into which she had so nearly surprised me.

I married another woman, a woman who supposed me already married, and who considered the ceremony proposed by me as an idle farce to quiet her own conscience.

It was no innocent victim whom I thus deceived, but a woman as wily, as full of passion, and as lax in moral strength as if she had been born twin sister of my Cousin Maud, instead of merely being her dressing-maid.

I do not care to linger upon this part of my story, or to give it in detail. It is not pleasant to remember the white face and steadfast eyes with which Maud listened to my boast of what I had done, or to remember the year that followed. If when I saw the only woman I had ever loved slowly dying of a broken heart and a bruised spirit, I found my own heart as slowly crushed beneath the weight of that dying woman's curse, my own spirit writhing and tortured beneath the burden of its almost accomplished revenge—if these things were, I will not tell of them, I will not satisfy the Nemesis which has overtaken me, by an admission that her work is accomplished. As I have lived, so will I die.

When I found that my real wife, still unconscious of her rights, was likely to become a mother, I sent her away, and after a time followed with the lady whom all the world but herself, myself and the wicked old mother supposed to be my wife. Returning to Cragness after some months, we were accompanied by an infant, who was introduced to the world as our second son, Alfred by name.

The lady's-maid had returned to England, where some years after she died, never having suspected for a moment that her generous protector was in fact her lawful husband, or that the brat whom she believed dead, was actually the legitimate heir of his father's name and property.

In less than a year after this my Cousin Maud died. Of this occurrence, or of my own feelings in connection with it, I will say nothing.

Years after I married again, my lady's-maid being as I supposed dead, although I have since found reason to doubt whether the date of the marriage or the death should be placed first. Nor did I particularly care, being in those days somewhat reckless, and more than somewhat contemptuous of life, and law, and my fellow-creatures, especially of women.

My son Reginald's mother was a pretty and innocent girl whom I loved as I did my dog, my horse, my tame doe. She loved me, too, as far as she was able, and respected me fearfully. We were happy together, and I was sincerely sorry when she died in childbirth.

Egbert and Alfred Vaughn as they grew up displayed the honest antagonism to be expected from their birth and antecedents. They hated each other cordially, and I hated both, the one for his father's sake, the other for his mother's. On my youngest child I centred such affections as I yet had to offer, and in my own heart recognized him as my only true son, and heir of such property as I felt at liberty to bestow upon any one; the estate of Bonniemeer, derived from my Cousin Maud, I had always destined to Egbert her only child.

With these arrangements in my mind, it was no cause of regret to me when my son Alfred announced his intention of leaving home forever, in consequence of the constant quarrels between himself and Egbert, and the harshness and injustice which he complained of having always received from me. I presented him with a thousand dollars, my malediction, and a plain warning to let me see or hear of him no more. He sailed for Europe, and was a few years after reported dead. I have since learned through a reliable but secret source, that this report was circulated by himself in a childish desire to annoy me, and to cut off all possible attempt at reconciliation on the part of his friends at home.

He little knew the utter indifference to his life or death which possessed my mind. I accepted the contradiction without taking the trouble to make it public, and for many years as completely set aside the memory of my son Alfred as I did that of the vicious and disgusting woman his mother.

But now arrives the time when failing Nature warns me to be done with the concerns of earth and resign myself to the great oblivion; and now I prepare the Parthian bolt, which even from my grave shall reach and punish, through their descendants, those who half a century ago stung and warped to boundless evil a nature formed by God for boundless good. The son of Richard Grant and Maud his wife, born and bred as the eldest son of the house of Vaughn, and heir to its wealth and honors, now in middle life, with all the pride, the prejudice, the luxury of his assumed station fastened irrevocably upon him, is now to learn, and to learn in face of the whole world, his own ignoble parentage, his mother's weak and criminal subterfuge, and the relentless hate and vengeance that even in his cradle prepared this grand finale to the drama in which he has played so important although unconscious a part.

Before my death I shall confide this paper to my son Reginald Vaughn, with peremptory orders to convey it at once to my solicitors, instructing them to take immediate steps for depriving Egbert Grant of his wrongfully assumed name of Egbert Vaughn, and of certifying the fact that Alfred Vaughn and his children are my only assuredly legitimate descendants. The estate of Bonniemeer pertaining to Maud, wife of Richard Grant, in her own right, devolves upon her son, but failing heirs of his body reverts to me, her nearest living relation, and in case of such reversion I hereby express my intention of bequeathing said property to my son Alfred and his descendants, and if sufficient time is allowed me, shall draw up a formal instrument to that effect.

My son Reginald, rest content with this decision. You alone are, and have ever been the son of my heart and my hopes. Whether the law would recognize your legitimacy or not I cannot say, and the question need never be agitated, as I shall leave to you by name the slender patrimony of Cragness, sufficient, if you are prudent, for all your needs, especially as I have striven to imbue you with so much of my distrust and aversion to womankind as shall keep you from the arch-folly called marriage. Over the property now called Bonniemeer I do not consider myself to have any control, as I never was legally married to its possessor. It descends, of right, to her son, Egbert Grant.

In concluding this confession, a model father would naturally deduce for the benefit of his son, various moral conclusions and warnings. I prefer to leave them to your own common-sense.

The characteristics of our race are almost unfailing in each generation. Their errors only vary in ranging from folly to crime, according to the constitution of each member. I have little hope that you will avoid them, but should you find it possible to do so, I earnestly recommend the course. The old age of lawless youth is not a comfortable one, even to a man *sans peur*.

CHAPTER XXXI.

THE ORGAN'S REQUIEM.

THE darkening sky was black with the approaching tempest now, and a low peal of thunder mingled with the deep tones of Fergus's voice as he pronounced the last words, and suffered the parchment to fall from his hands.

In the gloomy chamber seemed to have fallen an uglier shadow than all those crowding there before; the very air seemed thick with the passion and the wrong, the crime and the misery summoned from their uneasy graves by the recital just finished. Out from the record of that wicked life seemed to have emanated a curse ready to fall upon the heads of those, his luckless descendants already trembling in its presence. Already it had set its seal upon the wan face of the girl, the hard rebellious brow of the man. Each looked at the other through the gloom, as might the children of Cain have looked at each other when first they learned to read the sign upon their father's brow.

Fergus was the first to speak, and his tone was harsh and bitter:

"Allow me to congratulate you, Neria. You are, it seems, the only veritable Vaughn among us, although you have lost the name by marriage. Your husband, my uncle, has as little right to it as my mother had. I wonder where we shall find our relatives of the Grant connection."

"Richard Grant's wife was as much a Vaughn as her cousin, our great grand father," said Neria, timidly.

"Ah, yes, I forgot; we may claim cousinship still through that immaculate woman—that woman '*sans reproche*,' as her cousin so aptly called her," sneered Fergus.

In the growing gloom, Neria crept a little closer to his side, and put her hand in his, saying, softly:

"Dear Fergus, they are dead long years ago. Let their sin and their suffering rest with them. Let us live as if we had never learned their dismal secrets; let us hold ourselves in the sunshine and leave these mournful shadows to themselves. Why should we clasp them to our hearts to darken what should be all brightness. Let us look for our own faults which, with God's mercy, may yet be set right; and let us only remember this sad confession when we pray to God to forgive those who sinned before us, and to keep our own feet from the bitter path they trod."

"This paper directs that the children of Richard Grant shall no longer bear the name of Vaughn. It belongs alone to you," persisted Fergus; but his face brightened, his voice softened as Neria spoke and looked.

"Could he speak to us now he would take back that cruel wish. In the grave all is forgiven. Make peace with his memory, dear Fergus, as you yourself need pardon. Forgive and be forgiven."

As she spoke, the tempest, risen to its height, broke in a fearful thunder-clap directly above their heads; the bolt splintering the topmost crag of the Lion's Head, and sending its blackened fragments plunging into the flat and pallid sea at its feet. The old house rocked to its foundation, and the great organ in its recess quivered through every fibre. Then, like the swan who dies, its agony found voice, and from the long-silent pipes crept a strange wild sound, as fantastic and as thrilling as the supernatural tones of the Æolian harp. For one moment its wild waves filled the chamber, then sank, trembling through fine gradations to a whisper—a sigh faint as that of a dying infant, and were gone. "It is the answer to my words—it is the promise of peace and pardon," murmured Neria.

Fergus made no reply. His hard reason refused to accept this solution of the phenomenon, yet failed to furnish a better. While he still hesitated, another flash of lightning, yet more blinding than the last, filled the room, and in the same instant a clattering peal of thunder seemed to burst upon their very heads.

"The house is struck—quick, Neria!" cried Fergus; and, seizing her in his arms, rushed from the room, through the long corridors, and into the open air, leaving the storm, the shadows, the grim, golden knight, the confession of Egbert Vaughn, the memory of his son Reginald, of Lazarus Graves, of John Gillies, of Giovanna Vascetti, of all the sin and misery which a hundred years had gathered there, to hold revel together in the dreary house.

But the measure of its days was full; its heaped iniquities might no longer be forgiven. With a thunderous crash the western wall, riven stone from stone, fell out, and through the chasm Fergus pointed silently to the organ already wreathed in flame, whose agile fingers ran across the keys, whose waving garments fluttered from the choir, whose passionate breath crept through every tube, and flaunted, banner-like, from the desecrated cross at the top.

Neria looked and hid her eyes.

"Some attempt must be made to save the house or its contents," said Fergus, looking impatiently down the empty road.

"Do nothing; it is the hand of God," replied Neria, solemnly. "Let house and secret perish together, and let us trust that, with fire from His own hand, God has purged away the guilt of each."

CHAPTER XXXII.

ULYSSES REDIVIVUS.

THE tempest without was less terrible than the flames and ruin within, and the cousins resolved upon immediate flight. But Mrs. Vaughn's ponies had already decided the question on their own part, and tearing themselves free had dashed down the road and out of sight just as the last fatal bolt descended.

Nancy Brume, waiting only to satisfy her conscience by informing her employers of her intentions, had followed them, and Fergus saw no other course but to wrap Neria as securely as possible, and with his arms about her, to half carry and half lead her down the cliff, hoping to find some shelter at its base. But Neria, wrought upon almost to frenzy by the scenes she had passed through, was now inspired with a wild terror of the spot and its neighborhood, and refused to listen to any proposition of lingering, even for a few moments.

"No, no! Let us get on. Anywhere away from this," was her only answer to the expostulations of her companion, and when Fergus had marked the rigid pallor of her face, the wild light of her eyes, and the convulsive trembling of her limbs, he no longer resisted her entreaties, but led her on through the storm, shielding her as best he could from its fury, and silently longing to take upon himself the double of her pain, fatigue and terror, if so she might be spared. And still as they struggled onward through the tempest, the flames of the burning house shed a lurid light along their path, and as they turned to look shot upward in a torrent of fire and smoke, as if earth, refusing longer to conceal the ghastly secrets of the house, committed them once for all to the Prince of the Power of the Air, to do with them as he would. Then the fierce flame smouldered down to an angry glow, and a cloud of smoke and mist wrapped the ruin from sight.

The way was long and rough, and yet a mile from the gates of Bonniemeer, Neria's fictitious strength suddenly gave out, and she would have fallen to the earth but for Fergus, who hastily threw an arm about her waist, and found her in the next moment swooning helplessly upon his breast.

No human habitation lay nearer than Bonniemeer, but some rods from where they stood, Fergus remembered a ruined smithy whose broken roof might yet afford some shelter from the storm; and, tenderly raising Neria in his arms, he made his way toward it as rapidly as his burden, the blinding rain, and the approaching darkness would allow.

As they approached the shed Neria, recovering consciousness, struggled to regain her feet, and Fergus suffering her to so, supported her by an arm about her waist while with the other hand he drew the light shawl more closely around her neck. But as they gained the shelter of the smithy and paused, Fergus looking earnestly into the face of his companion was startled by its unearthly pallor and the vacant stare of the usually animated eyes. With a rare impulse of tenderness he clasped her to his heart and kissing her cold cheek, murmured:

"You are too nearly an angel, for the sin and trouble of this world, darling."

With a faint sigh Neria's head sank upon his breast, and he, not knowing that she had swooned again, bent his own above it in caressing tenderness.

At the same moment, a man who had, at their entrance, secreted himself behind the chimney of the forge, and thence attentively watched and listened to al that passed, stepped quietly through a chasm in the wall of the ruin, and with bent head and muffled form, made his way through the storm in the direction of Bonniemeer.

An hour later, Neria, leaning heavily upon her cousin's arm, reached the house, and was met at the door by Francia.

"Why Neria! How came you to walk in such a dreadful storm, and where is the carriage? But what do you think? Papa is here."

"Here!" exclaimed Neria, faintly.

"Yes, indeed. He came in the stage-coach, and one of Burrough's men drove him over about three o'clock. He wanted to go on to Cragness and meet you, but you had the ponies, and the carriage horses are both sick, John says, so—but you mustn't stand here in your drenched clothes. Go up stairs, please, and I will run and tell papa you are come home."

"No, no, not yet," cried Neria, catching at Francia's dress as she turned toward the library door.

"I am so tired and wet, he would be disturbed," pursued she, in answer to the look of surprise upon the young girl's face. "Let me go up stairs first and change my dress."

"Come then, I will go and help you. Let us be as quick as we can. Papa must be asleep or he would hear your voice."

"Wait a moment, Neria," interrupted Fergus, and drawing her a little aside, whispered,

"Shall you tell my uncle what we have discovered?"

"O no," returned Neria, in the same tone, "what need of disturbing him with it? Let us forget it, or at least appear to forget."

"Fergus, you shouldn't keep Neria now, she is very wet and will take cold. Besides, she wants to see papa," called Francia, from the foot of the stairs; and Neria obeyed the summons, while Fergus, with rather an angry glance at his cousin, sought his uncle for the double purpose of greeting him and of relating the catastrophe of Cragness.

Half an hour later when Neria, refreshed, but still pale and worn with her recent fatigue of body and mind, came to greet her husband, Vaughn met her with a grave and even pitiful tenderness very different from the fond devotion he had been wont to exhibit in the first days of their marriage. And as Neria raised her eyes to his face she was shocked to see how it had changed since their separation.

"You are not looking well, Sieur. Have you been ill?" asked she, kindly, and yet with a timid reserve in her voice, painfully familiar to her husband's ear.

"Not at all, only hard at work," replied he, releasing the hand he had taken as he kissed her cheek. "I have found plenty to occupy my time, especially of late, and I have only asked a furlough now for a week. I shall return to-morrow."

"So soon?" asked Neria, and to Vaughn's sensitive ear it was as if she had said, "It is well it is no longer."

He made no reply, but Francia's voice volubly filled the silence with regrets, entreaties and exclamations of dismay. Fergus standing in a distant window with his back to the room, took no part in the conversation. He had fancied his uncle's greeting to him strangely cold, and his manner repellant although strictly courteous; and Fergus, man of the world as he was, was still young enough to allow a slight he could not resent to obviously disturb his mind.

Tea was served, and under the genial influence of the brilliant table, the exquisite beverage, and the harmonious influence of social feeling, a certain superficial cheerfulness veiled for a time to each mind its substantial anxieties and troubles. But when in the great drawing-room they gathered about the smouldering fire, and looked each in the other's face, a shadow of reserve and isolation seemed to stand between, dividing those who should have been nearest, and replacing the fond confidences of a reunited family by the ominous sentence, " Every heart knoweth its own bitterness, and there is a grief with which the stranger intermeddleth not." Only Francia, in whose mind the necessity of concealing her feelings from Fergus was even more urgent than the feelings themselves, assumed a liveliness so forced as to border on levity, and without perceiving that no one listened, no one applauded, that Vaughn was abstracted and gloomy, Neria pre-occupied with her own thoughts, and Fergus with Neria.

The evening dragged wearily on, and at an earlier hour than usual Neria rose, pleading fatigue, and bade good-night. Vaughn accompanied her to the foot of the stairs, and taking her hand looked deep into her eyes.

"Sleep well to-night, pale nun," said he, sadly. "To-morrow I shall be gone."

"O Sieur! you do not think I wish it? You do not feel your visit unwelcome?" asked Neria, in pained surprise.

"My visit? You are right, Neria, I have no home, no wife. Good-night, child, do not be grieved at what I say, do not think I blame you. You have been as courteous to me as to any gentleman who might have been the guest of the house for a night. More, I did not expect, or if I did, I deserved to be again disappointed." He smiled as men have smiled while death tore at their hearts and drank their blood, and left her to wearily climb the stairs and sink forlorn upon the floor of her chamber, crying,

"O mother, broken-hearted mother, why did you not cast me into the sea before you died upon its brink? Cruel, cruel life, and O most merciful death!"

CHAPTER XXXIII.

NOBLESSE OBLIGE.

THE next morning, Colonel Vaughn, returning from his morning walk, was overtaken by a ragged boy, who thrusting a billet into his hand with the injunction, "Miss Rhee says you must look at it right off," turned and shot away in the direction of Carrick with a rapidity strongly suggestive of a reward in prospect.

Vaughn looked after him a moment in some surprise, and then opening the paper read,

"I am dying. Come to me once more for the sake of Francia's mother, if not for the sake of poor Anita."

As he read, Vaughn's haggard face grew yet paler, and he muttered:

"Does not the day bring its own troubles without calling back those of yesterday? Anita, Gabrielle, Francia, if I have wronged you, be content, for Neria revenges all."

Tearing the paper into atoms, he scattered them upon the fresh autumn wind and walked slowly homeward.

The unsocial breakfast over, Vaughn took his hat and left the house, but paused a moment on the terrace, doubting whether he should not mention his destination, and yet disliking to enter upon the subject of Mrs. Rhee with any member of the family who had been taught to avoid her name.

Standing thus, Fergus's voice reached his ear through the closed blinds of the library. "You look ill and worn, Neria. Are you disturbed at anything?"

"How can you ask, Fergus? This terrible secret crushes me to the earth. It will kill me with its shame and sin," murmured Neria in reply; and Vaughn starting as if a serpent had lain at his feet, sprang down the steps and struck toward Carrick, his brows drawn low above his glittering eyes, his mouth hard and white with the emotion he suppressed.

Arrived at the little cottage, he was admitted by the old domestic as an expected guest, and conducted at once to Mrs. Rhee's bedchamber.

"You have come!" exclaimed the dying woman, extending her wasted hands and fastening her eyes hungrily upon his face. "I was afraid you would not."

"Why should I refuse, Anita? If you indeed are dying, I shall lose in your death a heart that once, at least, loved me well."

And Vaughn, half bitterly, half tenderly pressed the thin hands to his lips; and, seating himself, retained them in his grasp. Upon the wan face of the dying woman came the flush and light of almost incredible joy, and the ebbing life seemed to rush back in a flood to her heart as she cried:

"And you say it! O Frederick, not once, but always—now—this very moment, I love you as no woman ever will or ever can love you. Believe that, and tell me you believe it before I die, for it is so many, many years that you have forced me to be silent, that you cannot know how unswerving my love has been from then till now."

"And has this love been joy or sorrow?" asked Vaughn, abruptly.

"A bitter joy, a cherished sorrow," replied Anita, after a pause.

"So is love always to one of the two it falls between," returned Vaughn, harshly. "Be content, Anita, your love is as happy as mine; happier, for it had its day, a brief one, perhaps, but bright while it lasted. You were content while we were abroad?"

"Content!" exclaimed Anita, while the flush upon her cheek deepened to a fever glow. "Each moment of that time has made tolerable a year of the life since. I die because those moments are expended."

"Pity me, then, Anita," groaned Vaughn, hiding his face upon the bed. "Pity me, for I have no such memories to support me, and I am a man and cannot die."

"She does not love you then, this pale girl, whom you have placed above all the queens of the earth by giving her your heart and your name?" asked the octoroon, fiercely.

"She does not love me! She loathes my presence, my voice, my face. If I touch her she swoons with disgust and terror."

As the bitter words dropped from his lips Vaughn would, if he could, have snatched them back, but it was too late. Anita's jealous ears had caught every one, and she murmured passionately, "If I could but live, if I could but live!"

Vaughn did not hear her. He was pacing the little room through and through, and already had forgotten the presence of the dying woman, when she said meaningly,

"There is good cause, no doubt, for such coldness. Does Fergus Murray remain at Bonniemeer since your return?"

Vaughn was at her side in an instant, her hands grasped in his, her eyes chained by the terrible inquisition of his gaze. "Anita! What does this mean? Explain yourself, or you shall die repenting that you had ever spoken."

"You should have learned in the old time that to threaten was to seal my lips," returned Anita sullenly.

"Yes, but speak! Woman, you will drive me mad! Speak out, for God's sake."

"For your sake, who are my God, I will speak. Do you not know that long before the fatal idea of making her your wife occurred to you, your nephew loved her and she him? She would have married him, but it was better to be mistress of Bonniemeer than the wife of a young man with his fortune yet to make—"

"No. There you are wrong, I will swear," interposed Vaughn, sternly. "She has nothing mean or calculating about her. She is above the world in her errors as in her virtues."

"O well then," sneered Anita. "Very likely it was some romantic idea of gratitude, of sacrificing her own wishes to those of the man who had been a providence to her when Providence deserted her. She offered herself a victim to your passion."

Again Vaughn started to his feet, stung to the heart by an explanation tallying so cruelly with the experiences of his married life. "And I, who loved her so far beyond myself, accepted the sacrifice."

"The sacrifice was incomplete it seems, for she could not conceal, even in your arms, her regrets for another," said she, cunningly.

Vaughn paused in his stride, looked at her as looks the wounded lion at the foe who has hurt him unto death and yet holds himself beyond his reach, and said nothing.

"It is not for myself that I speak," resumed Anita; "I am dying, and even though I lived, I have long since relinquished all hope of your love; but it is Francia—it is the child of my child who is the true sufferer, the real victim. Long ago, before you forbade her to visit me, I knew that she loved Fergus, and when I found her suffering and troubled, I drew from her the secret that was poisoning her life. She loved Fergus, and Fergus would have loved her, but that Neria stood between, and drew him to her with the wonderful magic of her smile. I tried to soothe and quiet her, but the child inherits the passions of her mother's race with the pride of yours, and she threw herself away upon a man whom already she despises. Neria married you, and now rewards herself for the sacrifice by indulging her passion for Fergus in your absence. "Do you know where they were yesterday?"

"At Cragness," replied Vaughn, briefly.

"Yes. The whole day alone in that deserted house. Even the woman who lived there was sent to Carrick, and it was night before they returned home."

"What scandal are you trying to make of this? The place was struck by lightning and burned to the ground. Mrs. Vaughn's horses were frightened and escaped, and she was forced to walk home; of course it was late when they arrived. Be careful, Anita, not to go beyond the truth."

"Beyond!" exclaimed the octoroon, with an evil laugh. "Be careful you, not to go so far as the truth if you still would hold to your idol. How engrossing the conversation or the business which took them there must have been, when neither the lady nor the gentleman perceived the tempest gathering in time to escape it! Nancy Brume had watched it for hours, and went to the library door to warn them of it, but, although she knocked loudly, no one replied. Mrs. Vaughn is a great business woman, I believe; probably she was engaged in settling old accounts."

"That is enough. Not one word more," groaned Vaughn, and his torturer, looking in his livid face and meeting the gaze of his burning eyes, saw that it was enough, and sank back upon the pillows exhausted with the vehemence of her own passion. When she spoke again it was in an altered tone. "Frederick, shall not I see Francia once more before I die?"

"To poison her ears with this?"

"No; I swear before God not to reveal one word of all that has passed between us. I only wish to bid her good-by, to kiss her lips and feel her pure breath upon my cheek. Remember, she is the only creature of my blood in the whole world. You will not deny my dying wish?"

"I dare not. She shall come, if you will promise also not to reveal yourself."

"I promise. When shall she come?"

"To-day." I shall not return to Bonniemeer, but you may send for her."

"You will not return! Will you not let them know that they are discovered?"

"Discovered? I do not comprehend you, Mrs. Rhee," said Vaughn, with a haughty coldness. "The scandalous suspicions you have suggested with regard to my wife and my nephew, inspire in my mind only a feeling of contempt for the slanderer who can utter them. They harmonize well with the anonymous letter whose author I now recognize."

Anita started to her elbow. "An anonymous letter relating to Neria and Fergus!" cried she, in tones of genuine surprise. "Have you such a one? It was not from me. I swear it by all that is sacred."

"It is sufficient. I believe you," said Vaughn, briefly.

"And this letter, from an entirely different source—does this also excite only contempt for the slanderer who wrote it?" sneered the octoroon.

Vaughn hesitated; but only for a moment, only until the chivalrous honor of his nature could assert itself. Then he said: "Yes; I will not believe Neria guilty of more than the fatal error of sacrificing herself to me, until my own eyes or her own tongue convict her."

"Such proof you will never have. She is too careful," muttered the baffled woman, bitterly.

"Such proof I shall never have, for a lie cannot be proved. To connect sin or shame with Neria is to drag the heavens down and trample on them." But as the words left his lips, a fiend's echoed in his ear those that Neria had that morning spoken to Fergus:

"This terrible secret crushes me to the earth. It will kill me with its shame and sin," and his proud heart quailed within him. He threw himself upon his knees. "My God, my God!" groaned he. "Let me not lose my reason, let me not lose my faith in her. Take life, take honor, happiness, all, but leave me my faith in her—let me die with her pure image in my heart." Never prayer was thus wrung from the centre of a tortured soul, and remained unanswered, never since He, hanging on the cross, called upon the Father and was comforted. Vaughn arose pale and serene. The temptress, looking at him, knew that her power was over, her work done, and with a bitter moan she turned her face to the wall and was dumb. Without another word Vaughn left the room, and an hour later was on his way to the great battle he knew to be approaching, and in whose front he now hoped to lay down the life he no longer cared to keep. He had not, however, forgotten his promise. In the hurried note of leave-taking, written to Francia, from Carrick, he had bidden her go to Mrs. Rhee as soon as possible, and had sent word to Neria that she would receive a letter from him in a day or two, explaining his abrupt departure in full.

CHAPTER XXXIV.

MRS. RHEE'S PARTHIAN ARROW.

TO Neria came Francia with her father's note. She found her in the library with Fergus, who reported the present condition of the ruins at Cragness, and the attempt he had, by his uncle's desire, put in progress to rescue such books, pictures or furniture as might have been spared by the flames. As Francia entered, Neria was saying—

"I am sorry anything is to be done. I had rather everything perished together."

"That is just of a piece with my news," exclaimed Francia, in a voice oddly compounded of grief and vexation.

"Here papa has run away without even coming back to bid good-bye, and only says it was impossible for him to see us again before starting, but he will write to you to-morrow to explain; and he says that poor Mrs. Rhee is dying and wants to see me again and I may go. Come with me, Neria, please. I don't know what to say to any one who is dying, and I shall be afraid."

"Afraid of what?" asked Fergus, somewhat contemptuously.

"Not afraid of being too tender with her, as you might be," retorted Francia, turning decidedly toward Neria, who sat pale and silent.

"Come with me, won't you?" pleaded she.

"To Mrs. Rhee? Yes, certainly; but show me your father's note. Gone!"

"Yes, actually gone. Here's the note, and I will run and change my dress. Shall I order the pony carriage?"

"Yes, please," replied Neria, absently, and as the door closed, turned to Fergus, her eyes full of perplexity and dismay.

"Why should Sieur have left us so, and why was he so strange while here?"

"I cannot tell, nor do I wish to speculate upon either question. It would be an impertinence toward my uncle. He promises to write and explain fully to-morrow, you see," replied Fergus, characteristically.

"Yes, but I feel that something is amiss. I had meant—I had hoped while he was here—"

She paused and Fergus would never have asked her to continue, had his curiosity been excited to its fullest extent. He only took her hand, kissed it lightly and walked away to the window, lest he should seem to watch the emotion she could scarce control.

The silence had not been broken when Francia returned, bringing Neria's hat and announcing the carriage.

Fergus, with silent courtesy, waited upon his cousins to the door, helped Francia to enter the carriage as carefully as he did Neria, and saw them drive away before re-entering the house. Upon the library floor he found Neria's handkerchief, wet with the tears she had been unable quite to repress. He put it to his lips and hid it in his bosom, whispering—

"Did she weep because she loves him and he is gone, or because she loves me and fears her own heart in his absence? And I—can I stay here loving her as I do love her? Did he read it in my face or in my heart? Is this the pure honor I have tried to guard before everything? I will leave this place tonight." And then, sternly suspicious of the tender weakness which had overtaken him, Fergus drew the little handkerchief from its hiding place, and denying himself even one more kiss, laid it upon the table, and taking a book, buried himself in its contents with all the force of his iron will.

The rapid drive to Carrick was almost a silent one. Neria, sad and grave, answered but briefly Francia's first attempts at conversation, and as they approached their destination the young girl herself grew grave in remembering their errand.

"You must go up-stairs with me," whispered Francia, as they stood in the passage of the little cottage, and she was informed that Mrs. Rhee would see her. Neria silently assented, and the two entered together the chamber of the dying woman and stood at her bedside. She was dozing, but opened her eyes as they approached, fixed them fondly on Francia and then turned to Neria.

"Since you have come here I have something to say to you, Mrs. Vaughn," said she, maliciously. "I did not send for you, but Fate has given me the opportunity. Francia, will you wait below for a few moments? I must see you last."

"Certainly, if you wish, aunty," replied Francia, moving somewhat reluctantly to the door, and casting wondering looks at Neria, who although much surprised at the request made no movement to contradict it.

"Sit here close by my bedside," continued the dying woman, as the door closed behind Francia.

Neria silently obeyed, and Mrs. Rhee gazed scrutinizingly upon the pure pale face with its fearless eyes and queenly mouth.

"I will move you from that proud calm before I am done," thought she, and then said, significantly, "Mr. Vaughn was here this morning and talked to me a long time of you."

"Indeed!"

"Yes. You think it strange that he should confide so much in one who has been no better than a servant in his house. But old habits are strong, and long before he ever saw you he found in me all that he required of friendship or love. Why should he not return to me in his disappointment and his grief?"

"I have not blamed him for doing so," replied Neria, calmly, as the other waited for an answer.

"But your lips grow white with mortification at finding that he confides in me what he hides from you. You would give that diamond off your finger to know what those confidences were," persisted the other.

"I would not allow you to tell me if you wished. What Colonel Vaughn desires to keep secret from me I have no desire to learn."

"You were always a hypocrite, but you never cheated me with your artful ways, nor do you now," exclaimed the octoroon, fiercely. "But you shall know, whether you will or not. You are found out, madam! Your husband has gone away without seeing you, because he has discovered your intrigues with Fergus Murray, and will not stoop even to reproach you with your unfaithfulness, he holds you in such contempt."

Neria rose and stood looking down upon the miserable woman who sought to insult her, with a sublime compassion, a lofty innocence.

"I do not know what you are saying, but I will not listen longer. You must be very unhappy to feel so toward me, who never harmed or wished you ill. It is not the first time you have hurt me. I knew that you tried to make Chloe poison me. I knew that you made Francia suspicious and jealous of me, but I knew, too, your own unhappy story and I forgave and pitied you, understanding how you should feel me an usurper both of Francia's place and of your daughter's. And even now, when you have done me this last great injury, I still can pity, and if before you die your conscience stings you for the evil you have done and tried to do to me, remember that I have freely forgiven all."

"Forgive! You forgive me!" screamed Mrs. Rhee, her face distorted, her eyes glaring with impotent rage. "You dare to stand there, accusing and forgiving me; you, whose husband has this very day left you forever because he knew you to be false and a wanton—"

"Stop!" cried Neria, and into her pale face flashed the seraphic power which had subdued Luttrell, which had drawn her secret from Chloe's reluctant lips; the power of a nature untouched by sin, though filled with the knowledge of good and evil.

"Stop! I will not allow you to add to the burden already on your soul. Do you not see that it is yourself and not me whom you injure? Do you think any words of yours could make such a monstrous lie look like the truth to a man like Vaughn, or do you think you could force me to believe that he believed it? You have failed, utterly failed, and I have no anger, only a profound compassion, a full forgiveness for you. Pray God to forgive you, also, and thank Him that you have not been suffered to succeed."

"Begone! Send me Francia," gasped the dying woman, upon whom her excessive emotion was telling fearfully.

Neria left the room without reply, and telling Francia that Mrs. Rhee was ready for her, added a caution against staying long, as she was already much exhausted. Half an hour passed while Neria, waiting in the little parlor, resolutely battled with the doubts and terror, inspired, in spite of her determination, by Mrs. Rhee's explanation of Vaughn's disappearance.

She was roused from her reverie by quick footsteps running down the stairs, and Francia's voice calling to her from the passage, as she hurried out of the house and seated herself in the carriage. Neria followed with some anxiety.

"Is some one with Mrs. Rhee? She should not be left alone," asked she, hesitating.

"Yes, I called the nurse from the next room. She did not wish me to stay," replied Francia, hurriedly; as she drew her veil closely about her face, and taking the reins drove rapidly homeward.

Neria looked at her in suprise. The voice, the manner, the reserve was so unlike Francia, especially toward herself.

"You are distressed at sight of your old friend so near her death, dear?" said she, inquiringly, when some moments had passed in silence.

"My old friend? Yes, and more of a friend than younger ones. If I had known her sooner—"

She stopped abruptly, as fearing to betray a secret, and with averted face urged the horses to a more rapid pace.

Neria leaned back in her seat, her eyes fixed upon the distant shimmer of the sea, lying like a lake of fire beneath the noonday sun, and the bitterness of wronged and repulsed affection surged irresistibly upon her soul.

"First Vaughn, and now Francia; she has alienated both with her wicked falsehoods!" thought she.

Reaching home, Francia threw the reins to the groom, sprang from the carriage without a word, and hurried to her own room. Neria did not follow her there, but still stood wistfully watching her retreating figure when Fergus, opening the library door, asked her to enter for a moment.

"I wanted to say good-bye, that is all. I must return to town to-night, and am about to start for Carrick now. Can John drive me over?" said he, with forced indifference of manner.

"You, too!" exclaimed Neria in a tone of sharp distress, and turning, she would have left the room, but staggering blindly against a chair sank beside it, her face hidden upon it, and broke into a passion of tears.

Fergus, not guessing the pain and doubt filling her heart to overflowing when she entered, stood thunderstruck for a moment, and then a strange wild joy throbbed through his veins. This uncontrollable grief, this emotion so rare in one so habitually calm; was it that Neria felt his presence a necessity, that she leaned upon him and could not lose him?

He stooped and raised her in his arms. "Darling! what is this?" whispered he, in a palpitating voice. "Shall I not leave you? Do you care to have me stay?" His lips sought hers and kissed them tenderly, but Neria wrenched herself from his embrace, crying:

"This! O this is worst of all! Leave me, cast me off as they have done, but do not make me despise myself and you! Such love is worse than the desertion, the alienation, the hate that others have heaped upon me!"

She fled out of his presence, and Fergus, guessing at his mistake, cursing his fatal error, and consumed with mortification at his own weakness and the injury he had done both to Neria's feelings and her opinion of himself, left the house abruptly, with no further leave-taking or explanation.

CHAPTER XXXV.

"NOT LAUNCELOT OR ANOTHER."

THE next day brought Vaughn's promised letter to Neria. It was this:

Pardon the seeming discourtesy of my abrupt departure, and my first signifying it to Francia. I could not see you again, Neria, I could not write to you of less than the whole.

Remember first and always in what I have to say, that I hold you above all women in my respect, and in my love, and that whatever unhappiness has come between us I trace wholly to my own folly, and would, if possible, keep wholly to my own heart, leaving you only the divine sorrow of an angel who has tried to become mortal for a mortal's sake, and has failed.

Dearest, this is a farewell and a petition. A farewell, for a great battle is approaching, and what one poor life can do to win it for our country shall be done. A petition, for I see now, as never before, the cruel wrong I did in accepting the sacrifice of your young life, and in giving it back to you, as I shall do in my death, I ask you to bestow it, hereafter, where your heart dictates. Become his wife, dear child, without too much regret for him who should never have stood between you, and be sure that such peace as my hereafter may know, is doubled by the assurance of your happiness.

Nor fancy, tender conscience, that you have wronged my love by showing, even to my eyes, the love, not for me, filling your pure heart. Love such as yours, Neria, is of God, and as holy and as sacred as all his gifts. You have subdued and hidden it, because the unholy bond between us two forced you to do so, but had there been sin and shame in its existence, that sin and shame should have been mine, not yours.

Now you are free, or shall be soon, and let the future recompense the past. But at the last, O love and life, hear me say that never one thought of blame, never one reproach for you has sullied my heart. Chief among women I have loved you, chief among women I have reverenced you, and do now, and shall, as I go out alone to fight and die, and win for myself the peaceful rest of a struggle past, the sweet dark night of the toilsome day.

As Neria read and read again these tender words, and felt the noble heart throb through them its devotion, its trust, its heroic abnegation, her own heart stirred within her as it never yet had stirred. Again and again she read them until her eyes shown bright, and her cheeks burned scarlet with the fire of a wild emotion.

"You, you yourself, my king! 'Not Launcelot or another,'" murmured she, pressing the letter to her brow, her heart, her lips. And then the passionate words of the great Idyl sprang to her lips, and with the guilty queen she cried

Is there none
Will tell him that I love him though so late?
Now, ere he goes to the great battle?

But at that woful word, the new-born human love gave way to human grief and terror, and Neria, for the first time in her married life, felt her heart shrink with the sudden fear that Vaughn might die and leave her desolate.

"Not before he knows that I love him, not before my lips have told him so! O God, not so!" cried she, upon her knees, with hands and eyes upraised to heaven. When she arose comforted, it was with a fixed resolve. She would seek her husband were it in the front of battle. If he died she would die with him; if he lived her love should make life another existence from what they had either of them known. And then her thoughts went back through her own brief history, gratefully acknowledging the tender affection, care, and honor with which Vaughn had crowned the life he had rescued; the chivalrous homage of his love, the passionate devotion, so coldly repaid, in the early days of their marriage. And now, at last, when he had traversed hundreds of miles to greet her, perhaps for the last time, to bid her, it might be an eternal farewell, he had found her preoccupied, cold, reserved. It was the shadow of the secret, she said to herself, it was the curse of that old-time sin and misery pursuing to the third and fourth generation the children of those who had so sinned and suffered; and she now regretted that she had not at once confided all to Vaughn, and by sharing with him the secret of her depression, prevented the misconception under which he evidently labored.

Still dreaming, with smiling lips and dewy eyes, Neria was startled by two soft arms laid tenderly about her neck, while Francia's lips sought hers. "Forgive me, darling; say that you forgive me," whispered she.

Neria's arm about her waist drew her to a seat upon her lap as she whispered back: "How can I forgive what has not offended me?"

"You should have been offended, or at least shocked and hurt, at my conduct ever since we left Mrs. Rhee's that day," persisted Francia; "but she told me, O little mother, she said such things of you, and, and—some one."

"Yes, dear, I know. And you believed them?"

"No, O Neria, I did not believe; but you know I felt—well I felt differently o you."

"Yes, dear, I know," said Neria again.

"And then she said papa believed—"

"You should have done your father more honor than to believe that he believed," said Neria, quietly.

"I know it; but at first—and then, Neria, she *told* me something else—something—"

The girl paused, and, drawing a little back, looked into Neria's face with such a dumb cry of appeal, such endless protest against the burden fallen of a sudden upon her untried shoulders, that Neria caught her to her heart, shielding and comforting her as if she were a little wounded child.

"Of your mother, darling?"

"Yes, and of herself. O Neria, my father bought her; she was a slave. I don't so much mind the negro blood; but I come of a race of slaves, of women who have been bought and sold for their beauty, of women who had no right to their own consciences, their own honor. Neria, Neria, speak out the truth! What can wipe away such disgrace? How can I ever feel myself what I was before? How could any honorable man ever trust—"

She hid her burning face again, and the passionate sobs that shook her frame finished the sentence.

"Make yourself such a woman, Francia, that an honorable man shall in loving you care for no past; shall trust the future as he does the present, because to doubt it were to doubt you."

"But, O, Neria, can I learn to be such a woman? Can I ever be such a woman that a man would say, 'I trust you in spite of all?'"

"Yes, Franc, such a woman you can be, and though the day may never come when the man you love best shall say this to you, it shall not be that you do not deserve it, but that our destinies are not for us to choose."

"You do not think he will ever love me, then?" broke from Francia's impetuous lips; but before Neria could answer, she hurried on: "I don't mean—that is—I wasn't thinking of what I said. I have a little note for both of us from dear papa. I did not give it you at first because I wanted to make up, and let you not have my ill temper to trouble you, too. Uncle Murray sent it down just now. It was directed to either of us, so I opened it. See!"

Neria took the scrap of soiled and torn paper and read these lines, hastily written in pencil:

I arrive just in time. My regiment is to move in half an hour. We shall be in action before night. A courier leaves for Washington at once, and I write one line to say good-bye, and God bless you both. My darlings, He only knows how I love you. I leave you each to the other's care.

FREDERIC VAUGHN.

"So soon! O, I shall be too late; I shall not reach him! O, Francia, why did you not give it me at once? I must go to him; I must go directly! If it should already be too late! My God, if it should be too late!"

Francia looked at her in astonishment. Could this be the calm and self-contained Neria; this wild-eyed creature, moving, looking, speaking with an impetuosity to which her own stormy moods were calm? And so resolute to seek, even upon a battle-field, the husband whose danger and whose absence had been hitherto so tranquilly borne? What could it all mean? But almost before the question was formed Francia's affectionate nature had set it aside for the more pressing need of sympathizing with and comforting even an undue affliction.

"I will go, too, Neria, darling, if you must go," said she, beginning with busy hands to arrange the clothes in a travelling sack that Neria was already packing.

"Come, then, but hurry; for every moment is a life now!" said Neria, ringing the bell violently to give the order: "Tell John to harness the horses as quick as possible to drive me to Carrick, and send Mrs. Barlow to me immediately."

A few moments later, the two young women were on their road; and that evening, as Mr. Murray and Fergus sat at their unsocial tea-table they were startled by the intelligence that Mrs. and Miss Vaughn were in the drawing-room, and would like to see the elder gentleman as quickly as possible.

Both answered the summons; both heard in silent astonishment the hurried announcement that Colonel Vaughn's wife and daughter were about to seek him upon the field of battle, and each replied in his own way—the father by a compassionate smile and a shake of the head so courteous as to be almost an affirmative, the son by the curt remark:

"I should think you were out of your senses, both of you. It is perfectly impossible."

"I must try it. I must see my husband at all hazards," exclaimed Neria, feverishly, turning from one to the other with hands clasped in unconscious appeal.

"If it could be done at any hazard, however great, Neria, you should try it, and I with you," said Fergus, coming close to her, and taking the clasped hands in his; "but we might not even be allowed to try. It would be impossible for any but a military man or a government agent to obtain a pass to the front now, and without one we should be turned back before we were within ten miles of the scene of action. It is quite impossible, believe me. Do you not say so, sir?"

"Of course, of course; Fergus is entirely correct, my dear, and you can only submit. In a few days, or whenever hostilities cease, it is very possible something may be done; but at present it is quite, O quite out of the question," replied Mr. Murray, in his silkiest manner, but with a determination in his cold eyes that smote Neria with dismay.

"Quite impossible?" echoed she, despairingly.

"Quite, my dear Mrs. Vaughn. In fact, the telegraph announces to-night that action has already commenced with the right wing of our army; and long before you could reach even Washington the whole force will have marched and countermarched, have moved this way and that, hither and yon, a dozen times. If my life depended upon it, absolutely my life, madam, I would not undertake to find Colonel Vaughn until this battle is well over."

Neria's head dropped upon her breast. "And when it is over he will be where I shall never find him!" muttered she.

The cool-blooded old man could not hear the words; but even he could not see unmoved the despairing attitude, the woful face of one so fair, so young, so delicately nurtured. He laid a hand upon her shoulder, and the dry white fingers quivered with a motion that was almost a caress.

"Don't be so much disappointed, my dear," said he, kindly, "Vaughn will be at home again before long, and that will pay for all."

Neria looked vacantly in his face, and turned to Fergus. "And do you refuse to help me, too, Fergus?" asked she, unconsciously using as a weapon in her extremity the very ove whose confession she had so sharply rebuked a few hours before.

"Refuse you, Neria?" exclaimed the young man, passionately; "it is not I, it is the fact that refuses you. I would do more than you think to satisfy you, if it were possible; but it is not. You can only wait."

"Wait! But while I wait he will be killed; and then—" She looked at him, at his father, at Francia. In every face she read denial, and a l the pity and the love covering it could not assuage the sharp pang that pierced her heart, the bitterness as of death borne in upon her soul by the mocking echo, "Too late! too late!"

To return to Bonniemeer in this uncertainty was impossible; and for the next four days the two ladies waited under Mr. Murray's roof for the almost hourly bulletins flashed over the wires from the scene of action, and regularly brought to them by Fergus, even before the public could receive them.

At last came the victory; but victory or defeat were one to Neria in the terrible anxiety devouring her. The returns from the regiments arrived, and hour by hour Fergus came with cheery step to say, "No bad news yet, Neria." At last he did not come until, as the suspense grew intolerable, and Neria was about to venture forth to seek him, she heard him slowly ascending the stairs. She met him in the doorway, looked into his marble face and pitiful eyes, and crying, "Too late! too late!" sank swooning at his feet.

CHAPTER XXXVI.
TWO STORIES.

A WEEK later, Fergus returning from "the front" with a companion, brought him to Bonniemeer, and into Neria's presence.

"This is Reuben Brume," said he, introducing him. "He was close beside my uncle when he fell, and he will tell you all."

Neria raised her dim eyes to the sergeant's agitated face. "Please tell me everything you can remember of him," said she, simply.

"Well'm, the kunnel seemed as chirk that morning as ever I see him. I took particular notice, as we come in sight of the enemy, and he turned round to cheer us on, how bright his eyes was, and how his mouth shet together as if there wouldn't be no two ways of settling with him that day. He didn't say much, only told us to remember any one of us might be the man to save his country, and he told us to fight for them we loved at home, who was a praying for our success, and then he sung out "Charge!" and we went in. What come next I couldn't say particular. The blood sort of got into my head like it does in a wild creter's, and I just let drive right and left on my own hook 'thout noticing the rest on 'em, till I found myself right cheek by jowl with the kunnel. Lord! how he did fight! He slashing away at a big fellow, a captain, I guess it was, any way, an officer, who was slashing away again at him, and the two mated so equal there's no knowing who'd have had the best of it, when up come a big brute behind the officer and with a yell and a cuss druv his bay'net square through the kunnel's breast, through the very heart of him, I reckon, for he just throwed up his arms and staggered back with one mortial cry, and was dead 'fore he reached the ground. No one heerd that cry but me; but I did—it was your name, ma'am."

Reuben Brume stopped and turned his face away; but though tears rained down his bronzed cheeks, and Fergus was fain to hide his face, Neria's eyes glittered cold and bright as winter stars, and her voice was unshaken while she asked: "And his body?"

"It had to be left there, ma'am. It wasn't a minute, hardly, just time for me to smash in that rascal's skull with the breech of my gun, which my bayonet was lost; when the order came to fall back behind the batteries. Before night we'd fell back five mile, and though we beat 'em in the end, the place where the kunnel fell was fur within their lines. The gineral asked leave to send in and bury our dead, but they refused; they said they buried 'em themselves, but—"

"Colonel Vaughn was dead when he fell?" interposed Fergus, hurriedly.

"Yes, I'm sartain sure he was," asserted he, stoutly. "The bay'net went in just about here, and that's right over the heart, and he wouldn't have fell as he did unless it had been a mortial wound. It touched the life for sartain, ma'am, and he never suffered no more after that. His eyes was shut, and his face turning white, in the last glimp I caught, just as we was falling back, and the enemy piling along after us."

"Over the bodies of the fallen?" asked Neria again, in that icy voice.

"Well'm, I guess they didn't stop to pick their way much, that's a fact," assented Reuben, reluctantly; and Neria turned her stony face toward the window and seemed to gaze at the far-off sea, smiling and dimpling in the gorgeous hues of sunset.

At a sign from Fergus the soldier followed him silently from the room, and from the house, and a few days later shipped on board a whaler for a long voyage, so careful was Fergus to remove from Neria's path all that might remind her of her loss.

It was the depth of an autumnal night. Driven before the hurrying wind the bewildered clouds drifted hither and thither, now huddling in massive groups, now breaking and fleeing to the four quarters of the heavens only to gather again, again to flee. The late moon rising through one of these cloud-banks looked out upon the scene, tipped with silver the crested ocean waves, flaunted her banner across the combat of wind and forest, and fell like a benediction upon the golden harvest fields already ripe for the reaper. But from one field the blessed moonlight shrank affrighted, upon one harvest fell no benediction, but rather a curse; for when climbing the mountain behind it, the moon hung where she might view it well, she hid her face and all earth remained in darkness. It was a bloody battle-field, it was the harvest of a violent and cruel death.

And yet the dying and the dead were not sole possessors of the field, for as the moon hurrying from the refuge of one cloud to that of another, shot a wild flood of light upon the scene, a human figure stole from the covert of the wood and crossed rapidly to the centre of the field, where, sheltered behind a rampart of lifeless bodies, lay the tall and stalwart figure of a man still grasping a broken sword, while on his breast lay congealed the blood that had flowed from wellnigh a mortal wound. He was alive, for in a death-pale face shone two resolute dark eyes, moving slowly from side to side as if to recall the scene or speculate upon the chances of help.

Between these wistful glances and the sky, came the dark figure of a man stooping to peer into the face of the wounded officer, who in seeing it involuntarily closed his eyes and shrank a little, brave soldier though he was, in thinking that the knife of an assassin and a thief was to end the life just creeping back to his frozen heart. But it was no assassin's hand raising that fallen head to a fairer position, no assassin's voice muttering,

"It's he, sure enough, but be he dead or not is more than I can say. Master, be you alive?"

Colonel Vaughn's eyes opened wearily, and his white lips whispered, "James! Is it you?"

"Yes, sir, and main glad to find you alive," replied the faithful servant, who having followed his master to the battle-field as he would upon any other expedition, made the cause in which he fought quite subsidiary to the service that had led him into it.

"How came you here?" whispered the white lips again.

"Why, sir, I saw you go down, and then our men fell back, as they called it, I should say ran, and the others after them; but my lookout was to keep near you, sir, to help you if you was alive, and to bury you if you was dead. So, passing through a wood back here about a mile, I just swarmed up a thick tree and waited till they'd gone by, both lots of 'em. Then I waited a spell longer till it was dark, and then made my way back here. When the moon rose I took a squint over the field and made out pretty nigh where you lay, and so come across, and here I be."

"Faithful fellow. But I will die here," murmured Vaughn.

"No, sir, you won't, if I may be so bold. I'm a bit of a surgeon myself, 'specially since I was in hospital last month, and I'm going to bind up your wound and then carry you on my back to a shanty up on the mountain yonder. There's an old black fellow lives there who's got the name of a wizard among the country folks. I heard all about it from one of our contrabands, but if he's the old boy himself he shall take you in and do for you, and when you can move we'll make a push for camp."

"Wait. You shall not stir me from this place, James, until you promise to obey my orders."

"Yes, sir. Of course, sir."

"You are not to tell this negro my name. Tear off my shoulder-straps, that he may not know my rank. If I die, bury me here, and go home to tell my wife. If I recover I shall volunteer as a private under another name. Meantime call me John Brown, and say I am your brother. You will do all this?"

"Yes, sir, if you say so, of course," assented the groom, somewhat reluctantly, but too well trained to express surprise or ask an explanation of what seemed an unaccountable whim upon his master's part.

"Support me, and I think I can walk. Have you a little brandy?"

"Here is your own flask, sir; it is filled with better stuff than they give us," said James; and after swallowing the cordial, Vaughn rose to his feet, and, leaning heavily upon the shoulders of his faithful servant, slowly crossed the field of death, and was presently lost in the rustling shadows of the wood.

CHAPTER XXXVII.

THE DARK HOUR.

THE days and the weeks and the months moved on. The golden autumn gave way to the majesty of winter, winter softened beneath the kiss of spring, like a hard old king in the embrace of his girlish bride; spring ripened into the trancéd glow of summer, and Neria's widowed heart mourned day by day more passionately, and more remorsefully. Remorsefully, for upon that delicate conscience lay the burden of a noble life sacrificed to her ingratitude. Not one of the weary days, not one of the fearsome nights since the news of Vaughn's death, but she had told herself that it was for love of her, for sorrow at her coldness, and remorse at the bonds he had placed upon her, that he had gone to his death so resolutely—that death and he could not fail to meet. Day and night she bowed herself before God and before His spirit for pardon and comfort, and day and night she rose uncomforted, for as the flow of Heavenly love warmed and expanded her heart, came with it the fresh consciousness of the earthly passion sprung full-grown to life within her soul, and clamoring aloud for the food she could not give it.

And Francia, the bright, the loving, the joyous Francia mourned also. Mourned the father she had adored, the joy that had passed from her life and from her home; mourned her own wasted youth and wasted heart; for this is the cruel nature of a great sorrow, that it does not absorb and negative the other sorrows preoccupying the heart where it comes to dwell, but rather stings and quickens them to new life, inhabiting with them not in peace or in harmony, but with a bitter fellowship.

To these two in their seclusion came occasionally Fergus or his father, with news of the great world, its battles, its progress, its interests, or its gossip. Thus they knew, or might, if they had cared to listen, how the elections went; how England and France stood waiting, one at either hand, to side with the stronger against the weaker party, so soon as victory should clearly declare itself in the family quarrel they so eagerly watched; how gold, and with it bread, and fuel, and clothes, rose day by day out of the reach of those who most needed them.

Heard, too, how Claudia, the gayest of the gay, shone starlike at all the festivities of not only her own city but the other great capitals of the country, and how, while her husband buried himself to the lips in the gold the misfortunes of the land was pouring into his coffers, Queen Claudia was forever surrounded by a cloud of courtiers and slaves whom she managed so well that rumor found no one among them to honor with the preference. And the hard old man, her father, in whose heart a certain admiration for this brilliant and evil child replaced all other emotions of tenderness to his kind, rubbed his dry white hands, smiled a covert smile and said,

"Claudia is a clever girl, a very clever girl. She enjoys herself and spends Livingstone's money after her own fashion, but the world finds nothing to take hold of. A cool head, and a cool heart, too, has Mrs. Livingstone."

But of all these, one subject alone had interest for Neria, and this was the war. Since Vaughn's death the only link holding her to earth had seemed to be the cause in which he died. She read all the news, listened to all the details brought her by the Murrays, traced through the desolate southern land the progress of our armies, but more especially the corps containing Vaughn's regiment, whispering to herself,

"He would have been here now," or "They need not have made this retreat had he been with them," and so, half persuading herself that he was still identified with the great struggle, she identified herself with it not only in interest, but by contributing of the means at her command, so liberally as to call down the censure of her advisers, and a recommendation on more than one occasion from Mr. Murray to regulate her donations somewhat upon the scale of those of other and wealthier patriots. But Neria, gentle and yielding in most matters of business, was here inexorable, saying, with serene decision,

"We need but little here at Bonniemeer, and all the rest goes to help his armies and his fellow-soldiers."

CHAPTER XXXVIII.

CLAUDIA.

It was the twilight of a summer's day, and Neria, from the shore beneath the ruins of Cragness, watched the curving waves slide up the sands, watched the glory dying from the western sky, watched the faint light of the young moon creeping down the wall and peering into the chasm whence had fled upon that fearful evening the secrets of the gloomy old home of her fathers.

The sound of horses' feet upon the sands broke upon her revery, and, looking around, she saw Mr. Livingstone dismounting from a carriage driven by one of her own servants; and rising hastily went toward him, smitten with a sudden terror by the pallor of his usually florid face and the gleam of his restless eyes.

"Mr. Livingstone!"

"It's me, Mrs. Vaughn."

Their hands met, and Neria's eyes asked the question her lips could not form.

"Yes'm," replied her visitor, nervously wiping the forehead where great drops of perspiration gathered, although the night wind was blowing fresh and cool— "yes'm, it's me, and I've come to you for help. O, Neria, she's gone, she's—"

His white lips quivered, and he stopped to swallow a great sob, while the clammy drops upon his forehead broke out afresh.

"She's gone?—who?" asked Neria, turning pale at sight of his emotion.

"Claudia, my wife, ma'am. The woman that I've worked and toiled for day and night, as you may say; the woman that hasn't had a want nor hardly a whim that hasn't been satisfied ever since I gave her my name. Money! she hadn't anything to do but sign a check; and all I had was hers, and shawls, and laces, and diamonds, and silks at her will. She didn't like the carriage I got her when she was married, and this very last winter I made her a Christmas present of a new one. She wanted her servants put in livery, and livery it was, though I lost one of my best customers, a New England man, by the means. She wanted to go to New York and Washington for the winter, and I never said worse than 'Suit yourself, my dear;' she wanted to go to Newport, and she went—"

"But how is it? what has happened?" asked Neria, stemming the torrent of words which seemed somewhat to relieve the over-burdened heart of the injured husband.

"She's gone, run off; and where, or who with, or for what, I don't know more than you," said Mr. Livingstone, pausing in the act of wiping his forehead again, and staring blankly into Neria's face.

"But what were the circumstances?" persisted she.

"All I know is that three days ago a letter from Newport came in with the morning's mail, and here it is. He drew from his letter-case a note written in Claudia's dashing hand upon the heavily-perfumed paper she affected, in these words:

Good-bye, for you will not see me again. You have been a good master and a good servant to me, and it was not your fault that you could not be more. I forgive your stupidities, and part with you upon the best of terms. No one here suspects more than that I travel to New York to-morrow; so arrange a story to suit yourself.

"It was just as she says there," continued Mr. Livingstone; while Neria handed back the note with a look of silent dismay.

"I went straight to Newport, of course, and, without letting on that there was any trouble, found that Mrs. Livingstone had taken the boat for New York the morning before, leaving word with the coachman to drive his horses back to the city, as she should not return that way. I went quietly round to all the hotels, but could not find that anyone whom I could suspect had been stopping in Newport, or, at any rate, had left about that time. Several people asked, rather curiously, if I expected to join Mrs. L. at Newport; and to all I said 'No, I only came down to settle up the bills and get a mouthful of fresh air.' Not a soul but her father and brother, and you and I know anything of it yet; and if I could only find her before it's too late I'd forgive her all—I would—and take her back cheerful."

"Would you?" asked Neria.

"Yes, I would; for somehow she's got such a hold of me, Neria, it seems as if I could forgive her if she cost me every cent I've got in the world. It hasn't seemed to me these three days as if I had got anything to live for. Actually, I didn't close a bargain with a good Western customer yesterday, though I might have with a little more talk; but, somehow, I didn't care. But where is she, and how am I to look for her? I've come to you to know, for you always could do more with her than anyone else, and you've got a way of looking right into matters that I never saw in any other woman. Besides I don't mind you knowing that my poor girl's gone astray, as I would another."

His voice faltered as he spoke the last words, and his anxious eyes grew dim. Neria, shocked and pained, assured him that there could be nothing she would not gladly do to aid him were it possible to do anything, but professing an ignorance as entire as his own of Claudia's probable movements or probable companion. She also agreed with him upon the expediency of keeping her imprudent, if not guilty flight secret as long as possible, and, finally, she promised, at Mr. Livingston's solicitation, to accompany him should he discover his wife's hiding place, and to persuade her to accept the forgiveness and opportunity for amendment so generously offered by her husband.

With this promise Mr. Livingston departed, refusing the hospitality of Bonniemeer even for a night, as he was eager to hear reports from the detectives he had already secretly put upon the track.

Toward night of the next day, however, he reappeared, with an excitement of manner and appearance, added to the disturbance of the previous day, that prepared Neria for his news.

"Read that, ma'am," said he, as soon as they were alone.

Mrs. Vaughn took the clumsily-folded letter extended to her, and read, in a scrawling hand:

Mr. Livingstone is by this informed that his wife and Doctor Luttrell are stopping in the farm-house of a man named Brown two miles west of the town of ——, in the Catskill Mountains. They call themselves Mr. and Mrs. Smith, and pass for a new married couple. The writer of this, thinking you might like to know, takes this way of telling; but if you will take his advice you'll let her go for a bad lot.

"There! What do you say to that?" asked Mr. Livingstone, meeting Neria's grieved eyes with a look of impatient questioning.

"Poor Claudia!" whispered Neria.

"Yes, but she's run away with that fellow, and she's passing for his wife; think of that; and this fellow, whoever it is, knows of it, and will tell the whole world. Then think of me showing my face on 'Change afterward. I'll have the law of him, if there's law in the land. I'll have damages out of him. I promise you—good rousing damages, too—if there's such a thing as a judge and jury to be had, and I wouldn't mind a thousand dollars divided round among 'em either, if they couldn't do me justice without."

"But yesterday you said you would forgive her—you said you would take her back if she would come," pleaded Neria, gently.

"Yes, but that was before I knew she was actually living with another man—Mrs. Smith, indeed!—and before I knew this fellow who writes the letter knew about it. He'll tell every one he knows, you see; there's where's the rub."

"Perhaps not. He seems to wish well to you by writing at all, and he surely would see that the way to serve you is to keep the matter as quiet as possible."

"If I only knew who it was I'd let him set his own price to keep it quiet, and pay it down, too," mused Mr. Livingstone, unable, more than the wily Walpole, to conceive of a man without a price.

"But Claudia? will you still forgive and shield her?"

"I don't know. It's worse than I thought. Living with another man, and she, such a figure of a woman, to fling herself away like that! Poor thing! where'll she get her velvets and laces now, I wonder. That fellow isn't worth ten thousand dollars, for all the fine property he got with his wife. That went like water as soon as she was dead. Poor Claudia; but it serves her right, it serves her right."

Neria looked at him in perplexity, uncertain whether to pity or to turn from him; but the struggle was a brief one. "Let us go and find her, and on the way we will speak of what we shall say to her," said she, with the angelic voice and look no one yet had ever resisted. And Mr. Livingstone, softened and refined in spite of himself, yielded to her gentle bidding.

Arrived at their destination Mr. Livingstone left Neria at the little inn while he made cautious inquiries as to the whereabout of Mr. Brown's farm-house and the character and appearance of his boarders. He returned after an absence of several hours quite excited.

"I have found her," exclaimed he, coming close to Neria, and speaking in a hoarse, quick tone.

"It is a lonely sort of place, no other house in sight, and I looked round among the trees and bushes until I saw her standing at a window. She looked pale and downcast, and as if she'd be glad to be off her bargain if she could. Poor girl! I can't but pity her, and if she's humble and sorry, and we can keep the matter hushed up, I will hold to my word and take her home again. She's a splendid creature at the head of my table, or receiving company, and if I separate from her there'll be a scandal at any rate."

"I do not doubt she repents already—it must be that she does," said Neria, eagerly. "And by forgiving her you may save a soul otherwise lost."

"I'll forgive her if she feels as she ought," replied Mr. Livingstone, stoutly; "I've said it and I'll do it. Of course, I shall make my conditions; she can't be quite as free with her check-book for a while, and I shall expect her to stay at home this winter. Washington isn't a good place for a woman like her, especially without a husband."

"It cannot be that she will wish to go," suggested Neria, considerably shocked at the nature of the conditions apparently considered satisfactory by the injured husband.

"I don't know that," returned he, shaking his head; "Claudia can hardly live without society and admiration, and she's always been where there was the most of it to be found. She won't like stopping in one place; but she's got to, if she comes back to me. I shan't trust her further than I can see her."

"And yet you will call her wife?" broke involuntarily from Neria's lips.

"Under conditions, yes. Why, she's no worse now than a dozen women I could name who stand as fair with the world as Claudia did last week, or does to-day, for that matter. Society's a queer sort of affair after all, Mrs. Vaughn."

"And shall we go at once to Claudia?" asked Neria, escaping from the discussion.

"Yes, they're harnessing a horse—here he comes now. Are you ready?"

"In one moment;" and as Neria possessed the rare feminine virtue of counting but sixty seconds to a minute, she was ready nearly as soon as her companion.

"Now, my plan is this," began Mr. Livingstone, as he drove down the bowery country road; "I'll show you the house and let you go in and get over the first with the poor girl alone. She might not feel quite so shamefaced with you as with me, and she'd be more likely to come round to do as she'd ought to. With me, like enough, she'd sort of straighten up and think I'd come to exult over her and all that, when goodness knows it's the last thought in my head. But she's a proud piece, and there's no such thing as driving her. She's got to be coaxed and no one can come near her half so quick as you, Neria."

"I'll do my best; but what shall I say from you, what offers or promises shall I make?" asked Neria.

"Why, say I know she's done what she hadn't ought to, but I forgive her if she's as sorry as she should be. Tell her I'm lonesome without her, and she's too handsome and too stylish a woman to go the way she's set out, and though it's a hard pill for me to swallow, still I love her well enough to overlook what she's done—and—you fix out the rest yourself. You know what a man had ought to say, and you can say it for me better than I can for myself."

"But if I meet Dr. Luttrell?" faltered Neria, as she left the carriage.

"Tell him, if he's wise, to keep out of my sight," growled Livingstone. "I won't take the law of him as I'd laid out to, but if I get hold of him I'll be my own judge and jury; yes, and executioner, too, may be. Flesh and blood won't stand everything, and though I'm a man of peace I'd shoot that fellow as quick as I would a dog."

With these instructions Neria walked slowly down the shady road, and stood presently at the door of an old red farm-house, nestling picturesquely among its lilacs and syringas. Her knock brought the blithe-faced housewife to the door, and as she nodded inquiringly at the visitor, a sudden perplexity arose in Neria's mind. How should she inquire for Claudia? She would not use the assumed name of Smith; she dared not speak the one sullied by Claudia's sin.

"Won't you walk in, ma'am?" asked the farmer's wife, finding that her visitor did not speak.

"Thank you. I wish to see the lady who is staying with you."

"O, Miss Smith. Yes, she's right in the parlor here. Come in." She threw open the door as she spoke, and Neria, entering, closed it behind her, for already she had caught the wild glance of Claudia's eyes, and shielded her from observation and scrutiny, while still she might.

"Claudia!" said she, softly approaching her, as cowering away, she hid her face in her hands.

"Claudia!" and the gentle hand upon that bowed head fell like a benediction. But the guilty woman shrank from that pure touch as sinners from the sunlight.

"What do you want with me?" asked she, sullenly.

"I want to call you back before it is too late," and Neria sank upon her knees beside her.

"Too late! It is too late already—too late for anything but to go on as I have begun—" exclaimed Claudia, half angrily, half piteously, but suffering Neria to take one of her cold hands in hers.

"Ah, no, dear Claudia, it never is too late for us to repent and amend; never too late for God to forgive."

"Us!" laughed the other, mockingly. "You do well, Neria, to put your name with mine. 'You who never since your birth had need of repentance or amendment, how will you judge for me?"

Neria's white lips quivered with the sharp pang at her heart, but she answered bravely—

"You cannot know it, but my sin is hardly less than yours. My whole life is a repenting; and, less happy than you, God does not offer me the opportunity of amendment."

"O, yes, you talk, you good women talk, but you know not what you say," exclaimed Claudia, writhing nervously away from Neria's arms. "Your sin is some fancied peccadillo, some trifle magnified by your own conscience, but it is not like this. And forgiveness, do you say? I do not know much of these matters, but do you think, Neria, it could ever be forgotten—I mean when I am dead?" She spoke softly, and woman though she was, seemed half ashamed of caring for what had always been her scoff.

"Better than forgotten—it shall be forgiven and washed away in the blood of the Redeemer. 'Though thy sins be as scarlet, they shall become white as wool,'" said Neria, solemnly.

"Does it say that in the Bible? I havn't been happy for many weeks. I ran away partly because I couldn't keep up a smiling face and easy manner any longer, but it is worse to be alone, and—" she stopped and looked about her— "worst of all to try and talk with him. But you, Neria, I can trust to you. You always were so true and good; there is something soothing about your very presence. I have longed for you so; but I thought you would not look at me. O, Neria, may I?"

She turned and laid her head upon Neria's bosom, clinging about her neck with a pitiful dependence, while she, her pale face and beautiful eyes irradiated with the joy of an angel, who leads back to the fold a soul almost lost forever, bowed her cheek upon that regal head, and whispered such words of promise and pardon and love, as God gave her to speak.

"But will he, will my husband—O, no, he cannot forgive, or shelter me from the world," moaned Claudia, at last. "It is too much. I must go away somewhere by myself and live out my life solitary and forlorn. If I might come to you, Neria; but no, they would not let me—I must not contaminate you. But I shall be so desolate!"

"Claudia, I would not tell you till now; but it is he that has sent me. It is that generous and forgiving husband who has bid me come and say to you that, if you so repent and amend that God forgives and receives you back, he will not refuse to do likewise. Can you hesitate in face of such clemency?"

"But can he forget? If he should taunt and reproach me!"

"I do not think it of him; but even if he should would not such humbling of your pride be a light penance in comparison to what you might suffer?" asked Neria, with some severity.

"True, true; I ought to be humble, and I will try; but you know, Neria, how ungoverned I have been," said Claudia, sadly. "He is generous and good to offer to pass it over, and so shows himself above me now; but you know it has always been I who have looked down upon him."

"Perhaps, dear Claudia, if you had done more justice to the really fine qualities of his disposition you would have developed others, and learned to love them so well that this could never have been," suggested Neria

"Perhaps; but now it is too late," said Claudia, wearily. "He may pity and forgive, and even receive me back; but if he is a man and human, he never will allow me the place I held before."

"Do you deserve it?" asked the clear voice, severely, yet so pitifully that the guilty woman did not shrink away as she answered, "No."

"Then, dear, should you not take as an unmerited alms such forgiveness as he tenders you,; and if reproach is mingled with it, take that, too; silently if not gratefully. Has he not a right to chide when he passes by his right to punish, as he might? And if he, being but human and a man, should mingle his pardon with the bitter draught of reproof and reminder, remember, Claudia, that He who is all love holds out a free and unqualified forgiveness to all who will seek it. He will forgive you, Claudia, and love you none the worse, so soon as you shall ask Him."

"It is you who must ask; I dare not," whispered Claudia.

"We will ask together," said Neria; and with the simple words of the petition went up to the Mercy Seat an offering of the scalding tears of a true repentance—the pure, bright drops of a holy sympathy, an angelic pity.

"Sit there, Neria; let me put my head in your lap and cry; it will do me good," moaned Claudia; and Neria did not resist the impulse of humility so significant in the haughty sinner. A half hour passed thus; and when the sobs had died away in sighs, and Claudia, pushing back the purple-black masses of hair from her face, smiled wanly up in Neria's face, she said:

"And now I shall call your husband to hear you say what I know you will wish to say to him."

"He—is he here?" asked Claudia quickly, while a deep blush burned over the face but now so pale.

"Yes; and he has waited all this time to hear whether he ought to see you."

"Then you would not have called him if—"

"If you had been hard and impenitent, no," said Neria, quietly. Claudia looked curiously at her.

"How is it you are so quiet and so resolute, so sweet and so severe, all in one?" asked she; but Neria, with a little smile and a shake of the head, waived the question, and hastened from the house.

Never in his prosperous life had Mr. Livingstone passed so anxious and miserable an hour as that since Neria had left him, and he now came to meet her with a trepidation of manner very unlike his usual placid self-satisfaction.

"Well?" asked he, briefly.

"She is waiting for you. You will be generous and gentle with her, I am sure," replied Neria, pointing toward the house.

"Aren't you coming with me?" asked he, nervously.

"No, you had better see her alone. I will wait here for you."

"Is Luttrell there?"

"No, he has gone away for some days."

"Well for him, and me, too, perhaps. Wait here in the shade of these trees, if you won't come. I shan't be long."

"Don't think of me, but go at once, and do not hurry back," replied Neria, pitying his agitation; and Mr. Livingstone with a fervent pressure of the hand, silently followed her advice.

Left alone Neria sat for a while in the shady nook selected for her by Mr. Livingstone, and then attracted by the tender gloom brooding in the recesses of a wood, bordering on the road, she wandered into it, satisfied that she should see or hear her companion whenever he might return. But absorbed in her own thoughts she soon lost sight of the road, and striking into a woodland path strolled slowly along it, pausing now and again to smile a recognition to some familiar flower, or to listen to the song of some forest bird, lovingly as to the voice of a friend. To pluck the flower no more occurred to Neria's mind than to kill the bird, or to wound the friend.

But at its height the harmony of this pastorale was broken by the baying of a hound, rapidly approaching, and while Neria startled, if not frightened, stood pale and still, he broke through the underbrush and sprang toward her. Timid, like most women, Neria's timidity took often the form of a blind courage, and she now advanced toward the fierce brute with the "good dog! poor fellow!" and similar expressions best suited to the canine perception. The hound, evidently surprised at this course of treatment, instead of the panic and flight on which he had counted, paused to consider of it, and like the woman who deliberates was lost, for Neria's little hand upon his head, her eyes meeting his, reduced him in one moment from her fierce antagonist to the humblest of her slaves, fawning at her feet, smiling up into her face, and lavishing such caresses as she would permit upon hands and cheeks.

A sharp whistle was heard from the wood. The hound paused, hesitated and listened. The whistle was repeated, and with an apologetic kiss bestowed upon Neria's hand, he bounded away, but was met at the turn of the road by a man with a gun upon his shoulder, who called him sharply by name and ordered him to follow more closely. Neria, already walking away, heard this voice, and caught her breath sharply. It did not need the hasty look she involuntarily cast behind to assure her that the gunner was Doctor Luttrell, the man of all others whom she most wished to avoid. He had recognized her also, and with a few strides was at her side, his tawny eyes glittering, his thin lips curling with malice.

"An unexpected pleasure, Mrs. Vaughn. May I hope that it is mutual?"

"It is no pleasure to me to see you, Dr. Luttrell, as you must be well aware," said Neria, coldly.

"No? *Je suis desolée;* but Mrs. Vaughn was ever cruel—to me. I believe Mr. Murray is more fortunate in gaining her favorable regards." The insulting tone pointed the words, and Neria suddenly stopped and looked at him.

"It was you, then, who wrote an anonymous letter to Colonel Vaughn," said she, contemptuously.

"Your sagacity is equal to your amiability, madam," replied Doctor Luttrell, coolly. "I thought it as well, since I had married into the family, to have an eye to the preservation of its character. You will remember, my dear, that I am your brother by marriage, and in that capacity found it a disagreeable duty to inform Colonel Vaughn of the use you were making of his absence. I did it anonymously to avoid disagreeable explanations when he should return home."

"Did you not know him to be dead you would not dare acknowledge such infamy," exclaimed Neria, indignantly.

"It is true, then, that you are a widow. Might I hope that in time I could conquer the repugnance with which you have ever repaid the admiration I have never concealed—" began Luttrell, mockingly, but Neria interrupted him.

"I have nothing more to say to you now or ever," said she, coldly; "except to give you a warning. Mr. Livingstone is with his wife, and intends to take her home with him. Her eyes are open to the sin and shame of the course to which you have tempted her, and she only desires to escape another interview. You will do well to avoid the presence of either."

Luttrell's lips grew white, and his eyes sparkled with rage as he fixed them upon Neria's. "Again!" said he, in a low voice. "You have dared cross my path again, dared grasp at another secret so nearly concerning my life and honor?"

"I dare anything for the right, even to meddling with Doctor Luttrell's honor," said Neria, roused to an impulse of bitterness.

"It is not safe. Believe me, Neria, it is not safe. I have a foolish admiration for your beauty and your character, or you never would have carried the secrets that you did from my wife's death-chamber. I tried to ruin your character in self-defence, fearing the harm you might some day do to me. But you had best not tempt me too far."

"I am not afraid of you, Doctor Luttrell," said Neria, quietly. "And you do not speak the truth. The reason you did not murder me, as well as my sister, was because guilt is always cowardly, and you knew that I had found you out. I spared you the ignominy of exposure, because the forfeit of your life could not give back hers, and you may yet repent and amend as Claudia already does."

"Nonsense. The reason you did not give your suspicions—for they were no more—to the world was, that you could not prove them; and if you could, would not have wished to introduce a gallows into the family history."

Neria looked at him a moment, and silently turned away. He overtook and detained her. "Stop; I have something more to say. You know or suspect too much of me to be allowed to go at large as my enemy. Be my friend, Neria. Keep my counsels and I will repay you amply—you do not know in how many ways. Speak your heart's desire, and you shall have it, were it even to summon the dead from his grave."

"Were you able to perform even that impious promise I would make no compact with you," exclaimed Neria, indignantly. "Any benefit you could ever render were insufficient to bind me for an instant as friend to my sister's murderer; my own slanderer; Claudia's seducer. Go; and if God gives you time, repent; but never think to be other than an object of pity and abhorrence to me."

She moved decidedly away, and Luttrell, gasping with passion and sudden hate, bounded after and grasped her brutally by the arm, but as he did so the imprecation upon his lips changed to a cry of pain and withdrawing his hand he clenched and shook it as in agony.

"What is this!" cried he, turning suddenly pale, and staggering to a seat upon a fallen tree.

His cry was echoed from Neria's lips, and as she wrenched her arm from his grasp the golden serpent bracelet fell from within her sleeve and lay coiling among the dewy grass, its diamond eyes and ruby crest sparkling with a malicious joy. The deadly purpose of Fiemma Vascetti had been fulfilled, and she in her century-old grave rejoiced at the vengeance wrought upon the enemy of her house.

"The bracelet! the poisoned bracelet!" cried Neria, pale with horror.

"Poisoned! Sorceress and murderess, you have wiled me to my death!" gasped Luttrell, sliding from his seat to the ground, where he lay writhing and moaning, his face livid, a light foam gathering upon his lips, his rolling eyes blazing with agony, and rage.

The hound, trembling all over, crept to his master's side, licked his cheek and hand, and then, with a piteous howl, darted away into the forest. Neria threw herself upon her knees beside the dying man, her eyes dilated with horror but shining with a holy purpose. "It is not I who have killed you," said she, solemnly; "It is the hand of God! O, repent, repent, before it is too late! Beg for His almighty pardon and He will give it you even now. Humble yourself before Him, quickly, before the agony of death seizes you. We forgive you— my sister, Claudia, I, we all forgive you—but it is nothing unless you gain His pardon. Say that you repent!"

"Why should I mock at God if there is a God?" gasped Luttrell, mastering, by a terrible effort, the convulsions trembling through his limbs. "If repentance could avail, it should have come sooner. Say no more of that, but listen; I did not mean to kill your sister. She was the victim of science. I had a splendid theory of a new mode of treatment. I experimented upon her. She could not have lived many years, at any rate. She had an incurable complaint. I never loved her, and I did love science. Claudia would have been none the worse for me if her own nature had not led her astray. I have done you no harm. Vaughn lives—I have seen him. Now go—I can no longer master this agony. O, my God, my God! The pains of hell have seized me before the time! Go, woman, go! I will not have you watch me! Go, I say!"

"Say that you repent. Ask God's forgiveness. One word, but one word, before it is too late!" persisted Neria, her whole frame quivering with horror as she knelt beside him, one hand pressed convulsively upon her heart, the other raised to heaven.

"Leave me, leave me! You shall not see me die like a dog. It is too late, I tell you—too late!" gasped the dying man, his face already grey with the awful pallor of death.

"Too late for human aid—never too late for God's mercy! I will not go, I will not watch you, but pray beside you till the last," said Neria; and with that guilty soul went to God such petitions for its pardon and peace as Neria could never have uttered had he for whom she prayed less bitterly wronged her and hers.

The soul was already sped, the prayer was ended, when, through the dim arches of the wood, hastened toward the scene, a man, conducted by the faithful hound. At sight of Neria he paused, hesitated, and would have turned, but was arrested by a warning growl from the dog, who seized him by the coat and dragged him on.

Neria looked up, too stunned for surprise. "Go for help, James," said she, quietly. "He is dead already, and they must carry him home. No, stay here, and I will go. She must not hear it too suddenly. Come to me afterward without fail."

"Yes, ma'am," said James, with taciturn obedience; and, leaving him standing with the dog beside the terrible thing so rudely marring the sylvan beauty of the scene, Neria hurried away, hardly conscious whither she went, hardly conscious of the joy that, buried deep beneath this weight of horror, began already to sing in the depths of her heart—"He lives! he lives!"

CHAPTER XXXIX.

SUNRISE.

FAITHFUL to every duty, Neria had prepared for that terrible home-coming; had broken the ghastly tidings to Claudia; had seen that Mr. Livingstone was able and willing to soothe the agitation into which her passionate excitement had subsided, and had singly told the story of Luttrell's death to the physician and magistrate summoned to meet his dead body at the farm-house, before she allowed herself a word with James, who, with the activity and tact of his class, had superintended not only the removal of the body from the forest to the house, but all the subsequent proceedings. Neria, released at length, found him sitting in a shady porch at the back of the house. She gave him her hand, while her eager eyes, asked as well before her lips:

"James, where is your master?"

"Up here, ma'am, among the mountains. We are camping in a log shanty we found there."

"But how—why—" She would not ask what wifely pride told her she never should have needed to ask; but her magical eyes spoke for her, and the man replied:

"I don't know, ma'am, except it was the Colonel's wishes that no one should know. He was left for dead down there in the Chickahominy; but I found him, and carried him off. He was sick a long spell; pretty nigh all winter, I might say; but an old darkey and I took care of him, and finally he pulled through. He hasn't been so as to enter again, and he never would have me write a line or send a message to anyone. This summer we came up here, and have been gunning and fishing for a living pretty much. I happened to find out about Dr. Luttrell and—and the lady, and so I thought it no more than my duty to let Mr. Livingstone hear where she was. I didn't say anything to the Colonel about it, because I thought he might be disturbed at the chance of some of the family coming this way, and think it best to remove."

Neria smiled slightly; for, indeed, the solemn twinkle of James's eye, and the elaborate innocence of his tone, in thus revealing his little plot for a return to civilization and identity, were too funny to be resisted. "I will go with you to him," said she, after a moment of thought.

"It's a long and rough way, ma'am. Can't I take a message or a note to the Colonel, asking him to come to you?"

"No; he might not—it is better I should go myself. Wait until I speak to Mrs. Livingstone," said Neria; and James submissively answered:

"Yes, ma'am;" while in his shrewd heart he thought—"She's afraid he'd be off and never come."

To Claudia, Neria simply said she must leave her for a few hours; and to Mr. Livingstone that she needed no other escort upon her errand than that of James, whose appearance in this place she did not attempt to explain. Absorbed in their own emotions, neither husband nor wife questioned or watched her, and just as the sun touched the tops of the tallest forest trees Neria passed under their shadows, and with a heart strangely vibrating between joy and fear followed her taciturn conductor toward the secluded hut where Vaughn had sought to bury his broken life, his despairing love. The path led by the scene of the morning's tragedy, and when James would have turned aside to avoid coming within sight of it, Neria checked him. "Let us go straight on," said she, quietly; and as they reached the place she paused and gazed unshrinkingly at the spot where the corpse had lain, while in her inmost heart she once more offered full and free pardon to the guilty soul thence sped, and prayed that even so might he be pardoned of God.

"Here is the bracelet, ma'am," interposed James, thinking that must be the object of her search. "I picked it up this morning, and would have given it to you before, but the Justice wanted to see it."

"Thank you, James; we will go on now," said Neria, taking the bauble in a reluctant hand, and hastily putting it out of sight, while its wicked eyes, catching a ray of the setting sun, shot out a green and crimson light.

"It's a very odd thing, ma'am, that the p'ison should have laid on that little spear so long and never got shot out before," pursued James, with respectful curiosity.

"It is very old, and no one understood its construction. I supposed it harmless or I should not have worn it," replied his mistress.

"Certainly, ma'am; and even now I can't make out how to start it, or how to hinder it. I tried it all sorts of ways, and so did the doctor and the squire; and finally the doctor said he didn't believe it was that killed him, or that he was p'isoned at all. He says he shall call it apoplexy in the report he's going to write out."

"I am glad if it is so," said Neria, quietly; and James, suspecting the subject a disagreeable one, said no more upon it.

The sun had set, and the moon—the moon that a few days before had shone upon Neria through the riven walls of Cragness—now shed silver light upon her head as she stood just within the edge of a clearing, half way up the mountainside, and looked at the picture to which her guide had silently pointed before he left her.

It was a sylvan lodge, such as hunters build of saplings, boughs, and bark ; and upon the flat stone at its door sat a worn and haggard man, his chin resting upon his hand, his elbow on his knee, as he looked wearily across the sea of foliage beneath him to the mountain peaks beyond, gleaming white and strange in the full moonlight. A lonely and a stricken man, said every line of his figure, said his attitude, and his mournful eyes, and yet a stately and a gallant figure withal.

But to Neria the picturesque side of the scene could not present itself. She saw before her the object of the love that since his reported death had risen to a vital passion ; the husband, whom, as she devoutly believed, God had given back to her incessant prayers, if not from the grave, at least from a living death. Heart and soul clamored for the joy and rest of his embrace, his kiss, his full, free pardon and love, and yet a nameless doubt, a womanly diffidence, a Nerean shyness held her back, would not let her run to fall at his feet as she would have done ; held her trembling and wavering there, a sweet statue of some wood-nymph smitten with love and awe at her first sight of humanity.

So, like the spirit of the night, the genius of the wood, she stood as Vaughn turned of a sudden and looked toward her, looked long and silently, and whispered, half aloud,

"It is her spirit—she is dead." Then, with bated breath and measured step, as one who treads a holy place, he came toward her, and she, blind and sick with the great joy swirling through her heart, stood mute and still awaiting him. A few feet off he stopped, and whispering, ".Neria !" held out his arms, imploringly yet hopelessly, as one holds them toward the heavens.

Then, with a great sob, the fountains of her heart broke up, and throwing herself into that longed-for embrace, she cried out, "My husband ; O, my love, my lord, my all ! "

"Not dead ! My Neria, mine at last, my very wife ? " incoherently questioned Vaughn, putting her away to look into the earnest, tearful face, all flushed with love and excitement, that so bashfully, yet earnestly, returned his gaze, and then straining her close, close and closer to the sad heart that had so longed to feel her there. But Neria, struggling from his arms, slid to her knees,

"Say, say that you forgive me for all I have made you suffer," murmured she. "I did not know it then, but since I have learned to love I have learned to feel."

"What ! You will kneel to me ? Nay, then ; will you now give me the first offence you have ever offered ? Here, here in my arms, and so near my heart that you may feel it beat the echo of my words, hear me say, sweet wife, that this one moment repays the past tenfold ; that I would not, if I might, abate one moment of that past if so I must abate one instant of this hour. It was right that I should wait and serve for you, my rich reward. It could not have been but that you must learn earth by slow degrees, my pure angel. I only feared that you should pine away in longing for your heavenly home, and so leave me desolate ; or that love, when he came, should point not toward me, but to another—"

"Stop, Sieur !" and in the bright eyes, whence the moonbeams flashed back into his, Vaughn read for the first time the sweet imperiousness born of a conscious love. He smiled, and would have kissed the clear, bright eyes, but Neria held him back.

"By one thing in all our life you have done me wrong," said she. "You have fancied that I, being your wife, could love another man ! O, Sieur, that grieved me much."

"That, and all the wrongs I have done you, my fairy princess, sprang from an incapacity upon the part of my grosser nature to comprehend your pure spirituality. But now, thank God and Neria, the love in my heart has reached to hers, and across that rosy bridge sympathies and perceptions shall travel so incessantly from the one heart to the other, that we may never say where the sweet pilgrims really dwell, the two shall so become one heart. O, darling, is this true, is it real? Can God have been so good to a sinful man like me? And how dare I accept such gifts, I who— Neria, here upon this lonely mountain-side, before we go back together to the world whence you have come to claim me, I must tell you the errors and mistakes of my early life, and, if it may be, gain pardon both for the concealment and for what has been concealed."

"No, Sieur, do not speak a word of what is past. I know all, and I have forgiven and forgotten all. Chloe, before she died, told me everything; and Mrs. Rhee—"

"Did she see you?"

"Yes. Hush, Sieur, she is dead, and with her the story of the past. Let us leave it all behind, and make our home in the future."

"But did she speak to you of what I afterward wrote?" asked Vaughn, anxiously. "Did she tell you that I believed—"

"She told me many things which I do not wish to remember or repeat. She told me that you believed them, and it was as if she had told me the ocean was dried up and the sun extinguished. I knew you too well even then to believe that you believed such tales of me."

"True woman and true wife! You but did me justice then, and yet I blush to think I could fancy even such innocent faithlessness as I did. But now tell me, sweet, how you came here, standing like a spirit in the moonlight, and watching me with your dreamy eyes, until I thought you indeed a thing of air or water or fire, altogether fashioned of the elements, and inspired with the pure soul of my pure-hearted Neria." He drew her toward his cabin as he spoke, and seating her upon the great stone where she had found him, stretched himself at her feet, gazing intently up into her face, while she related as briefly as she might, the strange chain of events that had led her hither.

"And so Master James was weary of our incognito, and laid a little plot to lead to its discovery," said Vaughn, gayly. "I may truly say to him, 'Well done, good and faithful servant,' for without his intervention I do not know, my Neria, how this tangled coil would have been undone. I could never resolve whether I should arise from the dead, as it were, or allow my name to go down to posterity among the killed of the battle of Seven Oaks. I think the leading idea was, to live here in the woods a sort of wild hunter life, until, at last, dying I should send for Neria to close my eyes, and give me one parting kiss. I always meant to see you again, at least once."

Neria looked at him with dim eyes and a quivering mouth.

"O, Sieur! You must have suffered so much before you could come to that!"

"Suffer? What is suffering? I do not recognize the word with my arm about Neria's waist, my head upon her knee, her eyes looking love into mine," whispered Vaughn, passionately; and then, man-like, he proudly smiled to see the rose-tint mount her slender throat, flush her soft cheek, and faintly tinge her brow.

"Neria, say 'I love you, Sieur,'" ordered he; and Neria, blushing yet more brightly, whispered,

"I love you, Sieur; I love you better than my life," and as he kissed her lips she kissed back with the first wife-kiss they had ever formed.

CHAPTER XL.

A NO-SAY AND A YES-SAY.

The moon that lighted Neria on her true-love quest had waned and faded, and a tender crescent hung in the west when Francia Vaughn, creeping from her father's house like a guilty creature, stole through the shadowy garden and on to the wood beyond, where lay the mere. But once within its friendly covert, and shielded from all eyes, even those of the stars just trembling into view, she paused, and throwing herself upon the ground, gave way to a burst of passionate grief; grief of which only an ardent temperament, an untried nature, and the first vigor of youth is capable. Later in life one's tears come more reluctantly, and from a deeper source, until at last it is its very life that the stricken heart distils in tears.

A firm, slow step came through the wood, and Francia, starting to her feet, resolutely composed her face and turned to meet Fergus. He extended his hand.

"I was looking for you, Francia, to say good-bye. I am going to Australia on business, and shall sail in a week. I am, of course, much occupied, and could only run down for to-night." The awkward sentence ended in a pause as awkward. Francia's cold fingers dropped lifelessly from Fergus's grasp, and she stood silent with averted face.

"Shall we walk as far as the lake?" asked he again. "I have not seen it in a long time." Francia mutely turned her steps in that direction, and walked beside him with eyes that, looking straight before her, saw nothing. They stood upon the border of the little lake watching the shadow of the hills, the duplicate crescent, the stars that momently showed more closely sown in the heaven below as in that above. Fergus, the iron Fergus, felt the influence of the hour, of his approaching departure, of the memories thronging the place and time, and turning to his cousin took her hand and softly asked, "Not one word of regret for me, Franc?"

She snatched her hand away, asking in turn, "Do you remember when we last stood here, Fergus?"

"Yes. You asked me if you should keep or break your engagement with Rafe Chilton."

"Yes, and do you remember that, when I, with full heart, brought my sorrow and my perplexity to you, you threw me off and told me that my affairs were not yours, and that you would not interfere. Do you suppose that one such rebuff is not enough?" The grief, so thinly cloaked by indignation, struggled up as she spoke, and turning to meet his eyes, her own suddenly overflowed.

"That was long ago, Francia. I have changed since then," said Fergus, moodily; and turning slightly from her, he bitterly reviewed the months of the last year.

"Yes, you have found what it was to love unwisely yourself since then," exclaimed Francia, hastily.

Fergus faced her, and, with his imperious eyes on hers, asked quietly, "What do you mean, Francia?"

"Nothing. I did not mean to say that," replied she, in confusion.

"Yes, but it is said, and now I must know what it means," said Fergus, with patient persistence.

"Well, then, I mean that when you thought my father was dead you loved

Neria," said Francia, softly, and turning from him to pluck the leaves from the rustling alder at her side.

Fergus was silent for some moments. At last he slowly said, "Some years ago, while I was gunning among the Berkshire hills, I climbed a crag to reach a gay tuft of flowers blooming there. As I drew myself up, a rattlesnake, basking on the rock, gave an alarm, and, before I could retreat, struck his fangs into my arm. I left the flowers where I had found them, and seating myself at the foot of the rock, took out my hunting knife, cut away the wounded flesh, and then, heating the knife at the fire I had just kindled, cauterized the wound. A scar remains that no time will efface, and it was long before I could forget the pain, but I was cured."

He was silent, and Francia, still plucking at the alder leaves, said, bitterly, "Yes, such a scar must remain through life."

"Better a life-long scar than a coward's lingering death," replied Fergus.

"Yes, your will decreed, then, that through torture you should retain your life; it decrees, now, that through other and finer torture you shall retain your peace of mind; but the body is forever maimed, the heart forever crushed," said Francia, gloomily.

Her cousin turned her face to his. "Franc," said he, "why did you escape through the window just now, when from behind the curtain you heard me tell my uncle that I was going abroad?"

Francia blushed in spite of herself. "You saw me then?"

"Yes, saw and followed you. I wanted to know why you escaped."

"To avoid the necessity of saying that I regretted your going," retorted Francia, desperate as any timid creature at bay.

"That answer deceives neither you nor me," said Fergus, coolly. "Francia, two years ago when I showed you that I loved you, or could love you, if you had met me frankly and generously, as my love demanded, how much would have been spared to both. You, too, wear your scars, poor child."

"Mine is not the scar of an unrequited love," interposed Francia, sharply.

"No, but of a desperate attempt to love an unworthy object. Tell me, now, Francia, why did you engage yourself to Chilton?"

"He loved me, and you—you had never said—I thought you cared for Neria."

"Impatient and jealous," pronounced Fergus, remorselessly. "Do you know now that you were wrong? Do you see now that by this course you so wounded my love—"

"No, your pride," interrupted Francia.

"Self-respect, I prefer to call it, and in my nature no love can be love that is at war with this quality. This self-respect, Francia, forbid me then to love you who had so doubted me, as it now forbids me to love the wife of another man. This is the knife which has cauterized my moral hurt, and well is it for me that I had it at hand."

Francia turned earnestly toward him. "But you have a terrible enemy, Fergus, in this darling self-reliance of yours. It is this that stands in the way of pity and generosity, and all the gracious virtues that you lack."

"After the cautery should come some blessed balm, and as it soothes the burning pain, the heart finds rest and room for these gracious virtues. They do not spring in the crisis of suffering and effort. Some such soothing balm as the love of an affectionate heart, Francia."

"And you would ask such love with nothing to offer in return but the pleasure of soothing the scar of an unforgotten passion?" said Francia, with spirit.

"Am I selfish? Remember, I am a man, and it is for you, a woman, to soften and refine my nature, nor look too curiously at the balance of benefit between us," said Fergus, somewhat sadly. "Come, little Francia, let us take what good is left to us, and be thankful for it. Perhaps we never can go back to the glow and glory of a first love; perhaps you never will be the woman, or I the man we once were to each other, but there may be better things in the future for us than we can now imagine. I need the influence of your warm and loving nature, your grace and gayety; and you, my wilful cousin, will be none the worse for a little training in law and order. Will you go with me to Australia, Francia, as my wife?"

Francia hesitated for a moment, and then facing him, frankly said: "No, Fergus. I do not like the way you have asked me to marry you, and although you seem so confident of my consent I will not give it on such terms. You say I love you, or you imply it. Well, I do not deny that I do, that I have always loved you, and that my engagement to Rafe Chilton was, as you called it but now, a movement of impatient jealousy. And yet with all this I value myself too highly to take the position you would assign me. My love shall never be used as a balm to heal the wound of another woman's indifference; I will not accept permission to give you my whole life, taking in return such scraps and fragments as are left when another has taken all that is best. If you cannot give me the 'glow and glory' of a full and honest love, be it first or be it second, I will have none. I will never follow you forlornly through the world on the chance that some indefinite future may reward me."

"And yet you own that you love me," said Fergus, somewhat bitterly.

"I love you so well that I would not have you marry a woman whom you could not respect, and I respect you so much I know you could not really love a woman who would accept the position you offer me. No, Fergus, I love you, and I refuse you."

Looking steadily into her face the young man read there a determination equal to his own; a dignity and self-respect as firmly based as those forming the foundation of his own character. Looking deep into the soul standing in that moment unveiled before him, Fergus saw there, qualities he had never before acknowledged, and the conviction flashed into his mind that should he lose the prize a moment before so undervalued and now so tantalizingly withdrawn from his grasp, the loss would be one that every day passing over his head should magnify until it became the lasting regret of his life.

"Francia, I am sorry to have hurt you—" began he; and Francia, turning to retrace her path, said quietly,

"I am sorry you did, but I forgive you Fergus. I am sure you will regret it."

She moved away with unaffected decision of manner, and Fergus, standing discomfited and humiliated, where she left him, watched the lithe figure pass out of his sight beneath the dewy arches of the wood, and felt, too late, the terrible mistake which he had made. And Francia, too, despite her proud and resolute bearing, did she not feel that this victory was almost more cruel than defeat? Reaching the first flight of steps leading to the terrace, she sank down upon them, faint and trembling, and, hiding her face in her hands, wished bitterly that she might never stir again.

Half an hour later somebody descended the steps and stood before her. It was Fergus, who, returning to the house by the more direct route, had seen her from the terrace and, after one sharp short struggle between love and pride, had come to say:

"Francia, I was very wrong, very much mistaken in what I said to you just now. I do not ask your love without return; I ask it as a great and precious gift, and I offer in return all the good of which my nature is capable. I love you more than I myself know; more than I ever have or ever can, as I now believe, love any other woman. If you will accept this love, and will return it, you need never fear that I shall forget how much it is for me to ask or you to grant. Do not judge me by my words, Francia; they are cold and hesitating; but you are able, as you showed yourself but now, to read the thoughts and feeling below the words. Read my heart, dear cousin, read it thoroughly, and you will be content."

He sat beside her, and the hands clasping hers were cold and tremulous as her own. In the dim light Francia saw how pale his face had grown, how earnest his eyes, how tender his mouth, and a great joy stirred at her heart. But the next instant, with a cry of sudden terror, she snatched away her hands.

"O, Fergus, you do not know!"

"Not know what, Francia? What is it, dear?"

"My story—my mother—"

"Good heaven, what is this! Francia, you alarm me inexpressibly. Speak out, I pray you."

Francia wrung her hands despairingly. "You do not know, and I had forgotten for one moment. I was so proud and glad that you should really love me at last; and now, good-bye, dear, dear Fergus, it can never, never be—never while we live." She would have sprung away like a wounded fawn to hide her mortal hurt in solitude; but Fergus seized her arm.

"No, Francia, you shall not go until you have explained these strange words. When you refused me just now, you gave your reason, and a good one. That reason is removed by what I said just now. You are satisfied on that point, are you not?"

"Yes, fully satisfied; but this other is a more terrible obstacle, for it can never be removed. Say good-bye, dear Fergus, and let me go. It must be so."

"Never, Francia. I demand an explanation; I demand it of your justice and your honor, and if you are what I think you I shall not appeal to them in vain," said Fergus, resolutely.

"Well, then," cried Francia, desperately, "have it, and be satisfied. Mrs. Rhee, my father's housekeeper, was an octoroon slave whom he bought at public auction in Savannah. My mother was her daughter by the master who sold her. My father married this free daughter of his slave, and I am her child. Now are you content?"

She struggled in his grasp, and when he would not let her go fell moaning at his feet in a passion of shame and grief too deep for tears. Fergus, grasping her wrists with unconscious violence, stood looking down at her in mute astonishment and dismay. Presently he raised her to her feet, and seating her again upon the step, asked, quietly:

"Will you promise to remain here until I return?"

"Yes," whispered the girl, her head falling helplessly upon her breast, her arms and nerveless fingers hanging straight beside her.

Fergus looked at her a moment; and then, with slow and measured steps, disappeared in the shadows of the grove. An hour had nearly gone when he returned, and seating himself beside Francia, who had never moved, put his arms around her, and laid her head upon his breast.

"So let me shelter you so long as we both live," said he. "I would not yield to the impulse that bid me say so at first, for I dared not trust an impulse. I would not risk wronging you by saying what I might repent. But that impulse came from the inmost chamber of my heart; it is as vital as my conscience. Francia, darling wife that you shall be if you will, never fancy that I remember this in the future. You could not but tell me, and yet I would have you forget that you have told me as soon as may be, lest at some time you may fancy me so base as to point at it should I treat you less tenderly than I ought."

"I never should suspect you of a meanness, Fergus. I know you too well."

"But this secret, Francia, calls for such added consideration and delicacy on my part, such thoughtful care and honor, that I fear my own harsh, hard nature; and yet if I understand myself at all, I do not think I can fail to make you feel how all my life and hopes and chance of becoming other and better than I am are bound up in you. Francia, will you trust me?"

"With my life, and my soul," whispered Francia.

> And on her lover's arm she leant,
> And round her waist she felt it fold,
> And far across the hills they went
> In that new world which is the old.

CHAPTER XLI.

L'ENVOI.

THE story is done, and in leaving these our friends and sometime associates to the chances of the future, we may please ourselves in remembering that each and all of them have learned at the hands of that stern mentor, Experience, lessons which rightly applied should insure peace, content and beneficent influences to the coming years.

Forestalling the secrets of those years, we may fancy Vaughn and Neria, in harmony at last with each other and with life, the noble, dignified and gracious heads of a well-ordered household, ruling their children and their dependents with such loving wisdom, such mild authority, that the law becomes delight, and obedience is as involuntary as affection.

We see Fergus and Francia, returning after years of exile, happy in themselves and in each other, the asperities of his character softened, as the weaknesses of hers are strengthened by the harmonizing influences of time and love, and we no longer fear lest harshness on the one hand, or levity on the other should destroy the happiness so long desired, so hardly won.

And Claudia? Yes, let us hope even for Claudia, for under the sin and passion and weakness that have hurried her to shipwreck, lies a great, strong heart, a heart whose deepest fountains were stirred while she lay upon her knees at Neria's feet that day in the lonely farm-house, and heard that the husband she had wronged would even yet forgive and grant her the opportunity for repentance that she had counted already lost.

Yes, Claudia, though thy sins were as scarlet, there is a Fountain wherein they may be washed white. And so, bidding them and you good-bye, O friend, let me hope that what has been told may have taught some lesson, however vague; may have won to momentary forgetfulness some aching heart, or solaced an idle hour for those whose hearts have not yet learned to ache; may have stirred an aspiration in the forecasting mind of youth, or a tender memory in that of age; or, failing all else, may have awakened one friendly feeling toward the narrator who lingeringly and regretfully closes this the happy toil of months.

THE END.

www.ingramcontent.com/pod-product-compliance
Lightning Source LLC
Chambersburg PA
CBHW020247170426
43202CB00008B/262